August 14, 2005
From Nay –

RIZZOLI
NEW YORK

THE COMPLETE MUSHROOM BOOK

savory recipes for wild and cultivated varieties

Antonio Carluccio the quiet hunt

special photography by **Alastair Hendy**

I should like to mention, and dedicate this book to, my dog Jan, who lived with me for thirteen years, giving me the best companionship one could desire, especially when out mushroom picking.

First published in the United States of America in 2003 by
Rizzoli International Publications, Inc.
300 Park Avenue South
New York, NY 10010
www.rizzoliusa.com

First published in 2003 by
Quadrille Publishing Limited
Alhambra House
27–31 Charing Cross Road
London WC2H 0LS

Library of Congress Control Number:
2003104762

ISBN 0-8478-2556-6

Printed in Singapore

WARNING: NONEDIBLE WILD MUSHROOMS CAN CAUSE SERIOUS INJURY OR DEATH. IN ADDITION, SOME PEOPLE MAY SUFFER ALLERGIC REACTIONS. MAKE SURE YOU DO NOT HAVE AN ALLERGY TO MUSHROOMS, AND EAT ONLY MUSHROOMS THAT HAVE BEEN POSITIVELY IDENTIFIED AS EDIBLE.

CONTENTS

INTRODUCTION
THE QUIET HUNT

I wrote my first book on the subject of mushrooms almost twenty years ago. At that time, I had about forty years' experience, having begun my mycological education at the early age of seven, for in Italy, you start to hunt from a very young age, either with parents or friends. It was in Castelnuovo Belbo, in the province of Alessandria in Piedmont, where my family was living, that I was initiated into the joys of the "quiet hunt," the collecting of wild mushrooms and truffles.

It wasn't until I was about ten, and by then living in Borgofranco d'Ivrea, that I started to learn properly about mycology. Still under the supervision of either my father or friends of the family, it always gave me great satisfaction to arrive back home with mushrooms I had collected after a day out hunting in the woods. The pleasure of eating them was just as immense for all of my family!

After having investigated all the hills and mountains near Borgofranco, I then decided to move abroad to Vienna to further my studies. Austria has very fertile ground as well, ideal for the growth of wild fungi, and the people have a good general knowledge of mushrooms. I continued the pursuit of my passion, and my "booty" was always very useful when feeding my friends. Students don't have much money, and wild mushrooms are free! After Austria I then moved to

Hamburg in Germany, where I stayed for the next twelve years, becoming a dealer in Italian wine.

I then moved to England in 1975, to continue my wine business, and have remained there ever since. I couldn't believe the attitude to fungi there was in England—a country so near to the fungi-lovers of the rest of Europe. There wild mushrooms have usually been regarded as something suspicious that only witches would collect and eat. But for me, the English soil was rich and full of wonderful examples of fungi just waiting to be picked. And often waiting until they faded and rotted, for no one had any interest. The British government apparently did consider publishing a booklet at the end of the World War Two, detailing edible mushrooms that could be picked in the British Isles, a result of there not being much food available due to rationing. Despite this, it seemed only to have been mycologists or Continentals who went mushroom-hunting in Britain at that time. And this idea that wild fungi are inedible has spread to most English-speaking countries since—America, Canada, Australia, New Zealand, and so on. Nowhere do they have the same enthusiasm as we do in Continental Europe.

But one cannot say that the British did not know anything about mushrooms, because when I arrived some books had already been published on the subject. The late Jane Grigson, a wonderful and erudite woman whom I had the good fortune to know, had written *The Mushroom Feast*, a very good cookery book. Roger Phillips, a botanist and photographer, had written and photographed an excellent scientific book about mushrooms (and other books on other aspects of nature).

Despite this, it is only in the last twenty years that mushrooms have started to become truly part of the British culinary scene, with both wild and cultivated sold in special markets and delicatessens. European countries, on the contrary, have had thousands of years of experience with these "jewels of nature." The Ancient Romans, for instance, were passionate about fungi, and would eat them regularly at banquets. The present-day Italians are just as enthusiastic, as are the Swedes, Poles, Yugoslavs, the Germans, and the French. In Russia there is actually a special train that departs every Saturday morning from Moscow, full of fungi-hunters bound for the country, who return in the evening with their baskets laden.

In all these countries you are able to buy fungi direct from markets. These have been collected by farmers, and are perfectly safe to eat as the authorities have checked them. But even in these places where people are quite knowledgeable, there are still deaths caused by over-enthusiastic pickers not checking the fungi properly before eating. I cannot stress enough how careful you need to be when picking mushrooms, and I shall repeat this warning many times throughout this book.

The most wonderful aspect of collecting and eating fungi is that people from all social strata can become "hooked." Drew McPherson, a Scottish friend of mine, started selling wild mushrooms collected in Scotland. Twenty years later, he has a multi-million-pound business, due to the demand for mushrooms increasing so rapidly, for there is no respectable restaurant that doesn't use wild mushrooms from time to time. The demand is now so great that Drew has to import mushrooms from all over the world, wherever

they are in season. Even supermarkets are selling cultivated mushrooms, which can compete favorably with wild varieties.

I'll never forget when I started to run my restaurant in 1981, that I had personally to collect all the mushrooms to be used in the kitchen! I used to go picking in the break between lunch and dinner service, and prepare the mushrooms before cooking them in the evening. I then put an advertisement in a Polish newspaper for expatriates living in Britain, asking for mushroom pickers. A queue of Poles with baskets laden with mushrooms turned up at the restaurant almost immediately. I trusted their expertise, and they earned good money, so this made for a frutiful partnership. For many years, too, I employed an Italian called Gennaro, who used to bring me baskets of mushrooms. I then gave him a permanent job at the restaurant, where he was responsible for collecting, cleaning, and storing all the mushrooms. I'm glad to say that he now has his own successful restaurant. It's always good to see people who have worked with you moving on and doing their "own thing."

It is due to the enormous surge of general interest, in both wild and cultivated mushrooms, that I decided it was time to update my twenty-year-old *A Passion for Mushrooms*. The present book's subtitle 'The Quiet Hunt,' comes from Mikhael Gorbachev, to whom I gave a copy of *A Passion for Mushrooms* when his private secretary was eating in my restaurant. I received a thank-you letter from Mr. Gorbachev, himself a passionate mushroom collector, and in it he referred to "the quiet hunt," an expression Russians use when going out to look for mushrooms in the woods.

The present book includes a Field Guide with a huge selection of my favorite mushrooms, both edible and inedible. It ends with a discussion of cultivated mushrooms, from east and west, which are now becoming familiar and are used more and more often in cooking in many parts of the world. Finally, there are my recipes—over a hundred of them from all over the world, not just from Italy.

My passion for mushrooms, despite the many years I have now lived in Britain, remains un-abated, and I feel a strong desire to pass on that knowledge and allow others to share the joys of collecting—and eating! This book is one result. In addition, there is my Neal Street Restaurant in London's Covent Garden, which is still a mecca for mushroom and truffle lovers, and which has now been joined by a series of Carluccio's Caffès that also offer exotic mushroom specialities. No one, in London at least, need remain ignorant of the wonders of wild fungi.

Finally I should like to mention, and dedicate this book to, my dog, Jan, who lived with me for thirteen years, giving me the best companionship one could desire, especially when out mushroom picking. The hunt was not actually that quiet with him around, though.

THE FIELD GUIDE
WILD MUSHROOMS

The world of fungi, from invisible micro-organisms to "higher" fungi with clearly visible fruit-bodies (such as mushrooms), is vast. Fungi differ from all other plants in that they do not contain chlorophyll, the green pigments by which plants synthesize carbon compounds from the sun's energy. (In fact, there has been an ongoing dispute as to whether fungi should be classified as plants at all.) Instead of "feeding" from the sun, fungi draw nutrients entirely from living organisms—plants, or even animals—or from decaying or dead organic matter.

To be honest, if we did not have fungi, many aspects of life would be difficult. A number of fungi perform a vital role in breaking down dead matter and assisting decomposition, and this clearing-up operation also provides further nourishment for the soil, new plants that will grow in it, and thus the habitat for new generations of fungi. Conversely, some fungi are parasitic in a less helpful way, attacking living plants such as trees, eventually killing them. Dutch Elm disease, which has destroyed so many beautiful trees across Europe, is caused by a microscopic fungus called Ceratocystis ulmi, carried by certain beetles.

And there are many thousands of microscopic fungi that have a significant place in our lives in one way or another, in important areas such as medicine and food. Perhaps the most significant discovery was that of the fungus developed into the life-saving antibiotic penicillin, while the Chinese (in their ancient wisdom) have known about the medicinal value of mushroom extracts for thousands of years.

The hallucinogenic fungus ergot (*Claviceps purpurea*), which infects several of our most important cereal crops, has been known about for centuries. Poisonings were frequent during the Middle Ages, and were considered to be God's punishment for sin. Known as "holy fire," and thought to be a contributory factor in the sudden appearances of "witches" in seventeenth-century Salem, ergot is now used medicinally in several compounds that are closely related to LSD.

Many of our basic foods are influenced by the action of fungi: sugar is converted into alcohol in wine- and beer-making, and breads rise because of the fungus that is yeast. A mold fungus is injected into young cheese to make the world's most famous blue cheeses (the French Roquefort and the Italian Gorgonzola, for instance), and molds are also used in the fermentation of many foods popular in the East, notably soybeans.

What are mushrooms?

The fungi we are interested in here are not microscopic. With mushrooms, we are concerned with a single stage in the life cycle of much larger and more evolved fungi—the "higher" fungi. The fruit-body that is the actual mushroom is only part of the story. Underlying this ephemerally visible part of the fungus is the more permanent mycelium. This is the important vegetative part of the mushroom (and should never be disturbed by inconsiderate collecting). It is formed of a complex of minute, hair-like filaments, invisible to the naked eye, called hyphae. These combine to form a cobweb-like mat that is the mycelium, which, when thick enough, can be visible. This mat spreads under the soil or leaf litter, forming an ever-more complex web, and often travels several feet to grow into and through, and to gain and absorb as much nutriment as possible from, the soil and other substances. When climatic conditions such as moisture and temperature are appropriate, a new fruit-body, a mushroom, rapidly develops.

The purpose of this fruit-body is not to give us mycologists pleasure, but to serve as the reproductive part of the organism. For as the fruit-body grows and matures, it produces millions of microscopic spores (seeds). At full maturity, these spores are discharged from the hymenium (the fertile spore-producing surface) to be dispersed by the wind or in other ways. Landing upon the ground in favorable conditions, the spores will germinate and form a new mycelium, and the whole process will start afresh. (Spore prints are useful in mushroom identification, see page 14.)

The main mushroom groups

The scientific study of mushrooms goes back many hundreds of years, and scientists throughout the centuries were keen to give names to newly discovered fungi, edible or inedible. The most useful step was in the classification of mushrooms with similar characteristics into groups. A Latin first name was given to the group—Amanita and Boletus, for instance—then a second Latin name was added to specify which particular member of the group was referred to. This second name reflects a more detailed characteristic of the individual mushroom: *Amanita caesarea*, the mushroom of the Caesar, the leader, is the edible best of the group, while the highly poisonous *A. pantherina*, which has white spots, is likened to a dangerous panther. *A. rubescens* —from the Latin for "red" or "redness"—is named for the pink tinge to its flesh.

It seems a fairly sensible and workable system, but confusion arises from the fact that various scientists in other countries began giving differing names to the mushrooms and mushroom groups. As a result, some mushrooms now have two or more names, and are often classified as being in more than one family. In this book I have given the primary or most familiar Latin name, followed by any alternative name or synonym.

And then, of course, there are the local names—nicknames perhaps—which are specific to each mushroom-collecting country. The "pre-eminent" quality of *A. caesarea* is reflected in the names used throughout Europe (see page 23), while the English for *A. rubescens* is straightforward—it's "the blusher."

In the present book I have followed the example of the late Bruno Cetto, a famous Italian mycologist who wrote five masterly and comprehensive books on the subject, with descriptions and photographs of no fewer than 2,147 mushrooms.

Another primary step in the classification of fungi was to further detail the type—whether saprophytic, parasitic, or mycorrhizal. Saprophytes live on dead organic matter like dying trees, decaying logs, tree stumps, even pinecones. Parasites do exactly what one might expect: they attack and kill living trees and plants. (*Armillaria mellea*, for instance, is typical, considered a pest by gardeners and arborists.) The fungi that are mycorrhizal live in a mutually beneficial relationship—a symbiosis —with the roots (the Greek "rhiza" means "root") of certain trees. They receive moisture and protection in adverse conditions, in exchange for which they give the roots of the tree phosphorus, nitrogen, and other elements the tree might not be able to obtain for itself. Boletes, russulas, and amanitas—as well as the highly valued truffles and matsutake—are

SPORE PRINTS

Spores are microscopic, and vary in shape and color from mushroom to mushroom. Even without a microscope it is possible to see the color of the spores *en masse*: all you have to do is leave the cap of a mushroom on glass or paper for a few hours. The spores will drop out, leaving a "print" clearly visible to the naked eye. (You could use a paper that is half white and half black so that the print is clearly visible whether the spores are light or dark.) Like a finger-print, the information contained in the spore is essential for correct identification. Although the shape of the spore itself can be seen only under a microscope, the color of the "print," plus all the other field characteristics, will help you name the mushroom you have collected.

all mycorrhizal fungi. Many saprophytic and parasitic fungi can now be cultivated, but the unique mycorrhizal relationship is much less easy to reproduce, in nature as well as in cultivation—possibly one of the reasons why many of these fungi are so rare, so highly valued, and so highly priced!

Yet another step in fungi classification was the division by mycologists of the larger fungi into two major groups—Ascomycetes and Basidiomycetes—according to the way they produce spores.

ASCOMYCETES

Ascomycetes, or "spore-shooters," develop spores internally within sacs called asci, from which they are violently discharged at maturity. The group comprises a diverse range of often bizarrely shaped fruit-bodies (and indeed some tubers, which actually grow underground). I have included only two Ascomycetes in my selection for the mycophagist (those of you who enjoy eating fungi). But as these are the highly prized morel and the even more highly valued truffle, their gastronomic importance considerably outweighs their numerical insignificance.

BASIDIOMYCETES

The mushrooms in this category are the most numerous in the wild and in this book. These are the "spore-droppers," which form spores externally on club-shaped cells (usually on gills or pores under a cap). These drop naturally to the ground, or are swept off and away by wind or rain. However, the spore-droppers, being such a large group, also encompass different types of mushroom. There are two principal sub-categories, gilled or pored fungi—conventionally mushroom-shaped with more or less convex caps and central stems—plus a motley crew of other edible Basidiomycetes.

GILL FUNGI The gilled category of mushrooms is extremely large and includes such familiar genera as Agaricus, Amanita, Armillaria, Cantharellus, Clitocybe, Cortinarius, Laccaria, Lactarius, Lepiota, Lepista, Pleurotus, Russula, and Tricholoma. They have a fruit-body that is fleshy, convex, and centrally stalked. Underneath the cap there are radiating gills, the lamellae, and the spores are produced on

the hymenium, which covers the gill surface. It is vital to study the color and mode of attachment of the gills to identify agarics properly, for instance. Some fungi in this group also have a volva—an egg-shaped membrane that encloses the developing mushroom, and which ruptures as the mushroom grows. Sometimes part of the volva remains on top of the cap of the mature mushroom in the form of flakes or scales, as happens with amanitas. Another characteristic of many agarics is the veil—the membrane that in young specimens encloses and protects the gills, but which, as the young fruit-body expands, is ruptured to leave a sort of skirt or ring around the stem, as in the case of Cortinarius.

PORE FUNGI The pored category of mushrooms includes the genera Boletus, Gyroporus, Leccinum, Suillus, and Tylopilus. They have a fruit-body that is fleshy, convex, and centrally stalked. The underside of the cap has a poroid, sponge-like appearance. Instead of gills, the surface is made up of closely packed little tubes that are invisible in the youngest fungi, but when they develop, hold the spores with which the mushroom can reproduce itself. The pores differ in their density and color from species to species, even from one bolete to another. In young boletes they tend to be cream, turning yellowish/greenish later, but they are of a reddish tone in some species. Bruising the pores also gives an indication of the type, especially if the color changes to blue or to black.

ODDBALLS Other edible Basidiomycetes are less easy to categorize. In hedgehog fungi the hymenium covers spikes or spines (instead of gills or pores) hanging from the underside of the cap. (*Hydnum repandum* could be confused with a pale pink mushroom or bolete until one sees the spiny lower surface.) Like boletes, bracket fungi have a poroid hymenium, but differ in their woody and leathery texture, their usually fan- or shell-shaped brackets, and their occurrence on wood. *Fistulina hepatica* and *Laetiporus sulphureus* are edible examples. *Sparassis crispa* is in a category of its own. Puffballs, whose spores are formed internally rather than externally and are "puffed" out when raindrops hit the mature fruit-body are, surprisingly, also Basidiomycetes, but are known as Gasteromycetes.

ABOVE A NAUGHTY LECCINUM QUERCINUM

IDENTIFYING MUSHROOMS

To identify a mushroom expertly you have to be sure of every single element. Checking physical characteristics observable in the field such as shape, color, texture, and smell is part of the procedure, as well as noting the habitat itself. (Completely accurate identification can ultimately depend on examining microscopic details, such as the precise form and color of the individual spores.) Fortunately, however, the wild mushrooms with which we are concerned are those with a clearly visible (and tasty) fruit-body, and if you systematically check a specimen against the descriptions in the Field Guide, you should go a long way toward establishing its identity. The surest safeguard is to consult a professional mycologist, who will identify specimens accurately, before you eat anything: you will often find such an expert if you take a field course organized by local naturalist groups or professional mycological societies. (Another alternative is to marry one, as my wife Priscilla did!)

Mycological experts themselves are slow to reach any agreement about the definitive classification of certain fungi, and this is why you will find the botanical Latin names varying from book to book (and why I have included some of the more widely used synonyms in this one). I recommend your buying two or more good books on identifying fungi (see my bibliography on page 220). Just as it is useful to have more than one to clarify the names (a giant puffball is a giant puffball whether known as Lycoperdon, Langermannia, or Calvatia), you get a helpful perspective on identifying a specimen by comparing both the descriptions and the illustrations in different books.

To start you off, though, look at all the different characteristics of the mushroom you are examining, and compare them with the details in the individual descriptions. If you are taking the mushroom home to be identified, you need to gather the entire fruit-body, base and all, preferably with both young and mature specimens to compare development. Carry them home wrapped in waxed paper to preserve their freshness. Keep these unidentified specimens well away from any you may be intending to eat.

CAP   Measure it, and note shape, color, and surface texture (is it shiny, scaly, and so on?).

GILLS/PORES   Look to see whether the mushroom has gills or pores, their color, how they are attached to the stems, and whether they change color when touched.

STEM   Measure its height and thickness, and note its color and whether there is a ring, veil, or volva.

FLESH   The color will be significant, as will the texture (dense, crumbly, fibrous). Does it exude milk? What does it smell like? And you can even taste most mushrooms as long as you spit out quickly and rinse your mouth out with water (but not, of course, with something like *Amanita phalloides* or any that are obviously poisonous).

HABITAT   Many of the edible species of fungus favor specific types of habitat and have particular requirements in terms of host nutrient. This not only means that it is worth making forays in likely looking places with the appropriate sort of vegetation, but that habitat can be a key element in identifying an unfamiliar specimen. Some fungus species grow on living or decaying wood, others on soil or dung. Certain mushrooms have a symbiotic relationship with certain plants, often trees and shrubs. Sometimes this mycorrhizal association is with a specific tree, sometimes with more than one.

As examples, *Suillus grevillei* (the larch bolete)—as its common name suggests—prefers larch trees. Leccinum mushrooms grow almost exclusively among birch. *Lactarius deliciosus* and *Suillus luteus* prefer pine trees, particularly Scots pines. *Boletus edulis* grows among oak, birch, beech, and pine. Morels, one of the first mushrooms to appear in spring, prefer the edges of broad-leaved woodland, but will also be found under poplar and in orchards, wasteland, and even burned ground. If you know your trees, it helps you to know your mushrooms. Meadow mushrooms and giant puffballs are found in open fields and meadows, and are the exceptions to the rule that mushrooms tend to prefer warm, damp, shady places. On the whole you will find most mushrooms in humus-rich soil, in places that are not too marshy, nor overgrown with thick, tall vegetation.

SEASON   The season varies according to the individual species. A few edible mushrooms (morels and St. George's among them) appear in spring, but most appear from mid- or late-summer on to autumn, and some continue after the first frosts. The right preconditions of temperature and humidity produce a flush of fruit-bodies: you can expect them to appear in warm weather following rain. Given optimum conditions—moist soil and a temperature of 68–80°F—the fruit-bodies of *Boletus edulis* can develop in four or five days, and you will know roughly when it is worth returning to the same spot for the new crop—if someone else has not beaten you to it. It is for this reason that you will often find me out hunting on a Wednesday. Mushrooming is a weekend activity for many people and the best places are often stripped bare of mushrooms by enthusiasts. By midweek there is often a flush of new growth, and the tiny specimens of the weekend are large enough to be worth picking.

THUMBSTICKS

A straight stick, preferably with a fork at the top, is a wonderful tool if you are a keen wild-mushroom collector. The fork is especially important, not only as a thumb rest, but to defend yourself against encounters with snakes, and to turn over leaf litter or ferns that might just hide a new mushroom.

Hazel sticks are straight with few side branches. Find the correct height by putting your thumb in the fork—your forearm should be at a 90-degree angle, resting horizontally. (Cut the base down if too long.) Then you can decorate the stick as I have done in the photograph overleaf. It's become a major, absorbing hobby of mine!

ABOVE THE RELIGIOUS CLEANING AND SORTING OF THE SPOILS

COLLECTING AND PICKING MUSHROOMS

Every year I wait for the right conditions for the mushroom season to begin with the impatience of a small child. Although I have a good "nose" for mushrooms, I am often a few days too early, and the first trip or two into the woods may not be very productive—not of mushrooms, at least. Instead I often come back with some consolation prizes in the form of new walking sticks to carve and decorate. Even in the height of the season my impatience has sometimes taken me to a mushroom spot in such good time that I have had to wait in the car for an hour or so before dawn breaks!

ANTONIO'S CODE OF CONDUCT

Because of the increasing popularity of collecting wild mushrooms, the authorities in most countries have intervened to regulate

picking to avoid the depleting and damaging of habitats by inconsiderate, greedy, or ignorant collectors. In France, Italy, Switzerland, and most other European countries, picking is regulated by law: local farmers can collect enough to sell to make a living, while occasional collectors have to follow strict rules (if these are not observed, they can be heavily fined or even imprisoned). Britain is probably the only country in Europe where foraging for mushrooms is not very popular, as is also the case in most of North America. I hope this book might help redress the balance.

I welcome the new rules in Europe, as they will help preserve fungi and their habitats. And, for much the same reason, I have created my own personal set of rules. I observe these myself when collecting, and I invite other collectors and lovers of fungi to do the same.

1 Before you start, make sure that you know enough about the habitats and the mushrooms themselves, either through expert tuition or through foraging expeditions organized by local mycological societies.

2 Preferably go with somebody, ideally an expert, and stay in contact with each other.

3 Be equipped with the right tools:
A WICKER OR WIRE BASKET This will safely transport the mushrooms and also helps to disseminate the spores while you are walking.
A MUSHROOM KNIFE to clean the stem of the mushroom on the spot, without carrying the dirt home, and to prevent the stem contaminating the gills and pores of other mushrooms in the basket. In Italy, special knives are available that have a curved blade and an inbuilt brush.
PROPER WALKING BOOTS.
SOME DRINKING WATER, something to eat, and hygienic paper.
A WALKING STICK OR THUMBSTICK.

4 Follow local codes of conduct and rules, paticularly in state or local parks. Check with your state's conservation department.

5 If you intend to forage in the country, you must ask for permission from land-owners, because almost everything is private property and you will be trespassing.

6 Respect the environment. It is the principal source of your pleasure, so be considerate. Take any refuse home with you, for instance.

7 When collecting in large woods or forests, be sure to remember how to come out of them again. More than once in Calabria, Italy, for instance, people have become lost and have never been found again. . . .

8 Collect only mushrooms that you actually know and don't experiment with those that you don't. (Don't even mix unknown mushrooms in your basket with your edible ones.)

9 Collect only enough for your own immediate use, unless you encounter an enormous crop that you would like to preserve (see pages 96–99).

10 Don't destroy any mushroom that you don't know, that you find ugly, or think is poisonous. All mushrooms have an ecological purpose.

11 If you want to identify mushrooms for your own scientific purposes, take only a few specimens at a time to compare with a comprehensive, scientific field guide. Avoid species considered rare or endangered.

12 Don't accept mushrooms given to you as a present by somebody you don't know.

13 Collect only mature specimens, leaving the very small ones to grow on, and the very old ones to decay, in their natural habitat.

14 Never use plastic bags or closed containers as you will spoil the quality of the mushrooms and possibly also alter the safety of the proteins. The mushrooms will sweat, lose condition, and become contaminated with bacteria.

15 Never collect mushrooms when it is raining or immediately after rain. They will have absorbed too much water, and you will have either an unusable mess or a mushroom that will exude too much water (and flavor) when you cook it.

16 Pick, pull, or cut the mushroom from the ground according to its species and my guidance. In general, try not to disturb the mycelium too much by tearing the mushroom out of the ground.

Finally, I can't emphasize enough how careful you have to be with mushrooms. Over-confidence may provide you with your last supper.

A few more tips

● Keep a note of your landmarks as you wander in search of mushrooms: it is easy to get disoriented.
● Once you have discovered a "good" place, mark it on your map so that you can visit it again next season. Since the mycelium is long-lasting, mushrooms can often be found in the same place year after year.
● As you search, keep your eyes open for local clues, such as scattered caps of boletes—the leftovers from a squirrel's meal—which tell you to look for others growing somewhere in the vicinity.
● Don't just look at the ground when you are on a mushroom hunt. Look up too, for you might find one of the beautiful and very edible bracket fungi.
● As you recognize more fungi you can use them as signposts. Where you see the beautiful but poisonous fly agaric, for example, look carefully: The king bolete enjoys the same environment, and is a good mushroom to start collecting. It is easy to recognize and the tastiest of all.
● And don't share your secret with too many friends, in case they turn into competitors.

Happy hunting!

The edibility of wild mushrooms

The wild mushroom is the only type of food in the world that offers equal doses of deliciousness or poisoning, depending on species. Perhaps it is this titillating frisson of danger that makes us appreciate the edible varieties even more. However, only six are lethal. The rest may be either very toxic or just mildly so, but still able to produce extreme symptoms.

To each description of a wild mushroom, I have added a word or two to describe its edibility—or the reverse.

The division of edible wild fungi is as follows:

EXCELLENT The mushrooms that are universally known as being of top quality.
VERY GOOD Mushrooms that are delicious but have a stem that may be less edible.
GOOD Good to eat, but their culinary appreciation depends on personal taste.
EDIBLE Various mushrooms containing toxins that disappear when brought into contact with heat, so they are safe only after cooking. They are inedible and toxic when raw.

The division of non-edible wild mushrooms is as follows:

NOT EDIBLE Mushrooms that either smell bad or are bitter, which would only spoil the dish without being necessarily poisonous.
TOXIC Mushrooms that can provoke intensive intoxication of the body. These toxins can accumulate over a long period of time.
POISONOUS These mushrooms actually poison. Symptoms are either immediate or develop within 4 hours, but only cause death sometimes. Promptly treated, they are curable.
DEADLY POISONOUS These are seriously poisonous, and ingestion usually results in death. The symptoms appear after 10 or more hours, after which organs such as the liver are destroyed. There is no antidote.

Should you ever eat a toxic mushroom, you will probably begin to suffer a stomachache, dizziness, and sweating. Seek immediate medical assistance, and if possible keep a sample of the mushroom you consumed so that the toxins can be identified swiftly.

To avoid all of the above, though, please keep to the basic rule of eating only mushrooms that you have identified as completely safe.

AGARICUS CAMPESTRIS

THE AGARICUS FAMILY IS LARGE AND FAIRLY COMMON THROUGHOUT
THE ENTIRE WORLD, AND IT IS FROM JUST ONE MEMBER, *A. BISPORUS*,
THAT ALL OUR FAMILIAR CULTIVATED MUSHROOMS ARE BELIEVED TO DERIVE.

Often when I talk to someone about my passion for mushrooms, I am amused to hear them say, "Oh yes, I know all about mushrooms . . ." meaning meadow mushrooms, and implying that everything else is a toadstool. This blithe assurance worries me because a non-expert might mistakenly collect the poisonous "yellow stainer" (*Agaricus xanthodermus*), which can be found in the same fields and meadows, as well as on lawns and in shrubberies. So when you find a colony of what looks like meadow mushrooms, avoid picking any with yellow stains on their stems or caps, especially if these stains are at the base of the stem and turn a deeper chrome-yellow when bruised. Above all, avoid look-alikes with white gills: they could be the deadly poisonous *Amanita verna* or *Amanita. virosa* (see page 27).

In the same family there is also *Agaricus augustus*—the Prince—wonderful to pick and eat, but rare.

RECOGNITION

CAP Round at first, very tightly attached to stem; becoming convex and expanding to 4 inches diameter. White, becoming cream/brown.
GILLS Adnexed, pale pink at first, deepening to dark brown when fully grown. Spore print: purple-brown.
STEM Relatively thick and short, $3/8-3/4$ inch in diameter and $1^1/4-3$ inches tall, with slight frill-like ring.

AGARICUS CAMPESTRIS

AGARICUS CAMPESTRIS

(SYN. PSALLIOTA CAMPESTRIS)
MEADOW MUSHROOM / FIELD MUSHROOM **VERY GOOD**

It pleases me that this wild mushroom and its close relatives can be recognized by a lot of people, and therefore picked and eaten with safety. The meadow mushroom (*Agaricus campestris*) and its larger cousin, the horse mushroom (*A. arvensis* syn.

Psalliota arvensis), can be found fairly extensively in their preferred habitat of well-manured fields, meadows, and grassy areas, when the summer weather has been wet and warm. Other relatives that are to be found in similar surroundings and situations are *A. bitorquis, A. macrosporus,* and *A. bisporus*. The latter is the one I have mentioned above, the commercially cultivated mushroom that is commonly found in every supermarket (see page 82).

AGARICUS MACROSPORUS

FLESH White, bruising slightly pink. Taste and smell pleasant and mushroomy.
HABITAT Fields, especially when richly manured, meadows, and lawns and other grassy areas. Meadow mushrooms usually grow scattered or in clusters, occasionally in rings.
SEASON Early summer to late autumn, later in milder areas.

AGARICUS ARVENSIS
HORSE MUSHROOM / PRAIRIE MUSHROOM **GOOD**

The main difference is in size: the horse mushroom is larger and more substantial, the cap growing to 8 inches diameter and the stem to 4 inches, with a distinctive cog-wheel-like ring. The caps of the bigger examples are fleshy and heavy, but the stems tend to become hollow. There is often a yellow tinge on the edge of the cap, so be careful not to confuse it with the poisonous *A. xanthodermus*, which turns yellow when touched. The gills and spore print are similar to the meadow mushroom. The flesh smells of aniseed. Meadow mushrooms are usually maggot-free, but larger horse mushrooms may become infested. They grow singly near stables and alongside paths. The season is the same as the meadow mushroom.

AGARICUS BITORQUIS
GOOD

This sturdy member of the agaricus family appears in small groups on very hard ground, sometimes erupting through tarmac, and even raising paving slabs on sidewalks. The cap is $2^{1}/_{2}$–$4^{1}/_{2}$ inches in diameter and white with an inrolled margin; the flesh has an almond-like smell. The gills are a dirty pink, finally becoming dark chocolate-brown (the color of the spore print). The stems are up to 3 inches long, white with two rings. *A. bitorquis* are found occasionally in sandy and manured soil, by roads, and beneath sidewalks or impacted ground, from late spring to autumn. They are good to eat, but when found at roadsides they can have absorbed pollutants from the traffic (as most fungi do). *A. bitorquis* can be mistaken for many of the amanitas—*Amanita verna, A. virosa,* and, sometimes, *A. phalloides*. Remember that all amanitas have white gills.

AGARICUS BISPORUS
GOOD

The "original" agaric, which is uncommon in the wild, is found on sale in supermarkets in its highly successful cultivated form. In the wild, *Agaricus bisporus* has crowded gills that are pinkish when young, maturing to reddish-brown. The spore print is brown. The wild version is found in manure heaps and garden waste,

AGARICUS ARVENSIS

and on roadsides, but rarely in grass, from late spring through autumn. *Agaricus bisporus* can be mistaken for many of the amanitas, as specified above under *Agaricus bitorquis*. See also the description of *Agaricus bisporus* in its cultivated form (page 82).

PICKING, CLEANING, AND COOKING

Cut the stems of agarics at the base with a sharp knife. Clean with just a wipe if necessary; there is no need to peel them. The whole mushroom can be used, although the older stems can be discarded if they are no longer fleshy and tender.

As these mushrooms are widely considered to be the only kind to be edible, it is not surprising to find them used in recipes everywhere throughout the world. They are delicious eaten raw in salads (especially the smaller, firmer young specimens), cooked in stews and soups, baked, grilled or broiled, and sautéed. They are also excellent dipped in batter or breaded and then deep-fried, and they can also be pickled and preserved to serve as antipasti.

Freezing and drying are not recommended, but since the very similar commercially grown species is so readily available throughout the year, this perhaps does not matter. I think the wild mushrooms are much tastier, though.

AGARICUS XANTHODERMUS
(SYN. PSALLIOTA XANTHODERMA)
YELLOW STAINER **POISONOUS**

Superficially similar to *Agaricus arvensis* and *A. campestris*, the yellow stainer (as its name suggests) stains yellow immediately when cut or bruised, and smells rather inky. Always pick out a piece of flesh from the stem base with the thumbnail. If

AGARICUS XANTHODERMUS

chrome-yellow, reject it. The meadow mushroom does not stain, and smells pleasant and mushroomy (as does *A. bisporus*); the horse mushroom may have a yellow tinge, but smells of aniseed; and *Agaricus bitorquis* smells of almonds.

Although not dangerously poisonous like *Amanita phalloides* (see page 25), *Agaricus xanthodermus* can give you a painful and unpleasant time, with serious problems of respiration and digestion that manifest themselves in cold sweats and stomach pains soon after ingestion. These symptoms can be remedied if they are quickly diagnosed and treated by a doctor. Strangely enough, some people are completely unaffected.

RECOGNITION

CAP Spherical when young, becoming flat with age, and growing to a maximum diameter of about 6 inches; dirty white, becoming yellow when bruised or scraped.
GILLS Pale pink at first, becoming brown with age. Spore print: purple-brown.
STEM White, staining chrome-yellow in bulbous stem base; $3/8-3/4$ inch in diameter, to 6 inches tall; with pronounced white ring or skirt just below cap; it is often infested with maggots.
HABITAT AND SEASON Much the same, in both senses, as the edible agarics.

In the Amanita genus you can find both the supremely edible *A. caesarea*, which i think is the most delicious of all, as well as *A. fulva* and *A. rubescens*, and the most toxic of mushrooms, including *A. phalloides* (death cap), *A. muscaria* (fly agaric), *A. verna*, *A. virosa* (destroying angel), and *A. pantherina* (panther cap).

AMANITA CAESAREA
EXCELLENT

History tells us that *Amanita caesarea* is so-named because it was the favorite of a Roman emperor, and the tradition lives on in the common names employed throughout Europe: the English "Caesar's mushroom," the

AMANITA CAESAREA

French "impériale," the Polish "cesarski," and the German "Kaiserling." The Italians, on the other hand, call it "ovolo" because when it is very small it looks like an egg in size and color. Even in the Mediterranean region, the mushroom is fairly rare (it is found mostly in the hills of northern Italy), and because of its demand as a delicacy, the price can become

astronomical ($90 per kilogram in the 2002 season). One of my all-time favorite dishes (tasted in Milan some years ago) consisted of raw ovoli with raw porcini (*Boletus edulis*), topped with some freshly sliced white Alba truffle. A truly unforgettable dish for a mycophagist like me!

So far this mushroom has never been found in Britain, and it is not found in North America: the fungi known as "Caesar's mushroom" in the U.S. is, in fact, *A. jacksonii*.

It is quite extraordinary that in this genus you can find both the deadliest and the most delicious of all wild mushrooms. Fortunately identification is easy, and there is no danger of mistaking the mature edible rarity for all the poisonous amanitas, including *A. phalloides, A. muscaria, A. virosa, A. verna,* and *A. pantherina* (but see pages 25–27).

RECOGNITION

CAP The egg-like volva splits to reveal the deep red cap; as it expands from hemispherical to convex, the cap pales through orange-red to become light orange when fully grown (diameter to 8 inches). Edges slightly cracked, and showing the yellow gills. Sometimes traces of the volva remain on the expanded cap.

GILLS Crowded, free, extremely fragile; an unmistakable rich yellow (this is the main identification characteristic—no other European amanita has yellow gills). Spore print: white to pale yellow.

STEM To $1^1/_4$ inches diameter and 6 inches high. Yellow, normally still with yellow ring. The stem base is encased in the bag-like volva.

FLESH Orange-yellow under the cap, becoming white toward the center and in stem. Firm-textured. Pleasant smell; sweet mushroomy taste.

HABITAT Open deciduous woodland in warm climates, especially with oak and chestnut. Occasionally under pine, particularly in Mexico (though it is not confirmed that the New World

AMANITA CAESAREA

AMANITA RUBESCENS

fungus is identical to that from Europe). They grow in little groups.
SEASON In Italy and France, and other southern Mediterranean countries, from early summer to the beginning of October, especially after hot summery weather.

🍴

AMANITA RUBESCENS
THE BLUSHER **EDIBLE**

This mushroom, a close relative of *A. caesarea*, is called "the blusher" because of the definite pink shade of its gills and stem. In fact, this is the only visible difference between it and the other amanitas, which are entirely white underneath, with the exception of *A. caesarea*, where the flesh and

gills, etc. are yellow. The cap is 2–6 inches in diameter, and is brown with white spots, which are the remains of the volva. The stem is 3–8 inches by $^3/_8$–$1^1/_4$ inches and cylindrical; as it ages, it becomes hollow. The flesh is white and very tender, but it, too, becomes pinkish when cut and exposed to the air. There is no discernible odor. The spore print is white.

One has to be very cautious when this mushroom has just opened or is still small, because the solid egg shape is similar to all the other amanitas. The actual differences between this and its poisonous counterparts are only possible to detect when the mushrooms are more open or more mature, or when you cut it in half. The habitat is similar to

A. caesarea, although it is common under pine, and it is found from spring through autumn.

Another peculiarity of *A. rubescens* is that it can be riddled with larvae and insects very early, when it first appears. Cut the mushroom and check inside for small black points, which are the head of the larvae. Perfect stems should have the characteristic pink tinge and the flesh should be immaculately white inside.

Eastern European and Russian people are very fond of this mushroom. It's not a great culinary delight, but is considered extremely useful when all the other mushrooms have been picked and the choice has been reduced! It must be cooked before eating, and any cooking water should be discarded.

RIGHT AND
BELOW
AMANITA
FULVA

AMANITA FULVA

TAWNY GRISETTE **EDIBLE**

This extremely small and delicate member of the family grows singly in the same type of mixed wood-land habitat as *A. muscaria* and *A. pantherina*. The cap is 1¹/₂–4 inches across and pale orange-brown, with striped see-through "ridges" from the center to the grooved edges. The stems are white, very long, and thin (3–5 inches by ¹/₄–⁵/₈ inch), and have no ring. When you collect it, any time between button and open, just take the cap. The fragile white flesh cooks very quickly because of its delicacy, but to make a meal out of it you will have to collect a huge amount! It is found from summer to autumn.

PICKING, CLEANING, AND COOKING

Just cut the mushrooms at the stem (or *A. fulva* at the cap), using a sharp knife. Don't peel the cap, just wipe the surface if necessary, and brush any foreign bodies out of the gills. In *A. caesarea*, if egg-shaped, pluck

whole from the ground, and simply trim off the first layer of the whitish volva. (Don't take the *very* small ones, those smaller than hens' eggs.) Check the stem for maggots: the base in particular may be infested and can be cut away, but the upper part is usually clear. Keep all these mushrooms, especially *A. fulva* when open, separately in the basket, as they are rather delicate and could be damaged.

Because *Amanita caesarea* is so rare, I recommend that you eat small ones raw, but you can cook them, in sautés and stews. Always cook the other two edible amanitas. The large caps are excellent grilled and served with freshly made pasta.

Amanita caesarea keeps relatively well for up to a week in a refrigerator, but eat the others right away.

AMANITA EXCELSA

(SYN. *A. SPISSA*) **NOT EDIBLE**

Although I classify it as inedible, this mushroom is considered to be edible by many people (although not of high quality). As it can easily be confused with *A. pantherina* (see page 27), I think it is best avoided if not positively identified. "Spissa" is from the Latin meaning "massive" or "huge."

RECOGNITION

CAP 4–4¹/₂ inches in diameter, dark brown to grayish-ocher with grayish, mealy patches.
GILLS White and crowded. Spore print: white.
STEM 4¹/₂ inches long, white with a persistent ring and a bulbous, almost rooting base.
FLESH White and firm. Smells unpleasant and slightly of radish.
HABITAT AND SEASON It is usually found in broad-leaf and coniferous woodland from summer through autumn.

AMANITA EXCELSA

AMANITA PHALLOIDES

DEATH CAP **DEADLY POISONOUS**

Most of the fatal cases of mushroom poisoning in the western world can be attributed to this mushroom. It bears no resemblance to the edible mushrooms mentioned here, but it is included because it is all too easy for it to end up in your basket of edible mushrooms, through innocence or ignorance. Even if you don't eat any, it can cause illness, possibly serious, if its spores "infect" your other mushrooms. If you ever find yourself in this situation, throw them *all* away, including the edible ones. Wash your hands thoroughly after even touching this mushroom. It is so dangerous that you cannot afford to take a single chance.

The trouble with *Amanita phalloides* poisoning is that, despite years of research, there is no simple antidote. In a simplified account, after ingestion the toxin passes through the digestive tract into the liver and kidneys, which it attacks; however, it is not passed out of the body with other waste matter but is recirculated into the blood-stream to begin its journey all over again. Symptoms (severe diarrhea,

stomach pains, and vomiting) start from 6 to 24 hours after ingestion, which is already too late: although the victim may appear to recover, death from kidney and liver failure shortly ensues. The only consolation I can think of is that it is quite rare to find it in the mixed woodland where it grows from late summer to late autumn, usually with oak. Unless you are accompanied by an expert mycologist and want a specimen for studying gill structure and spores, I warn you—DO NOT TOUCH IT!

indisputable facts are that its toxins will attack the central nervous system, producing such effects as intoxication, hallucination, euphoria, hyperactivity, coma, and possibly death. I've heard that people dry the skin and use it to gain effects rather similar to those of LSD, but caution has to be taken as there are dangerous after-effects.

The only edible mushroom with which it would be confused is *Amanita caesarea*. The difference in mature specimens is clear, but the danger comes in trying to identify young specimens where the caps are just beginning to emerge from the egg-like volva from which all amanitas grow. In this situation, cut one in half lengthwise and check the color of the

gills and flesh: if these are white, then it is *Amanita muscaria*; if they are yellow, it is *A. caesarea*.

RECOGNITION

CAP Grows to a maximum height of 10 inches including cap, which reaches 8 inches in diameter. Bright red with scattered spots (the remains of the volva), but these can be washed off by rain, leaving cap plain. In older specimens cap may fade to pale orange; there is a pale orange variety in North America.
GILLS Pure white.
STEM Pure white, scruffy, with remains of volva attached to it, and white ring just below cap. Height as above.

AMANITA PHALLOIDES

RECOGNITION

CAP Grows from egg-shaped volva, which remains at the stem base. To 4¹/₂ inches diameter, round at first, becoming flattened; silky pale green to olive color.
GILLS White, sometimes somewhat cream to pale green. *A. phalloides* var. *alba* is entirely white and equally devastating.
STEM To 5¹/₄ inches and ³/₈–³/₄ inch diameter, with white ring just under cap that turns green with age.
HABITAT AND SEASON It grows in deciduous woods and forests, often with chestnuts and hazel as well as oak, but not in fields. It is rarely found with conifers. It grows singly, perhaps two to three together. The season is from August until October.

AMANITA MUSCARIA
FLY AGARIC **POISONOUS**

Amanita muscaria, or fly agaric, is perhaps the best-known poisonous mushroom, depicted by illustrators throughout the centuries to conjure up the mysterious world of toadstools. There are stories about this mushroom from all over the world, but the

AMANITA MUSCARIA

AMANITA MUSCARIA

HABITAT AND SEASON Grows from summer through autumn in mixed woodland, preferring birch and pine, and is extremely common.

AMANITA PANTHERINA
PANTHER CAP **POISONOUS**

This mushroom is likened to a panther both because of its spotted cap and because of its potential danger. In fact, it is very dangerous indeed, containing a substance called muscimol (the same as in fly agaric). This has an incubation period of 30 minutes to 2 hours, and the poison causes dizziness, sweating, delirium, and hyperactivity that can last for up to 2 days. If a great many are ingested, the results could be fatal.

AMANITA
PANTHERINA

RECOGNITION

CAP 2¹/₂–4 inches in diameter. Russet-brown to milky coffee color; covered with small, pyramidal, pure white, warty fragments. It can occur in a yellowish form in North America.
GILLS Pure white, unchanging, and crowded. Spore print: white.
STEM 3 inches long. White, tapering at the top, with a membranous white ring and a basal bulb that often splits into two or three rings.
HABITAT AND SEASON One of the most common amanitas in parts of the U.S.; widespread yet uncommon in Britain and Europe. Often found in groups in deciduous and coniferous woodlands from summer to autumn.

AMANITA VERNA
DEADLY POISONOUS

A lethal and deadly mushroom, this could be mistaken for one of the agarics. It contains a substance called amanitin, which produces toxic poisons. These cause severe vomiting and diarrhea for 12 to 24 hours, followed by a brief remission and, finally, the onset of kidney and liver dysfunction or failure. Symptoms appear after 8 to 12 hours, and death usually occurs in 4 to 8 days.

RECOGNITION

CAP 2¹/₂–4¹/₂ inches. White, silken, and sometimes ocher at the center.
GILLS White and crowded. Spore print: white.
STEM 4¹/₂ inches long. White and silky-smooth with a membranous ring. It also has a basal sac or volva.
HABITAT AND SEASON It has a preference for growing in broad-leaved woods, and occurs mainly in the autumn, but can also appear in the spring. Usually found in warmer regions. It is rare in Britain and in North America.

AMANITA VIROSA
DESTROYING ANGEL
DEADLY POISONOUS

The common name says all there is to be said about this beautiful but lethal mushroom. I personally regard this as more dangerous than A. *phalloides*. This is not because it is more poisonous, but because, being all white in color, it could be confused with some white edible mushrooms by a beginner. The poison is very similar to that of A. *phalloides* and it should be avoided with the same meticulous care.

RECOGNITION

CAP White, to 4¹/₂ inches in diameter.
GILLS Crowded and white (distinguishes between this and agaricus species, whose gills are pink, turning brown with age). Spore print: white.
STEM White, with fibrous surface and fragile indefinite ring; to 4¹/₂ inches tall, and ³/₈–⁵/₈ inch in diameter.
HABITAT AND SEASON In mixed or deciduous woods in big groups from late summer through autumn.

AMANITA VIROSA

There are many varied mushrooms in the Armillaria family, poisonous and non-poisonous. The most common are here, and the edible ones must be cooked before ingestion. (See also *Lentinula edodes* in the Cultivated Mushroom section.)

ARMILLARIA MELLEA

HONEY FUNGUS / BOOTLACE FUNGUS **EDIBLE**

I first started to gather *Armillaria mellea* when I was only eight, the beginning of a lifetime passion. A man who worked for my father showed me where to collect "famigliola," the local name for this mushroom, which grows in tight little "family" clusters. The farmers had no objection to my tramping across their land, because the mushrooms I was gathering grew at the base of young trees, and would otherwise have killed them. *A. mellea* is a lethal parasite of most trees, but in particular of the willows that divided the fields and whose supple young branches were perfect for tying up the newly pruned grapevines in spring. It was a great thrill for a young boy to gather the mushrooms, and I would return home with full baskets, proud that I was saving trees as well as contributing to the family larder. My mother always used the mushrooms to make a wonderful meal for us.

In autumn you can always find the inexpensive "famigliole" at markets in Italy and France, alongside the very expensive porcini, ovoli, and tartufi.

The name "honey fungus" describes the color rather than the smell or taste. The mushrooms grow in small, tight clusters, with the caps very close together. The fungus spreads vegetatively by means of black rhizomorphs resembling bootlaces, hence the alternative name. White

ABOVE Armillaria mellea, chunky form; left Armillaria mellea, slender form

etc., and on stumps of trees and submerged roots.

Season Summer through late autumn, later in milder areas. In Britain, I used to look for this mushroom starting on October 15th.

Armillaria tabescens
RINGLESS HONEY FUNGUS **EDIBLE**

This differs from the true honey fungus in that it does not have a ring on the stem. Some also say that it is bitter in taste compared to its cousin *A. mellea*. However, it is quite useful in the kitchen, and when I find it I certainly don't throw it away! The cap is 1$^1/_2$–3$^1/_4$ inches in diameter, and ocher-brown with dark, cottony scales. The gills are whitish, soon becoming pinkish-brown and running down the stem. The spore print is white. The stem is $^3/_8$ inch thick and 4 inches tall. *A. tabescens* is found growing in clusters at the base of deciduous trees, especially oaks, or on dead roots. Season is from late summer through early autumn.

Armillaria
tabescens

gills distinguish honey fungus from its poisonous look-alike, sulfur tuft (*Hypholoma fasciculare*), whose gills are dull sulfur-yellow to greenish.

A distant relation of *A. mellea* is *Lentinula edodes*, the cultivated and highly regarded shiitake.

RECOGNITION

Cap Variable, 1$^1/_2$–8 inches, and hemispherical becoming flattened, with a depressed center. Pale honey-yellow to brown, or ocher to dark brown, with stronger concentration of color at the center. Young specimens usually have a few, rather fibrillose scales in the center.

Gills White, becoming creamy with age; adnate to slightly decurrent. Spore print: creamy-white.

Stem Tall and thin in relation to cap, $^5/_8$ inch in diameter but up to 8 inches tall. White in young specimens, later becoming yellow. Becomes woody with age. Yellow, cottony "ring" just below cap.

Flesh White, with mushroomy but not particularly pleasant smell. Taste is slightly bitter and astringent. (After blanching, both smell and taste improve dramatically.)

Habitat Parasitic, growing in large clusters at the base of deciduous trees, including olive but mainly beech, willow, poplar, mulberry,

Armillaria tabescens

AGROCYBE CYLINDRICA

AGROCYBE CYLINDRICA
(SYN. PHOLIOTA AEGERITA) **EDIBLE**

This mushroom has been popular in Italy for centuries, especially in the south. It is known as the "pioppino" or "piopparello," because it is commonly found at the foot of poplar trees. In the United States, the related *A. acericola* grows near maples. The cap grows from 1/2 inch to 3–4 inches in diameter, and is first semi-round, becoming flatter when mature. The dark brown color of the little heads becomes paler noisette when open, but they are still dark in the center. The gills are quite tight and small, with smaller ones between them. They are whitish when young, becoming darker—to pale brown— with age. The stem is quite meaty and solid, with a strong ring at the top. It is quite tall, up to 6 inches high, and 1/4–5/8 inch in diameter. The flesh is white, smelling slightly of flour. It grows in clusters as above, from springtime through autumn. This mushroom is now being cultivated.

PHOLIOTA MUTABILIS
(SYN. GALERINA MUTABILIS) **EDIBLE**

This is one of the best of the family, and is very similar to *A. mellea*. The cap is 1 1/2–3 1/4 inches in diameter,

brown-cinnamon, dirty, becoming ocher from the center with age and in dry weather. The two colors distinctly zone the cap. It absorbs a lot of moisture. The gills are annexed and tight, and slightly yellow, becoming cinnamon. The spore print is rust-colored. It is not to be confused with *Hypholoma fasciculare*. The stem, up to 2 1/2 inches high and 1/8 inch thick, has a ring, with small scales underneath. The flesh is whitish, with an excellent mushroomy smell. It grows on tree stumps, in large groups, especially in the summer.

PICKING, CLEANING, AND COOKING

Armillaria mellea is really rewarding for collectors, because when you do find it, it is usually in large quantities. When very young and growing tightly together, just detach chunks of the clusters and cut off the bottom part of the stem, which is tough and inedible. When it is more mature and open, just cut off the cap, because the stem will be woody. Wash if it is full of earth, and cut the stems off. You don't need to be too gentle: remember, it is a parasite and endangers the trees it grows on. The same applies to the others in this family.

A. *mellea* is one of my favorite mushrooms to eat with spaghetti. It is delicious sautéed in butter and garlic, and excellent in stews and soups or cooked with other mush-rooms (as are the other members of the family). Good for preserving as a pickle, cooked in vinegar

and kept under oil or put in a jar and sterilized. None of the family is recommended for freezing (apart from *Agrocybe cylindrica*) or drying.

Do not eat any of the edible armillarias raw—they are mildly toxic —but once cooked they are perfectly safe. Blanch for at least 5 minutes at a high temperature, and discard the cooking water.

HYPHOLOMA FASCICULARE

(SYN. NAEMATOLOMA FASCICULARE)
SULFUR TUFT **POISONOUS**

Sulfur tuft is an accurate description for both color and manner of growth. This poisonous mushroom can cause symptoms that vary from a severe stomach upset to death in people with compromised immune systems. Fortunately, its bitter taste is a deterrent to eating any quantities.

Though there are other differences, the simplest and surest way of ascertaining whether a cluster of mushrooms growing on an old stump is the excellent *Armillaria mellea* (honey fungus) or this poisonous mushroom is to look at the gills. In honey fungus these are white; in sulfur tuft they are a dull sulfur-yellow, becoming green with age. There are many more mushrooms that grow in clusters on wood, in

HYPHOLOMA FASCICULARE

HYPHOLOMA FASCICULARE

PHOLIOTA SQUARROSA

similar conditions to those of sulfur tuft and honey fungus, and a good identification guide will describe the others in detail.

RECOGNITION

CAP To 3 inches when fully grown; yellow, with more orangey center; sometimes remains of veil attached to rim.
GILLS Turn from yellow to purplish-green, and finally become dark purplish-brown (the color of the spores).
STEM Thin, $\frac{1}{8}-\frac{1}{2}$ inch in diameter; varying from sulfur-yellow when young to rusty-brown when mature; with slight, insignificant ring zone on upper part of stem.
HABITAT AND SEASON Grows in clusters on old stumps, preferring decaying wood of deciduous trees,

sometimes pine. Occasionally appearing to grow on soil, but in fact on buried stump or root, and is becoming more common in gardens, growing on wood chips. Grows all year round, but most frequent in autumn.

PHOLIOTA SQUARROSA

SHAGGY PHOLIOTA **TOXIC**

This fungus can cause severe gastro-intestinal upsets that generally occur some 30 minutes to 2 hours after ingestion. Symptoms may last for up to 2 days. It could be mistaken for *Armillaria mellea* to the untrained eye. It does seem inviting, I agree, when you see a large group of this mushroom, with its wonderful color, and its

apparently meaty flesh. But, as with many things in life, beauty is not the only consideration. Don't destroy it, because it is useful for insects.

RECOGNITION

CAP 4–6 inches in diameter, fleshy and shaggy with bright russet-brown, upturned scales on ocher background. The margin of the cap remains inrolled.
GILLS Crowded and pale yellow at first, then maturing cinnamon. Spore print: rust brown.
STEM $\frac{5}{8}$ inch thick, 6 inches long. Scaly and like the cap in coloration below a membranous ring. Above the cap, smooth and pale yellow.
HABITAT AND SEASON Found in clusters on the base of living trunks, especially in the autumn.

$^1/_{16}$–$^1/_8$ inch, while the diameter can reach 4 inches. There are no gills or stem. Its color is pale to dark wine or brown.

FLESH This is a gelatinous mushroom. The outside varies from pale to dark brown in color and is almost velvety, while the inside is definitely soft and wet. It doesn't smell particularly of mushroom, but has a certain scent, almost of iron, when just collected.

HABITAT It grows on dead branches of elder trees, sometimes on elm trees, sycamore, ornamental acers, etc., in colonies, one attached to the other.

SEASON All year round, provided there is enough moisture or rain.

PICKING, CLEANING, AND COOKING

The mushrooms can be collected and either used right away or dried. I sometimes collect them when they are dried, shrunken and black, and still attached to the branches, and get them to normal size by leaving them in water for a few hours. Just detach them whole from the tree by hand and cut off the little hard bit where it was attached to the tree. Wash in cold water (they don't absorb much when fresh, unlike when dried!) They very seldom have maggots.

If drying at home, the process is very simple. Check that there are no impurities or insects, then spread the mushrooms on a woven, flat basket-type of container to allow air through —anywhere will do. When completely dry, keep in a linen or cotton sack.

Great care has to be taken when frying the mushrooms in hot oil, because they may literally explode, causing the oil to spatter.

I usually cook it first in stock to give some flavor, and then use it together with other mushrooms in mixed stews or soups. It can also be cut in julienne strips and sprinkled on salads as an exotic addition.

You can buy the dried mushrooms from Asian markets. Let them soak in water for 30–40 minutes before use.

THERE ARE NOT MANY IN THE AURICULARIA FAMILY, BUT THE SINGLE REPRESENTATIVE DISCUSSED HERE IS FOUND ALL OVER EUROPE, AND IS THE LONGEST CULTIVATED AND MOST APPRECIATED FUNGUS IN CHINA.

AURICULARIA JUDAE
JUDAS' EAR / JEW'S EAR / CLOUD EAR **GOOD**

A very curious mushroom indeed. Although it is a Basidiomycete, it doesn't have any pores or gills in which the spores or seeds are produced; instead they are produced on the surface of the fungus. This gelatinous fungus grows in the shape of an ear, usually on stumps and branches of elder trees. This is how it acquired one of its common names: Judas is said to have hanged himself on an elder tree.

The Chinese call it "cloud ear fungus," because it looks like the clouds depicted in Chinese paintings, and "black fungus," because it becomes that color when dry—and it dries very

successfully. When rehydrated from dry it absorbs so much liquid that it completely regains its original shape and texture. Its culinary uses are limited because it is not as flavorsome as other wild mushrooms. However, it has a value for its texture and look, especially in Chinese and Japanese cooking (in which gelatinous textures are more appreciated than in the West). It is the wild counterpart of *A. polytricha*, the oldest cultivated mushroom (see page 83).

RECOGNITION

CAP There is actually no cap—a cup rather, as the shape is that of a human ear, flat and round to oblong, with sections inside. It's soft to the touch, almost like membrane, because inside it is gelatinous. It may be as thick as

THE LARGE BOLETUS FAMILY CONTAINS THE PORCINO OR CEPE (*B. EDULIS*), PROBABLY THE PROTOTYPE MUSHROOM OF IMAGINATION—AS WELL AS THE MOST SOUGHT AFTER—WITH ITS CURVED MEATY CAP AND PLUMP STEM. MOST MEMBERS OF THE FAMILY ARE EDIBLE, BUT A FEW ARE TOXIC, AND ONE IS POISONOUS.

BOLETUS BADIUS

BOLETUS BADIUS
BAY BOLETE **VERY GOOD**

This relative of the more popular *Boletus edulis*—by no means a "poor relation"—is very rewarding, not only for the frequency with which it grows, but also for its versatility in the kitchen. It is found in all European countries with a moderate climate, and in central and northeastern North America. I used to take dried specimens with me when I went back to Italy to visit my family. (Once after a successful "hunt," my wife and I had to make piles of them at the side of the path and pick them up later. We filled the trunk of the car with them, and still left plenty for other people to gather.) My mother always found plenty of uses for them, although her local porcini had—and still have—a more intense flavor. It is called the "bay" bolete because of its color, that of a bay horse, and possibly also because it looks leathery when dry.

Not every year is so productive, but you very often find some of these boletes growing in woodland—especially beneath pines, where the forest floor is relatively free from undergrowth. Sometimes they are difficult to find because of the camouflage of pine needles, cones, and dead branches; sometimes ferns hide the mushrooms beneath their fronds, but where these are not too dense you can brush them aside with your stick. The clue to their whereabouts has been given to me many times by the caps the squirrels leave lying on the forest floor after they have consumed the stems.

I well remember a mushroom foray some years ago in the grounds of Blenheim Palace in England. It was organized by Paul Levy and Roger Phillips. We collected quite a few *Boletus badius* there, but I had brought a big basketful of magnificent specimens with me just in case (I'd raided one of my favorite locations earlier in the day). After the foray I sautéed the mushrooms in butter with garlic and parsley, and we followed this with a wonderful apple pie baked by the late Jane Grigson. It was a day to treasure.

There are a couple of other boletes that are closely related to *B. badius*, and which can be collected and cooked similarly.

BOLETUS BADIUS

RECOGNITION

CAP Nearly spherical at first, almost merging with stem. Very small specimens have a deep brown, velvety sheen, which becomes slippery when wet. When fully grown, cap flattens and color pales to ocherous brown,

BOLETUS CHRYSENTERON

but retains its leathery feeling. When very old, cap tends to curve slightly, particularly at the rim, exposing more of the pores. Diameter usually $4^{1}/_{2}$–$5^{1}/_{2}$ inches, occasionally larger.
PORES Cream to pale yellow in young specimens, turning yellowish-green with age. In older specimens the pores can be seen quite distinctly, and turn blue-green when bruised. Spore print: yellowish-brown.
STEM Usually paler than cap, with vertical streaking; cylindrical, sometimes curved, and tapering at base.
FLESH Firm, creamy white to pale yellow. In mature specimens, turns sky blue when cut or touched. Delicate aroma, and the taste is mushroomy and sweet.
HABITAT Singly on soil, in coniferous and deciduous woodland.
SEASON Midsummer through late autumn. The ideal weather conditions are three to four days after some rain that has followed a warm spell.

BOLETUS CHRYSENTERON
RED-CRACKED BOLETUS **EDIBLE**

This fungus is found quite commonly, but is not so culinarily valued as the other boletes (it must be cooked). The cap is hemispherical then convex, rather irregular, $1^{1}/_{4}$–3 inches in diameter. Very characteristic are the red cracks in the dark brown of the cap. The pores are golden-yellow at the start, becoming green-yellow later, and the spore print is olive-brown. The stem is reddish, very thick ($^{3}/_{8}$–$^{5}/_{8}$ inch), and up to 4 inches high. When a little older, the entire mushroom is quite damp to the touch. The flesh is white-yellow, and under the cuticle is reddish. It smells fruity and has a sweetish taste. It is found under pine and deciduous trees, also in parks; more common in the lowlands than in the mountains. It is good to eat when young, spongier when more mature. Cook it with other mushrooms.

BOLETUS PIPERATUS
(SYN. CHALCIPORUS PIPERATUS)
PEPPERY BOLETE **EDIBLE**

This bolete, one of the smallest in the family, is actually edible, but I think it should only be used in tandem with other mushrooms, to lend a peppery flavor, as the taste is really rather sharp (in many countries it is actually used as a condiment). It should always be cooked. The cap is $1^{1}/_{4}$–$2^{1}/_{2}$ inches in diameter, orange-fawn or rust-colored, hemispheric, and sometimes slightly viscid. The flesh is a lemon-yellow color. The pores are

medium-sized and copper-orange, a deeper color than the cap. The spore print is snuff-brown to cinnamon. The stem is $1^{1}/_{4}$–$2^{1}/_{2}$ inches high and $^{1}/_{4}$ inch thick, concolorous with the cap. It is bright yellow inside when cut. It is often found on sandy soil with conifers, but also with beech and oak trees, and between woods and fields in groups. Common in Europe, from late summer to autumn.

PICKING, CLEANING, AND COOKING

The blue discoloration of the flesh of *Boletus badius* is one of the reasons many people avoid eating this mushroom, believing it to be poisonous, but it is, in fact, quite delicious, especially if your specimens are young, with firm flesh and a fresh aroma. Remember to collect only specimens where the pores under the cap are not too spongy or dark green. You have to inspect older specimens with some care as they can contain maggots, though in general the species is remarkably maggot-free. (As long as there are no maggots in them, the large, older ones are ideal for slicing and drying, see page 96.) Cut the stems near the base with a sharp mushroom knife. You should avoid washing them, because the pores soak up water: just wipe if dirty.

  Boletus badius can be found on the market stalls of most European countries, and its uses are very similar to those of *B. edulis*. Small specimens are delicious eaten raw, sliced very thinly for salads. They also make a wonderful accompaniment to any sort of meat or fish, and are exceptionally good sautéed in butter with garlic and parsley. They can be frozen or pickled, and dried specimens, which have a very delicate and subtle flavor, can be used in all sorts of soups and sauces. *B. badius* is the only one that can be eaten raw.

A GOOD WHOLESOME CROP OF FRESHLY PICKED WILD FUNGI

OF THE BOLETUS FAMILY, *B. EDULIS* IS PROBABLY THE MOST REPRESENTATIVE, AND ALSO THE MOST VALUED THROUGHOUT THE WORLD.

BOLETUS EDULIS

PORCINI / CEPE / KING BOLETE / STEINPILZE **EXCELLENT**

Boletus edulis represents the wild mushroom par excellence—it is what most people mean when they talk about "wild mushrooms." *B. edulis* was popular enough in Victorian Britain to be given a nickname—it was called "penny bun," because of its well-baked color and round shape. The Romans called this mushroom "suillus," the Latin for "pig," a name echoed in the contemporary Italian porcino (or plural porcini). Some say this is because pigs like them, some that the young specimens look like fat little piglets. In Germany, the common name means "stone mushroom"—descriptive like "penny bun"—but in Austria, it is known as "the gentleman's mushroom," and in Sweden, "Karljohan" (from the king).

Some mycophiles may claim to prefer the rare *Amanita caesarea* or the morel, but the porcini remains the safest to collect, the tastiest, and the most rewarding in the kitchen of all wild mushrooms—quite simply, the best. Since it is commercially collected and sold both fresh and dried, it is one of the most sought-after wild mushrooms. Because of the delicacy of its flavor and its versatility, this is the mushroom that the world's leading chefs make most use of, creating many wonderful dishes.

RECOGNITION

CAP At first hemispherical, becoming flatter when mature. Usually 3–8 inches in diameter; occasionally to 12 inches. Cuticle smooth, color varying from pale to dark brown.

PORES Closely packed and off-white at first, turning pale to dark yellowish-green in older specimens, with tubular pore structure clearly visible. Spore print: olive-brown.

STEM In very young specimens stem and cap seem to merge together in almost spherical shape; later, stem grows to club-like shape, slightly broader at base, to 5 inches in diameter. No ring. Sometimes the stem develops larger than the cap, and tends to become riddled with maggots. Color below cap is pale brown, becoming almost white toward base, with surface covering of white reticulum or network. To check that it is not *Tylopilus felleus* (see page 38), put a tiny bit of flesh or stem on your tongue. If it is bitter, discard swiftly.

FLESH In cap, off-white and firm; no discoloration when bruised. Stem flesh whiter, becoming woody and fibrous with age. The aroma is delicate and musty, though less intense in mushrooms found in temperate climates than in those in hotter areas. It has a sweet, nutty, and intensely mushroomy taste (when dried, it is the most perfumed and flavorful of all mushrooms). Sadly, it can be attacked by another fungus, which changes the characteristics of smell and taste.

HABITAT In grass in or near mixed woodland (pine, oak, beech, birch, and chestnut); usually singly, sometimes in groups of two or three. One of the

BOLETUS EDULIS

BOLETUS EDULIS

thick and 3–6 inches high). The surface of the stem is creamy with a network of lines. It grows in mixed deciduous woods, from the center of Europe and south, appearing from May until October.

BOLETUS AESTIVALIS
(SYN. B. RETICULATUS)
SUMMER BOLETE **EXCELLENT**

This bolete is as good as *B. edulis*, but is often riddled with maggots. The cap is 4–8 inches in diameter, pale brown with a mat surface. This is often covered with a cracked network, especially when more mature or the weather is dry, which is why its synonym is "reticulatus." The pores are white then greenish-yellow, small, and round. The spore print is olive, becoming snuff-brown with age. The stem is 1 inch thick and 6 inches high, spindle-shaped, and reddish-brown, covered in a fine white network from the cap to the base. The flesh is white and has a sweetish taste. It grows mainly with beech and oak, from very early summer to autumn. It fruits earlier than *B. edulis*.

most likely places is along a golf course, especially where the fairways are bordered with heather that in turn gives on to woodland. I have found porcini on pure sand and on bare soil—but never far from the roots of at least one of the trees that are supposed to nurture them.
SEASON Early summer to first frosts. Many Italians believe firmly that the mushrooms appear at the time of the new moon. I am much more scientific than that. . . .

BOLETUS AEREUS
EXCELLENT

Many Italians think this is the best of the boletes, even better than *B. edulis*. The scientific name comes from the Latin for "bronze," for from the very earliest stages the cap is a very dark

brown, almost black (in Italian it is known as "porcino nero"). The cap is 2½–8 inches, convex, flattening when mature. The dark coloring has paler zones, and the surface is slightly velvety, not too dry. The pores are grayish-white at the beginning, becoming yellow with maturity. The spore print is olive-brown. The stem is hard and bulbous, becoming elongated (1¼–2½ inches

BOLETUS AEREUS

PICKING, CLEANING, AND COOKING

Hold the stem near the base and twist to ease it away from the mycelium. If you cut it free with a knife there is said to be a danger that the part left in the ground will rot and destroy the mycelium, thus preventing any more fruit-bodies from growing in that same spot. Do use your knife, though, in order to clean the dirt from the stem base before you put the mushroom in your basket.

Don't peel porcini and their close relations, and certainly don't wash them—just wipe off any dirt. Some people discard the pores if they have become soft. Cut larger mushrooms in half to check for maggots. If you intend drying them, don't let a few maggots worry you: they will just disappear when the porcini are sliced and dried. Dry the bits and pieces as well as the good slices, to make into savory powder (see page 97). To avoid the larvae hatching eventually into moths (which can happen, amazingly, even after drying), keep your dried mushrooms— home-dried or bought—in the freezer.

Smaller specimens are suitable for pickling and freezing as well as cooking fresh, and can be thinly sliced and eaten raw in salads. Whole caps of mature porcini are good grilled, as in Italy. The older specimens are best sliced and fried or used in stews and sauces. Porcini are excellent dried, and give a very distinctive aroma to sauces and stews; adding a small quantity to blander mushrooms enhances their flavor immensely and is an economical way of using expensive bought dried porcini. See page 96 for information on how to dry mushrooms.

BOLETUS SATANAS

BOLETUS SATANAS
SATAN'S BOLETE **POISONOUS**

Fortunately this undesirable representative of the large family of delicious boletes is decidedly rare, and its distinguishing characteristics are so distinctive that there is little chance of making a mistake. Its appearance— especially when young, when it is very solid and bulbous—is similar to *Boletus barrowsii* or whiteking bolete, a form of *B. edulis* found in North America growing under oaks. Another similar fungus is *B. rhodoxanthus*.

Boletus satanas is said by some people to be edible after a long cooking process has destroyed the toxins, but what is the point of risking severe stomach upsets when you can safely eat the other species? Generally I would advise you to leave alone any red-pored bolete you find that bruises blue. Also avoid *Boletus calopus*, a close relation. This bolete is not poisonous in the lethal sense, but— like *Tylopilus felleus*—it is inedible due to its bitterness, which does not disappear on cooking.

RECOGNITION

CAP At first off-white, becoming gray or greenish-gray; at first round, becoming flat and sometimes cracked with age; to 12 inches in diameter.
PORES Very tightly packed, at first deep red becoming orange later, especially around the rim; turning bluish-green when bruised.
STEM Enlarged below and onion-shaped; can reach 3 inches in diameter even when young, sometimes being fatter than the cap. Saffron-orange to bright lemon-yellow above, but red toward the base and with a red network, especially on upper half.
FLESH Straw-color in the cap, paler to whitish or lemon-yellow in the stem, changing to sky blue.
HABITAT AND SEASON Grows beneath trees such as beech and oak from late summer through autumn; solitary, or in small groups of three or four.

TYLOPILUS FELLEUS
(SYN. BOLETUS FELLEUS)
BITTER BOLETE **NOT EDIBLE**

This bolete is not strictly poisonous, but it is so terribly bitter that including a specimen in a dish will spoil the whole thing. The possibility of mistaking it for *Boletus edulis* is more likely to occur in younger specimens, but if the mushroom is a little more mature, then the pink pores of *Tylopilus felleus* will distinguish it from *B. edulis*, which has creamy-white pores. When people bring me mushrooms to identify, this is very often the most common one in their baskets.

After going through all the identification points below, as a last resort, taste a little piece of the cap (and then spit it out). If it is very bitter then it is definitely *T. felleus*, and you will have to throw it away.

RECOGNITION

CAP At first round, becoming flat later; light brown, and to 4$\frac{1}{2}$ inches in diameter.
PORES Off-white in very young specimens, becoming pink with age and bruising brownish.
STEM Sturdy and fleshy; diameter to 1$\frac{1}{4}$ inches at top and 2$\frac{1}{2}$ inches at base; to 4$\frac{1}{2}$ inches tall. Net pattern on stem surface is another major identification point, particularly in comparison with *Boletus edulis*.

T. felleus has a dark brown net pattern over a lighter background, while *B. edulis* has a white net pattern over a slightly darker background.
HABITAT AND SEASON In conifer and deciduous woods, summer to autumn.

THREE OF THE CANTHARELLUS FAMILY
ARE PARTICULARLY WELL-KNOWN.
C. CIBARIUS IS PROBABLY THE MOST
SOUGHT-AFTER MUSHROOM IN
GASTRONOMY, AND *C. LUTESCENS* AND
C. TUBIFORMIS ARE EXCELLENT TO EAT
AS WELL.

CANTHARELLUS CIBARIUS

CHANTERELLE / GIROLLE /
PFIFFERLING **EXCELLENT**

The delicate aroma of apricots and
wonderful golden-yellow color make
the chanterelle a beautiful and graceful
mushroom. Like *Boletus edulis* and
B. badius, this is one of the most
popular edible wild mushrooms, well
known to leading chefs all over the
world. The French love these mushrooms
particularly, epitomized in their
Omelette aux Girolles (they call
C. cibarius "girolle," and apply the name
"chanterelle" to the two others). The
color, texture, and shape of *Cantharellus
cibarius* are unique, and in North America
there is a look-alike of a deep blue
color (*Polyzellus*). Can you imagine what
a wonderfully exotic sight a dish with
both colors would make? (Incidentally,
there is also a black version, *C. cinereus*.)

My wife, Priscilla, is a natural
chanterelle detector when we are out
on forays, and usually spots them long

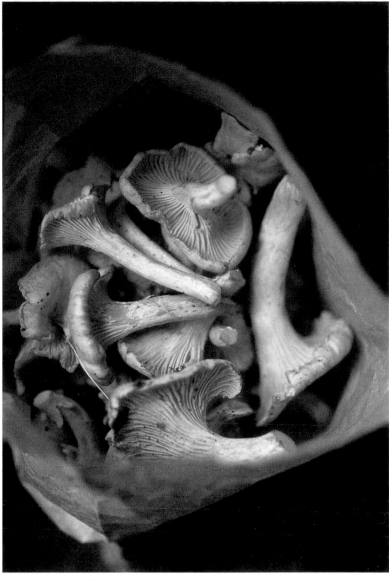

ABOVE AND BELOW CANTHARELLUS CIBARIUS

before I do, even in autumn when the
task is made more difficult by the
yellow and brown leaves that have
fallen from the birch trees. It is a fairly
common mushroom, especially in
Scotland, where I believe that they
sometimes literally cover the ground.
I have heard of many young boys
who increase their allowance quite
substantially in the season by
collecting large quantities and sending
them to France, where people are
prepared to pay a great deal of money
to enjoy them. Sometimes the woods
are bright yellow with them, as they
grow so gregariously, especially in

Scotland (and in North America). I still remember with sorrow, every time I drive that way, watching my best chanterelle ground disappearing beneath the ferocious teeth of an excavator preparing for a highway.

RECOGNITION

CAP In small specimens at first convex and minute, becoming funnel-shaped when mature, with thin and irregular rim. To 3 inches in diameter. Deep yolk-yellow to pale yellow in color, fading with age.

GILLS Resembling irregular branching folds or veins, decurrent from top almost to base of stem. Not crowded, quite irregular. Concolorous with cap. Spore print: pale yellow.

STEM Thick and wide ($^3/_4$–$1^1/_4$ inches), tapering toward base to form narrow lower part of funnel; up to $2^1/_2$ inches tall.

FLESH Pale yellow and firm, with a peppery taste. Fresh smell, faintly of apricots. No discoloring on bruising and usually maggot-free.

HABITAT In mixed woods, often among moss, solitarily or in groups on soil.

SEASON Summer to late autumn, later in milder areas. Wait to collect after rain has fallen.

CANTHARELLUS CIBARIUS

CANTHARELLUS
LUTESCENS

**CANTHARELLUS
LUTESCENS**
VERY GOOD

**CANTHARELLUS
TUBIFORMIS**
VERY GOOD

These two Cantharellus members are extremely easy to find in northern Europe and North America. They are the so-called autumn alternative to the normal chanterelle (in Italian, known as "giallo'"or "finferla"). The dark brown caps are $^3/_4$–$2^1/_2$ inches in diameter, trumpet-like in shape. The stems are 2–3 inches tall, and both are yellow: bright in *C. lutescens*, less bright in *C. tubiformis*. The gills are quite pale: almost yellow in *C. lutescens*, yellow-gray in *C. tubiformis*. The flesh is not very meaty, quite thin in fact, but excellent to eat. *C. lutescens* has a beautiful fruity smell, unlike *C. tubiformis*. They grow abundantly and gregariously under conifers, mostly in moss, from summer to late autumn.

PICKING, CLEANING, AND COOKING

Cut these mushrooms at the base with a sharp mushroom knife. They can be pulled as well, but then cut off the earthy part before putting them in the basket. Because they lose some of their flavor if washed, I suggest you clean them thoroughly with a brush when you collect them, to prevent sand or grit from getting lodged in the gills.

All these mushrooms are very versatile, and the color of the chanterelle is a fabulous decorative addition for a recipe. It is always good if eaten fresh, but also keeps well in a refrigerator for up to four or five days, in a basket covered with a damp cloth. It can be eaten raw, but its rather peppery taste disappears when it is cooked. It tastes at its best with scrambled eggs and is excellent for sauces; it can also be used in soups and stews. It is good for pickling, but does not freeze or dry satisfactorily.

OMPHALOTUS OLEARIUS

OMPHALOTUS OLEARIUS

(SYN. CLITOCYBE OLEARIA)

DEADLY POISONOUS

This poisonous look-alike of the chanterelle is fortunately rare in Britain and North America (I have never seen it myself), and only occasional in central and southern Europe. In Mediterranean countries it generally grows on olive trees—hence the name "olearius"—though when seen in America or Britain, it grows on hardwood stumps. If in springtime you visit a country where olive trees grow, don't get too excited by the sight of these mushrooms: they are not chanterelles—close inspection should show you the difference—and they should be left alone.

RECOGNITION

CAP The size of *Omphalotus olearius* is much greater than that of true chanterelles: it can reach 6 inches in diameter. From dark orange to bright yellow, as in the chanterelle. Convex in the center, with margin inrolled.
GILLS Very tight, unlike chanterelles, and concolorous with the cap. Incidentally, this mushroom may be seen glowing in the dark—mature specimens have phosphorescent gills.
STEM Meaty, 6–8 inches tall, and tapering toward the base.
FLESH A bit thin, and saffron-yellow, darkening with age.
HABITAT AND SEASON The fact that it grows on trees is the final disqualifying factor in its comparison with the chanterelle. It grows in groups and clumps at the base of stumps of various broad-leaved trees, especially olives. The season is summer to first frosts.

HYGROPHOROPSIS AURANTIACA

FALSE CHANTERELLE **NOT EDIBLE**

This was originally classified as poisonous, was later declared edible, but recent findings tell us that ingestion of a large amount can cause digestive complaints. Beginners often mistake this common mushroom for the true chanterelle, *Cantharellus cibarius*. It is a worthless look-alike.

RECOGNITION

CAP To 2$^1/_2$ inches in diameter, varying from orange-yellow to darker orange in the center. Margin at first inrolled, then flat.
GILLS Concolorous with cap; decurrent, as in the true chanterelle, but finer, and not extending so far down the stem.
STEM Less funnel-shaped than in the true chanterelle; concolorous with cap or slightly darker; to 2 inches tall.
FLESH Not as substantial as in true chanterelles.
HABITAT AND SEASON Grows in late summer and autumn in mixed wood-land, preferring conifers.

HYGROPHOROPSIS AURANTIACA

FROM THE SAME FAMILY AS CANTHARELLUS, CRATERELLUS (ONCE ACTUALLY KNOWN AS CANTHARELLUS) HAS MANY DIFFERENCES.

CRATERELLUS CORNUCOPIOIDES
HORN OF PLENTY / BLACK TRUMPET **VERY GOOD**

Of all the names for this mushroom, I like the English "horn of plenty" best. This fragile mushroom does indeed look like a cornucopia—or, perhaps, a trumpet—but it is black instead of gold. Most of the other descriptions sound too funereal to suit the mushroom. Although it is indeed gray to black in color, it has none of the connotations of death that so many of the names suggest—"trompette de la mort" in French; "trombetta dei morti" in Italian. It is, in fact, a very good and tasty mushroom that can be widely used in cooking. There is no edible or poisonous counterpart.

When I first introduced it on the menu in my restaurant, clients were somewhat reluctant to eat it because of its black color. Now, however, it has become a firm favorite, especially in dishes with a delicate white fish such as halibut, sole, or monkfish.

RECOGNITION

CAP Very similar to the bell end of a trumpet: deeply funnel-shaped, with irregularly lobed and wavy margins; initially pale brown, then gray, and finally black. To 4 inches in diameter.
GILLS Almost non-existent; the forming of spores takes place on the hymenium situated on the ridged outer sides of the tubular stem. When ripe, the pores color the stem white to gray, giving a velvety sheen.
STEM An irregular tube $3/8 - 3/4$ inch in diameter and up to $4^1/2$ inches tall, with very thin walls.
FLESH Externally gray, turning black when wet; internally darker gray. This mushroom is not very fleshy because of its thin, cartilaginous, and fragile

walls. A distinctive pleasant smell and particularly delicate taste and texture—in fact, it is known in some parts of Italy as the "poor man's truffle."
HABITAT Gregarious in leaf litter, especially in frondose woods, but preferring the presence of oak and occasionally beech. Don't forget to mark on your map where you first find them, because they usually grow in the same spot every year.
SEASON Summer through late autumn. Don't collect it on rainy days, but wait until the sun comes out.

PICKING, CLEANING, AND COOKING

The best way to collect it is to cut with a knife at the base. Pay maximum attention to cleaning these mushrooms, as small insects and other impurities

find their way deep into the funnel. If they are not dislodged by shaking, it may be best to cut the mushrooms lengthwise to clean them. This is one instance of a mushroom where washing is possible if the specimens are particularly dirty, but dry well with a cloth before using.

The horn of plenty is ideal for sophisticated dishes requiring its black color and delicate taste. It is delicious just sautéed in butter with parsley and chives, excellent for sauces, and also very good in soups and stews. It is not recommended for freezing unless first cooked in butter. Ideal for drying and reducing to powder, which is then used to improve the flavor of sauces. It is not particularly good for pickling, nor does it keep very long in its fresh state as it tends to dry out and become rather leathery.

CRATERELLUS CORNUCOPIOIDES

COPRINUS COMATUS

COPRINUS IS A SMALL GROUPING IN THE AGARIC FAMILY, OF WHICH ONLY ONE MEMBER, WHEN YOUNG, OFFERS GOOD EATING. THE TASTE AND FLAVOR OF *C. COMATUS* IS NOT DISSIMILAR TO MEADOW MUSHROOMS.

COPRINUS COMATUS

SHAGGY INK CAP / LAWYER'S WIG / SHAGGY MANE **GOOD**

The shape of *Coprinus comatus* always reminds me of the bearskins the guards wear at Buckingham Palace. Once I glimpsed a glorious troop of the mushrooms growing in luxuriously rich grass just outside the main gate of an army barracks, looking as if they were standing on guard. I stopped my car far too suddenly (a hazard of fungus collecting, I'm afraid), and started to collect the mushrooms, much to the astonishment of the onlooking drivers behind me and the genuine soldiers on guard.

The various English names appropriately describe different characteristics. The scales on the cap indeed resemble the curls on an English lawyer's wig, and the cap has a tendency to deliquesce into a black fluid, which in past ages was used as a source of writing ink.

This mushroom is a very delicate-tasting member of the Agaric family and, in my opinion, is perhaps underestimated by chefs. I have cooked it frequently over the years, with excellent results, and I find it quite versatile. Only the small specimens are of any value, while the gills are still white; once the cap and gills start to darken, the mushroom is of no use.

RECOGNITION

CAP Acutely ovate or cylindric in young specimens, growing $1^{1}/_{2}$–6 inches tall and $^{3}/_{8}$–$2^{1}/_{2}$ inches in diameter, closed toward the stem; the white cuticle is covered in large white scales with brownish tips, with a touch of light brown at the top. As the mushroom matures, the cap opens to a bell shape and the off-white cuticle becomes first gray and then black from

ABOVE AND BELOW COPRINUS COMATUS

later in milder areas. This mushroom can go from button to deliquescence in two days, even less in warmer conditions.

PICKING, CLEANING, AND COOKING

Cut the stem of small, firm specimens where the cap is still closed around the stem, using a sharp mushroom knife. Mature specimens would be too mushy in texture, and the ink would color black everything with which it came into contact. The caps quickly open out and mature once cut, so do not keep them too long. To avoid this you can pull the stem from the cap. If you are not able to use them straightaway, I suggest blanching them so they can be kept for a bit longer. You can wash closed caps to remove sand.

Coprinus comatus is simply delicious however you prepare it. Deep-fry the smaller "buttons" after dipping them in beaten egg and rolling them in bread crumbs. They are very good for stews, soups, and sauces, and for sautéing in butter with chives and parsley. The lack of a distinct flavor/aroma means they are not really suitable for the freezing or drying processes.

the rim upward, as auto-digestion takes place and the cap turns to an inky black pulp.

GILLS In young specimens visible only by cutting the cap lengthwise. Very crowded and tightly packed. At first white, turning pink, then gray, and finally black. Spore print: brownish-black.

STEM Long, thin, and hollow ($3/8$–$2^1/2$ inches in diameter and up to 10 inches tall). White. Membrane protecting young gills remains on the stem in the form of an irregular ring, or breaks loose and falls to the base.

FLESH When very young the stem and cap form a sturdy body with very

firm, delicate white flesh. Smell and taste very fresh and mushroomy, not dissimilar to that of old meadow mushrooms. Much to the delight of the gatherer, insect larvae do not seem to infest this mushroom, as the caps disappear too quickly and the stem is hollow.

HABITAT Occasionally isolated, but usually gregarious—sometimes in huge groups. Occurs almost anywhere—on hard soil along country lanes and bridleways; where soil has been disturbed; on lawns and in fields.

SEASON Summer through late autumn, especially in warm weather,

COPRINUS ATRAMENTARIUS
DARK FLAKY INK CAP TOXIC

Although it is edible when young, I am listing this mushroom as toxic because of its violent reaction when consumed with alcohol (this has been known to lead to death). Nausea, palpitations, and hot flashes not only can occur when beer, wine, or liquor are drunk at or just after the same meal, but to some extent are likely if alcohol is taken at the next meal, some hours later. Indeed, a chemical substance with similar properties is used to treat alcoholics. I strongly advise that you avoid collecting this mushroom.

It has an inky cap like *Coprinus comatus*, but the two are easy to distinguish.

COPRINUS ATRAMENTARIUS

COPRINUS TRAMENTARIUS

RECOGNITION

CAP At first ovate, then conical when mature; color grayish, brownish toward the top, growing darker with age and blackening at margin when autodigestion takes place (as with *C. comatus*).
GILLS At first white, turning gray and then inky-black with autodigestion.
STEM To 6 inches tall; thin (only $^3/_8$–$^3/_4$ inch in diameter); hollow.

HABITAT AND SEASON Grows gregariously in tight clusters on stumps near cultivated areas, on lawns, in gardens, and along roads, from late spring through late autumn.

COPRINUS PICACEUS
MAGPIE INK CAP NOT EDIBLE

A member of the ink-cap family, this is not regarded as being edible. In fact, it is slightly unpleasant to eat. Young specimens may resemble *C. comatus* because of the similarity of the cap shape.

RECOGNITION

CAP $1^1/_2$–$2^1/_2$ inches in diameter, oval in shape becoming bell-shaped. White, then gray, and finally black spotted with white patches.
GILLS White, then pinkish, and finally black, when they rapidly dissolve to an inky fluid. The spore print is black.
STEM 3 inches, whitish, fleecy with a woolly, bulbous base.
HABITAT AND SEASON It usually grows with beech from late summer through autumn in little shaded groups, in the Midwest of the United States.

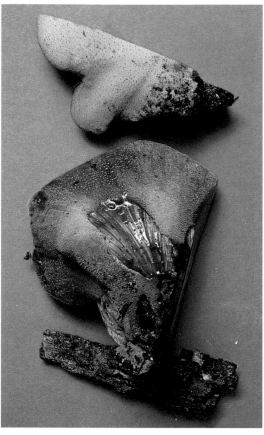

FISTULINA HEPATICA

OF THE MANY BRACKET FUNGI OR POLYPORES
(SO-CALLED FOR THE MANY PORES ON THE
UNDERSIDE OF THE CAP, FROM WHICH THE
SPORES ARE RELEASED), ONLY A FEW ARE
EDIBLE. *FISTULINA HEPATICA* IS ONE.

FISTULINA HEPATICA
BEEFSTEAK FUNGUS / OX TONGUE
VERY GOOD

Most polypores have a destructive
effect on the trees they parasitize, but
there are fringe benefits. As well as
being appreciated gastronomically,
Fistulina hepatica produces a
particularly fine coloration of the oak
wood on which it usually grows and
which it eventually destroys. This rich
mahogany-red coloration is valued by
furniture-makers.

Bracket fungi are so named
because they look like a bracket or
shelf attached to the tree from which
they obtain their nutrition. Hunting

mushrooms does not always mean
keeping your nose and eyes to the
ground: although these mushrooms
are sometimes found at the base of
the trunk, they can grow anywhere on
the host tree, so I'm afraid you will
have to look a bit higher from time to
time. See also *Laetiporus sulphureus*,
page 53, another fine example of a
bracket fungus.

RECOGNITION

CAP To 14 inches in diameter and
$2^1/_2$–3 inches thick. It is broadly
tongue-shaped and, when young, is
very soft and juicy with minute warts
covering the top of the cap. Color is
brick-red, so the whole is very similar
in appearance to an ox tongue.
Margin rounded at first, becoming
thinner and very sticky as it ages.
PORES Pinkish, closely packed.
Pores visible and separate (unlike
most polypores where they are fused
together), bruising darker when
touched. Spore print: yellowish-pink.
STEM Either sessile, or attached by
a short, thick, almost indiscernible
stem.
FLESH When cuticle is peeled away,
flesh appears wet and of a brilliant
red that deepens with age. Cutting
reveals pale pink, veinous streaks
similar to some steak (hence "poor
man's meat" or "liver"); flesh is heavy
for its size and extremely succulent.

Aroma pleasant, strong, and mushroomy; taste slightly sour when raw.
HABITAT Deciduous woodland;
prefers oak, sometimes sweet chestnut;
on living trees or stumps. Sometimes
singly, sometimes in small clumps.
SEASON Late summer through late
autumn. It does not need particular
weather conditions, because it gets
its nourishment from the living tree.

PICKING, CLEANING, AND COOKING

Just cut it off at the base where it is
attached. As the fungus grows on
trees it is usually fairly free from dirt
and will just need brushing off. Don't
collect sticky old specimens, which
will be dry inside.

I have spent many years trying to
find ways of using this mushroom in
the kitchen, as it is full of proteins and
vitamins. Because it can be slightly
sour-tasting, I once advised that it
should always be cooked, to remove
possible bitterness and ensure
digestibility, but very succulent young
specimens can be used raw in salads
(see page 120). The fungus is similar
to real meat in texture, and so it can
be prepared as such.

Fistulina hepatica turns black when
cooked, because of its acidity. Take this
into account when cooking—it makes
a good accompaniment to fatty or rich
food such as sweetbreads or brains.

FISTULINA
HEPATICA

GRIFOLA FRONDOSA

GRIFOLA IS A SUB-SPECIES OF THE MERIPILUS OR POLYPORUS FAMILY, TO WHICH THE GIANT POLYPORE AND THE DRYAD'S SADDLE BELONG (SEE PAGE 69). OF THE MANY POLYPORES, THESE ARE THE MOST DELICATE. THEY ARE NOT VERY COMMON, AND ARE UNDERGOING INTENSE STUDY FOR THE PURPOSES OF COMMERCIAL CULTIVATION (SEE PAGE 84).

GRIFOLA FRONDOSA

HEN OF THE WOODS **EDIBLE**

When you talk about "chicken of the woods" (*Laetiporus* or *Polyporus sulphureus*, see page 53), you have to ask yourself if there is an equivalent "hen of the woods." Indeed there is, and it is one of the best wild mushrooms when young. It is also one of the most satisfying and exciting mushrooms in the wild, because when you find it, it is usually large and round, and really resembles a brooding hen sitting on her eggs! The word "frondosa," from "fronda" ("leaf" in Italian/Latin), denotes that these special mushrooms grow from one stem, expanding in many leafy lobes, one on top of the other. Because *Grifola frondosa* is a polypore, it has pores, not gills. It is found in most northern regions, in forests from eastern North America to Europe and Asia. The Japanese have learned how to cultivate it, as "maitake" (see page 84), which makes it more accessible to markets throughout the world.

RECOGNITION

CAP There isn't actually a cap, as the fruit-body consists of hundreds of leafy lobes that grow from a many-branched nucleus attached to the tree. The cuticle, which is smooth, is of a brown to gray color, with darker circles. It develops pale and dark stripes as it matures.

PORES White, not too tight, round, and 1/8 inch long. Spore print: white.

STEM The supporting stem to the cluster of "leaves," which grow like a fan, is thick and tender when young, of a white color. It can reach a height of 12 inches and a diameter of 8–20 inches. Tender when quite young, chewy when older.

FLESH White and dense, slightly fibrous when old. Smells of wheat flour, becoming cheesy when old.

HABITAT On stumps or at the base of dead or dying hardwoods like elm,

the ground by the roots of broad-leaved trees, especially oak, willow, and beech. It is uncommon in North America.

PICKING, CLEANING, AND COOKING

Cut with a sharp mushroom knife, check for insects, and brush clean before cooking. They could actually be washed as well, because they take up so many impurities from the soil. Both are excellent mushrooms, beloved by chefs, but should not be eaten raw. They can be sautéed with egg and bread crumbs, stewed, and even preserved. One specimen can serve five to six people.

ABOVE AND BELOW GRIFOLA FRONDOSA

oak, beech, maple, or even pine.
SEASON Early summer through autumn. These mushrooms don't need very wet weather to grow (although it helps), as they draw moisture from the tree.

GRIFOLA UMBELLATA
(SYN. POLYPORUS UMBELLATUS)
EDIBLE

This edible fungus is very similar to, and could be mistaken for, *Grifola frondosa*. However, it is very rare, and authorities in Europe suggest it should not be collected. It is used in China as a stimulant for the immune system. The fruit-body—as with *G. frondosa*, this is more descriptive than "cap"—can be up to 20 inches in diameter. A thick, fleshy base gives rise to numerous umbrella-like caps, each $1^1/_2$–$2^1/_2$ inches. They are gray-brown in color and covered in small scales when young, fading to beige with age. The pores are angular and whitish, and running down the stem. The spore print is white. The many-branched stems are white, very thin, and merging into a common base. It grows on

THE LARGE HYDNUM FAMILY HAS ONE DISTINGUISHING CHARACTERISTIC: INSTEAD OF GILLS OR PORES UNDER THE CAP, THERE ARE THOUSANDS OF LITTLE SPINES. OF ALL THE HYDNUMS, THESE TWO ARE THE EDIBLE ONES. MOST OF THE OTHERS ARE COMPLETELY INEDIBLE, EVEN EXTREMELY ACIDIC AND EMETIC, SO BE SURE TO GET IT RIGHT!

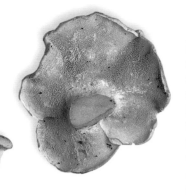

ABOVE RIGHT HYDNUM REPANDUM

HYDNUM REPANDUM

(SYN. DENTINUM REPANDUM) SPREADING HEDGEHOG MUSHROOM **GOOD**

This excellent mushroom, found throughout North America and Europe, has one distinctive characteristic: instead of gills or pores, which most other edible mushrooms have, the spore-producing hymenophore consists of spines pointing downward from the underside of the cap—hence the name "hedgehog." It is also known as "sweet tooth." As far as texture and taste are concerned, it is very similar in character to the chanterelle. It is quite common and relatively easy to find, even in seasons when other mushrooms may not be so plentiful. Because of its spines, this mushroom is one of the easiest to recognize. There are similar mushroom species with spines, but with darker coloring, making the "hedgehog" quite easy to distinguish.

HYDNUM REPANDUM

RECOGNITION

CAP Irregular, very fleshy, brittle, convex to fat; from almost white through pale yellow to orange, depending on location. Up to 6 inches in diameter. Cuticle very smooth, not viscid, but with a suede-like quality.
SPINES Very crowded, growing perpendicular to the underside of cap, decurrent, reaching up to $^1/_4$ inch. Extremely fragile, breaking at slightest touch. Usually concolorous with cap. Spore print: white.
STEM Large, more pronounced toward the base, often eccentric to cap. Surface smooth and color paler than rest of mushroom. To 3 inches high and $1^1/_2$ inches in diameter.
FLESH Fleshy and quite firm, but brittle; whitish yellow, and slightly bitter in taste: when cooked, bitterness disappears and mushroom is tasty with pleasant aroma. Smell pleasant and gently mushroomy.
HABITAT Gregarious, sometimes in rings or strips, under trees in coniferous or broad-leaved woodland.
SEASON Midsummer through late autumn in mild weather.

SARCODON IMBRICATUM

(SYN. HYDNUM IMBRICATUM) SHINGLED HEDGEHOG / SCALY TOOTH **EDIBLE**

Although this relation of *H. repandum* is edible, it is not much sought after because of its bitterness. Its cap is 4–10 inches in diameter, covered in coarse, gray-brown scales raised at the tip, on a pale russet cap that becomes funnel-shaped. The spines run down the stem, up to $^1/_2$ inch long; tight, decurrent, and whitish, darkening with age to brown. The spore print is brown. The stem is 3 inches tall and $^3/_4$ inch thick, whitish, becoming gray-brownish with age. The flesh is dirty white, becoming a pale sepia. Solid, but chewy. The smell becomes strong with maturity, and the taste is sour and bitter. It is found in coniferous woods, especially on sandy soils, late summer to autumn. Abundant in North American and European ancient woods.

SARCODON IMBRICATUM

PICKING, CLEANING, AND COOKING

Just cut at the base with a sharp knife. *H. repandum* is one of the mushrooms least likely to be infested with maggots, and is easily cleaned with a scrape of a knife or a light brushing. It can be kept in the refrigerator for a few days.

Younger specimens are very rewarding, as the whole mushroom can be used, including the spines; in older specimens the spines should be removed, as they can add to the bitterness. Both should always be cooked before eating, to remove any hint of bitterness. They can be eaten by themselves, stewed or fried in butter with onions, and also with other mushrooms. The flesh of *H. repandum* is firmer than that of the chanterelle, making it good for drying and using later in sauces and soups. It is also excellent pickled, and once cooked can be frozen. *Sarcodon imbricatum* is not a mushroom for gourmets, but is useful cooked in a mixture.

THERE ARE NOT MANY MEMBERS OF THE LACCARIA FAMILY, BUT OF THE MANY SMALL, EDIBLE MUSHROOMS YOU MIGHT FIND WHEN MUSHROOM HUNTING, THIS IS THE BEST FOR ME.

MYCENA PURA

LACCARIA AMETHYSTEA

AMETHYST DECEIVER **GOOD**

This is a much underrated mushroom so far as cooking is concerned, perhaps because of its color, but it is one that gives me great pleasure, both in collecting and cooking. It is very small and delicate, but I actually love it for its color! It is said to "deceive" because the fruit-body changes color as it ages. Alternatively, you could use *L. laccata,* a reddish-brown relation, which is edible.

ABOVE AND BELOW LACCARIA AMETHYSTEA

RECOGNITION

CAP Very small, ¹/₂–3 inches in diameter. Bright amethyst-violet in color, but fading with age and drying to a pale lilac-buff. Sometimes scurfy at the center.
GILLS Distant and irregular, at first bright violet, but becoming powdery white with age. Spore print: white.
STEM To 3¹/₄ inches tall and ³/₈ inch in diameter, concolorous with the cap. The base is covered with lilac down.
FLESH Tender and delicate in young specimens. The taste is sweet; there is no significant smell.
HABITAT Coniferous and deciduous woods, usually with beech, in many small groups. (*L. laccata* will be found everywhere there are trees, from sea coasts to mountain tops, where it grows with dwarf willows.)
SEASON Late summer to early winter.

PICKING, CLEANING, AND COOKING

Just cut at the base, and brush off any soil. I usually use both *L. amethystea* and *L. laccata* as an addition to salads—where they can be eaten raw—or for any dishes I want to embellish. They lack culinary quality and so are best used in a mixture of mushrooms, but *L. amethystea* goes especially well with the yellow of chanterelles.

MYCENA PURA

INEDIBLE

Although once described as edible, this small mushroom is now thought to contain cumulative toxins, which, if eaten regularly, can cause immune deficiencies. It has also been said to be hallucinogenic. I should try to avoid it. It can resemble *Laccaria amethystea*, but is generally much paler.

RECOGNITION

CAP ³/₄–2 inches in diameter. Purple to pale lilac and lined at the margin when wet.
GILLS White fading to pink. Smelling of radish. Spore print: white.
STEM 2¹/₂ inches tall and ¹/₄ inch thick, concolorous with the cap. It is also tough, leathery, and hairy at the base.
HABITAT AND SEASON Gregarious in all types of woodland. Growing in leaf litter and moss from summer to winter.

As the names "Lactarius" and "milk cap" suggest, the members of this genus exude a milky substance when broken or cut; this liquid may be white or colored, or may turn wine-colored or orange, depending on species.

RIGHT AND BELOW LACTARIUS DELICIOSUS

LACTARIUS DELICIOSUS
SAFFRON MILK CAP **EXCELLENT**

Two major features clearly distinguish *L. deliciosus* from other members of the family: the milky fluid exuded immediately becomes a deep reddish-orange, and the saffron-orange flesh slowly turns green when bruised.

There are many other edible species of Lactarius, especially in North America (around 200), ranging from purple to indigo-blue in color, but in Europe, *L. deliciosus* is one of the few considered worth collecting. Many people, including the French, Germans, Poles, Swedes, and Russians feel passionately about this mushroom. I love it for its nutty taste and firm texture, but above all for the brilliant color, which looks wonderful in special dishes. Timothy Neath, my "Scottish man," supplies me in season with wonderful specimens of milk caps, porcini, wood blewits, and chanterelles—and occasionally sends me some wonderful candles, made with pure beeswax collected from his own hives.

When collecting, take extra care not to confuse this mushroom with the poisonous *L. torminosus* (see page 52).

RECOGNITION

CAP At first convex, with a small depression at the center becoming larger and deeper as the margin, which is initially rolled, expands to form a large, shallow funnel. Smooth cuticle first orange-saffron (often with concentric narrow zones alternating lighter and darker saffron, which fade with maturity); later paler and rather dull; tending to turn green when bruised. Diameter to 6 inches.

GILLS Same color as cap, turning green when bruised. Very crowded, slightly decurrent, fragile. Spore print: pale yellowish.

STEM Hollow, relatively short, and thick, to 3 inches in diameter. Color paler than cap or gills, and flecked with orange depressions, especially toward base; also discoloring green.

FLESH When cut or broken, all parts exude a milky latex that rapidly turns carrot-orange in contact with air. Slight bitter taste (disappears on cooking); the milk is slightly sweetish. It smells of fruit and acid, like candy.

HABITAT Among short grass in coniferous woods, often nestling beneath pine needles (with stem hidden and only the characteristic "zoned" cap visible). Occasionally solitary; usually gregarious.

SEASON Late summer through late autumn.

PICKING, CLEANING, AND COOKING

This mushroom has an al dente texture and a not-too-distinctive flavor. To my palate it is delicious, given some attention in its preparation. Cut with a sharp mushroom knife. First of all, check for maggots: older specimens may be infested, so cut these lengthwise down the stem for closer inspection and cleaning. These mushrooms are firm enough to rinse in water if they are particularly dirty or gritty. Next, blanch for 2–3 minutes to remove any bitterness.

After this, use the blanched mushroom raw in salads; steam, stew, or

LACTARIUS TORMINOSUS

fry; or use in sauces for pasta, meat, and fish. It freezes well. The Russians preserve this mushroom in salt (see page 97).

LACTARIUS TORMINOSUS
WOOLLY MILK CAP **POISONOUS**

Of the many Lactarius species, some are edible, many are inedible due to their taste, and some are distinctly poisonous. Mistakes are made between *Lactarius deliciosus* and its poisonous counterpart *L. torminosus*, but the key differences are easy to spot. There are parts of northern Europe and of Russia where this mushroom is eaten after special treatment, but I recommend you to play it safe and leave it alone, if you don't want to suffer a severe colic.

RECOGNITION

CAP The most obvious difference between *L. torminosus* and *L. deliciosus* is the woolly, fluffy filaments covering the cap of the former. The latter is smooth. The cap can reach 4$\frac{1}{2}$ inches in diameter. The general color is pinkish-orange, while the general tone of *L. deliciosus* is orange. There are the same concentric circles of dark and pale.

GILLS White. Spore print: cream.

STEM Flesh-colored, and roughly same size/height as *L. deliciosus*. The primary difference is that the stem and flesh of this mushroom, when cut, exude a milk that is and remains white (it is reddish-orange in *L. deliciosus*). It is peppery in flavor (if you wanted to taste it!).

HABITAT AND SEASON Grows singly in birch woods, not conifers as its edible counterpart, from summer to autumn.

LAETIPORUS IS A BRACKET
FUNGUS GROWING ON LIVING
TREES. FORTUNATELY, THE
WORD "SULPHUREUS"
APPLIES ONLY TO THE COLOR
OF THIS SPLENDID FUNGUS,
NOT TO ITS TASTE!

LAETIPORUS SULPHUREUS

(SYN. POLYPORUS SULPHUREUS)
SULFUR SHELF / CHICKEN OF
THE WOODS **VERY GOOD**

Like *Fistulina hepatica*, this is a
bracket fungus, a member of the
polypores, and it parasitizes older
trees, from which it gains its nutrients.
So, when you go mushrooming,
always remember to look up as well
as down! Years ago I employed an
Italian to pick wild mushrooms for
me. On one occasion he found
a wonderful specimen in rather a
precarious situation, suspended from
a huge willow bough overhanging a
lake. He had to borrow a boat and
a ladder in order to collect it—a hair-
raising experience, since the boat was

small and he was large. We managed
to pick the fungus, though, and greatly
enjoyed it later on.

It is called "chicken of the woods,"
or "chicken mushroom," because its
tender white flesh is similar—when
young—to chicken meat in texture.

RECOGNITION

CAP   Brilliant sulfur-yellow, the
cuticle very smooth and suede-like
when young, becoming leathery later.
Sessile, attached by growth to bark of
host tree. Shape at first bud-like, later

fan- or bracket-shaped; sometimes
singly but often in tiered clusters
that assume grotesque shapes and
proportions. Fully mature specimens
can reach 28 inches in diameter and
weigh up to 50 pounds, although they
are too tough to be edible at this stage.
PORES   Visible only under magnifica-
tion; concolorous with or slightly
paler than cuticle, depending on age;
bruising darker. Spore print: white.
FLESH   Extremely succulent, with
fibrous structure similar to chicken
meat. Young specimens exude
moisture when squeezed (you sometimes see droplets of liquid—known
as "fungal guttation"—exuding from
surface, giving an aura of extreme
freshness); flesh becoming white
and crumbly with age. Aroma very
mushroomy, sometimes even pungent;
taste usually excellent, though
sometimes sour.
HABITAT   Deciduous woodland:
prefers oak and willow; common on
wild cherry and yew. Sometimes
singly, sometimes in small clumps.
SEASON   Late spring through
autumn. This mushroom continues
to grow and appears fresh and
succulent even in dry spells, as it
takes moisture from the host tree.

PICKING, CLEANING, AND COOKING

Cut away the base of *Laetiporus
sulphureus* where it was attached
to the tree, since splinters of bark
are occasionally absorbed into the
fruit-body and must not be eaten.

Large slices from a tender specimen
can be broiled or sautéed in butter.
When the specimen is more mature
and the color deepens to orange-
yellow, it is excellent for soups,
stews, and pickling—but is not
recommended for freezing (unless
first cooked in butter). Although I
haven't tried it, it is said to be a
good flavoring when dried and then
reduced to a powder (see page 97).
It is better to cook this mushroom, as
some people are allergic to it raw.

ABOVE AND BELOW LAETIPORUS SULPHUREUS

LECCINUM
VERSIPELLE

THE BOLETES OF THE LECCINUM FAMILY CAN BE VERY CONFUSING FOR
BEGINNERS, BUT ONCE YOU HAVE CRACKED THE RELATIONSHIPS OF
NAME, COLOR, AND SHAPE, YOU ARE DEALING IN FACT WITH THE SAME
TYPE OF MUSHROOM.

LECCINUM
VERSIPELLE

(SYN. BOLETUS VERSIPELLUS /
B. AURANTIACUS) ORANGE BIRCH
BOLETE **GOOD**

The Leccinum family is still confused
in the minds of mycologists, who tend
to give different Latin names to the
same mushroom. Many experts say
that *L. versipelle* is synonymous with
L. aurantiacum, while others say it is
synonymous with *L. testaceoscabrum*
and even with *L. quercinum*. In North
America, *L. testaceoscabrum* is
mostly known as *L. manzanite*, while
L. versipelle is known as *L. insigne*
(the aspen bolete). Do you see what
I mean?

Anyway, the main similarity is
that every single one of them is
edible, and I love them all. Although
they are not exceptionally good
culinarily, they are extraordinarily
satisfactory to pick because they are
solid, large, and heavy.

On the left you can see all the
aspects of *L. versipelle*, and on the
right, in my hand, is an example of
L. quercinum (*L. testaceoscabrum*).

L. scaber, the common birch bolete
or carpini, is the poor relation of the
family, but nonetheless also useful.
This again comes in many different
colors, from pale gray and brown to
dark brown, and it is slightly smaller.
If any mushroom can be considered
to have a "phallic" image, the young
specimens of Leccinum possess this
quality par excellence, sometimes
even assuming grotesque
proportions! You can usually spot the
orange cap of *L. versipelle* from quite
a distance, and on parting the grass
to pick it, you may be surprised by
the length of the solid stem. In a
good season my basket can be full in
minutes, and the problem for me then
is to carry them back to the car, since
they are very heavy indeed.

If you discover a secluded place
that people rarely visit, you may find
mature specimens with caps as large
as 12 inches in diameter. These are
usually so soft and spongy (and so
infested with insect larvae) that the
only useful thing to do is to break
them up into pieces and scatter them
around in the hope of assisting in the
dissemination of spores. I have a
fabulous place for hunting this mushroom, which likes to grow beneath
birch trees.

Poles and Russians in particular
love this mushroom and cook it in
many ways; some of them even
prefer it to *Boletus edulis*.

RECOGNITION

CAP Hemispherical at first, growing
to maximum 12 inches in diameter
and becoming largely convex. At first
very solid and a rich reddish-orange,
becoming quite soft and paler orange
on maturing.
PORES Minute in young specimens,
dark gray to ocherous, becoming

paler later but also very spongy. Spore print: yellow-brown.

STEM   Almost as distinctive as cap: off-white with brown or black scabrous scales. To 2 inches in diameter and 10 inches tall, tapering toward cap. *L. scaber* is smaller altogether.

FLESH   Both cap and stem in young specimens are very firm, almost hard, but tender. When mature, the flesh of the cap becomes white and slightly spongy, and the stem becomes more fibrous, both turning grayish-blue when cut. The smell is freshly mushroomy and the taste pleasant.

HABITAT   Usually solitary, sometimes in groups, among rich ground vegetation beneath birch and oak trees.

SEASON   Early summer in humid weather through end of autumn.

PICKING, CLEANING, AND COOKING

Cut with a sharp mushroom knife. Always peel the stem with a sharp knife and discard the scales. Check for any insect larvae present, and discard any older specimens whose pores have become watery.

   As the Leccinums are fairly moist and lack a particularly intense aroma, I would not suggest drying them. They are, however, good for freezing from the raw state, and they pickle well, though the color turns dark gray. Above all, I recommend them sliced and sautéed in butter and garlic, or stewed; they are also extremely good for soups and sauces. Don't worry if the mushrooms turn almost black after cooking—they will still be delicious. They are good "bulking" mushrooms, useful for quantity rather than quality.

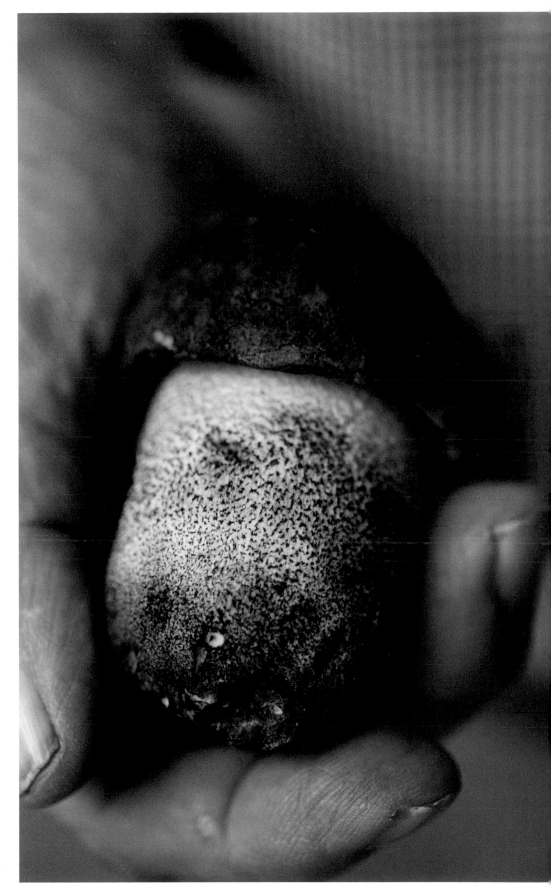

A NICE PLUMP EXAMPLE OF LECCINUM QUERCINUM

some gastric upsets in sensitive stomachs, so it is best to keep to the simple parasol, *L. procera*.

RECOGNITION

CAP At first ovate, with a veil sealing the rim to the stem. When the cap opens, the veil breaks away and remains loosely on the stem as a whitish-brown ring. Fully grown cap has concentric brownish scales around the center, where there is a definite nipple, or umbo, and underlying color is whitish. To 10 inches in diameter.
GILLS Free and crowded, white, very broad (accounting for two-thirds of the cap's thickness); resembling pages of an open book. Spore print: white.
STEM To 12 inches tall and $3/4$ inch in diameter ($1^1/_2$ inches at bulbous base). Ridiculously thin, apparently not strong enough to support the cap, but tough, because woody and fibrous, and hence inedible. Initially grayish, becoming white later, with brownish scales or snake-like markings. Veil remains loosely on hollow stem as large, double ring.
FLESH Thin flesh of cap is white, at first firm, becoming soft with age. No color change on cutting or bruising. Pleasant smell and taste.

ABOVE AND BELOW LEPIOTA PROCERA

LEPIOTA OR THE PARASOL MUSHROOM IS PROBABLY THE TALLEST OF ALL, AS ITS STEM CAN REACH 12 INCHES. THE WORD "PARASOL" DESCRIBES IT PERFECTLY!

LEPIOTA PROCERA

(SYN. MACROLEPIOTA PROCERA)
PARASOL MUSHROOM **VERY GOOD**

While the Italian name for this mushrooms means "drumstick," after the similarity between the young specimens and the drumsticks that drummers in brass bands use, all the other countries name it "parasol" after the mature specimens, which look just like huge sun umbrellas. Considering the differences in the weather, and the British love of brass

bands, I would have thought the Italian and English names would be more apt if reversed.

The parasol mushroom is an agaric with a distinctive appearance, and is quite easy to find and to recognize. It is one of the best and tastiest of the edible mushrooms, and is quite safe to collect if you follow the exact description. You need to distinguish it from its relative *Lepiota rhacodes* (see page 57), which has more woolly scales on top of the cap, a shorter stem, and red-staining flesh. This species is believed to have caused

HABITAT Solitarily on soil, some-times in small groups; in drier parts or margins of deciduous woods (with no particular tree preference); also open fields, paths, and lawns.
SEASON Periodically from summer through autumn, later in milder areas.

LEPIOTA RHACODES
(SYN. MACROLEPIOTA RHACODES)
SHAGGY PARASOL / WOOD PARASOL **GOOD**

This parasol mushroom is regarded as edible and good, but it is known that some people have an allergic reaction, which can cause a minor gastric upset. It differs from *L. procera* in that when the stem is cut, the flesh reddens immediately. The cap is 2–6 inches in diameter. It has a woolly texture, eventually leaving a beige-brown central patch surrounded by slightly reflexed concolorous scales. This gives it its shaggy appearance. The gills are white but bruising red, also turning red with age. Spore print: white. The stem is 4¹/₂ inches tall and ⁵/₈ inch thick, with a broad basal bulb that is creamy white, becoming orange to red when cut. It has a double membranous ring. It is often seen in coniferous woodland, from summer to late autumn.

PICKING, CLEANING, AND COOKING

Cut with a sharp mushroom knife. This mushroom is usually free from any insect larvae—unless the specimen is too old for picking anyway. When cleaning, just brush away any residual earth or sand from the cap. Avoid washing, since it readily absorbs water and this dilutes the flavor.

The stem is too tough to be edible, but, depending on the stage of growth, the cap can be cooked in many different and delicious ways. When it is small and still closed (at the "drumstick" stage), it can be

dipped in batter and deep-fried. When it has opened into a sort of cup, it is ideal for stuffing prior to stewing. When it is completely flat, like an opened parasol, it can be coated in beaten egg and crumbs and then fried, making a tasty meal in itself.

Parasol mushrooms are not particularly good for pickling or preserving, so I suggest that you eat any you find fresh.

LEPIOTA CRISTATA
STINKING BABY PARASOL
POISONOUS

This mushroom produces an amanitin-like poison that takes from 5 to 15 hours to incubate. Symptoms may include muscular cramps, sweating, and intestinal congestion, and the

duration is not properly known. Many of the small lepiotas are poisonous, and for that reason all except those you have very firmly identified should be avoided.

RECOGNITION

CAP ³/₄–2¹/₂ inches in diameter, mainly white with a reddish central patch and similarly colored concentric scales.
GILLS White and well spaced. Spore print: white.
STEM 2 inches long and ¹/₈ inch thick. White becoming vinaceous red at the base, and with a slight ring.
FLESH Thin and white, with a very strong and pungent smell of rubber.
HABITAT AND SEASON Found growing in woods, garden refuse, leaf litter, and soil. From summer through autumn.

LEPIOTA CRISTATA

MEMBERS OF THE LEPISTA FAMILY ARE PALE TO DEEP VIOLET IN COLOR, AND TASTE MEATY WITH A WONDERFUL AROMA, WHICH MAKES THEM QUITE SOUGHT AFTER.

LEPISTA NUDA
(SYN. TRICHOLOMA NUDUM)
WOOD BLEWIT **EDIBLE**

Mushrooms do not contain any of the chlorophyll that gives plants their green coloring, but they do have a wonderful assortment of other colors instead. *Lepista nuda* is one of the commonest and most exquisite edible wild mushrooms, and its colors range from bluish-lilac and violet to pale brown and buff. It is a very satisfying mushroom because it grows abundantly, is quite easy to recognize, and is excellent to eat. This is *after* cooking, however, which is why I have had to classify it as only "edible": avoid the temptation to enjoy the beautiful color raw in a salad, because *Lepista nuda* contains a toxic substance that can cause gastric upsets if eaten in large quantities. This mild toxicity is removed during the cooking process, after which the mushroom is perfectly safe and absolutely delicious.

LEPISTA NUDA

LEPISTA NUDA

These mushrooms often grow in large groups over a wide area, so that you can gather a substantial amount very quickly—though fallen leaves in the deciduous woods make them more difficult to find. Their season is later than that of many other mushrooms, continuing well into the winter.

They are now cultivated quite easily and commonly (see page 88).

RECOGNITION

CAP At first convex, expanding irregularly until the margin curls up exposing the gills. To a maximum 4$\frac{1}{2}$ inches in diameter. First lilac-colored, then brownish. The cuticle is very smooth, giving a moist impression even in dry weather.
GILLS Free or slightly sinuate, crowded, darker than the cap, soon fading and becoming buff. Spore print: pinkish.
STEM Surface at first lilac-speckled or fibrillose, becoming pale with age. When cut, darker at the edges and paling toward center. To 1$\frac{1}{4}$ inches in

diameter (tapering slightly toward top) and 4 inches tall.

FLESH In young specimens, thick and firm; violet, becoming more grayish with age. When cut, the flesh in older specimens has the appearance of being impregnated with water. Pleasant, fruity, almost perfumed aroma; extremely tasty.

HABITAT In small or large groups, sometimes covering a wide area, in deciduous woodland, along paths, often on compost heaps and in deep leaf litter.

SEASON Relatively late, sometimes starting in September and continuing into December, or even through to March in milder locales.

LEPISTA SAEVA
(SYN. L. PERSONATA)
FIELD BLEWIT **EDIBLE**

Lepista nuda's close relative, the field blewit, can—as the name suggests—be found in fields, meadows, and well-manured pastureland, often growing in rings or little groups. It is more difficult to find than *L. nuda*. It differs in having a very pallid, cream to brown, cap; only the stem is a brilliant violet, hence its other common name of "blue leg" ("pied bleu" in French). It is more or less the same size as its relation, in height and cap diameter. Its season is slightly earlier, from autumn through early winter. The taste is very similar—and, like the wood blewit, it must be cooked before eating.

PICKING, CLEANING, AND COOKING

Cut at the base of the stem with a sharp mushroom knife, and clean before putting in your basket. Sometimes leaves stick to the caps, so wipe them if necessary. Blewits are usually fairly insect-free and clean, but check the stems particularly for any signs of infestation. Discard the tougher stems of older specimens.

Since blewits tolerate cold weather, they will keep well in the refrigerator for a few days.

Both lepistas are excellent mushrooms: the very thick, moist flesh means that a satisfying meal can be made from just a few specimens. They are wonderful by themselves, simply cooked by frying in butter with a little garlic and parsley. You can use them in stews or sauté them with other mushrooms, and they are particularly good in sauces to accompany meat or fish. They freeze well after initial cooking, and are very good for pickling and for preserving in oil. I dry them in my purpose-built mushroom-drying machine (see page 96). In fact, these mushrooms are of the few that can be used in any culinary process, but do remember that they must be cooked.

MUSHROOM HUNTING WITH MY THUMBSTICK AND BASKET

To the Lycoperdon or Calvatia family belong those mushrooms that have neither gills nor pores, but instead expel their tiny spores in the form of a cloud coming from the inside. Just a light sprinkling of raindrops can start the process off.

LYCOPERDON GIGANTEUM

(SYN. CALVATIA GIGANTEA)
GIANT PUFFBALL **VERY GOOD**

The photograph shows the typical open fields where puffballs grow, and indeed when they grow, they do so in great profusion. However, they sometimes grow in more unexpected places. Years ago, I was walking through an autumnal Hyde Park—in the very center of London—with my dearly loved dog, Jan, when I glimpsed what I thought was a white soccer ball partly hidden among some shrubs near the path. There were no children around who

LYCOPERDON GIGANTEUM

might have lost it. My attention was then drawn to a smaller ball next to the big one, which immediately gave me the clue that maybe this was a giant puffball. And, of course, this is what it turned out to be: a superb example of *Lycoperdon giganteum*, whose habitat, according to the books, is open fields.

Once on the M25, the circular freeway around London, I saw that the middle section between the opposing lanes was covered with millions of puffballs. I mentioned this shortly afterward in an

interview with a news-paper, and was then severely reprimanded by the police. Apparently people who had read the story were slowing down and stopping to look at the puffballs, thus threatening to cause accidents. Needless to say, the M25 has since expanded, and the prolific puffball ground is now covered with tarmac.

Of the many species of edible puffballs, the giant one is obviously the most rewarding as well as the most distinctive; one prime specimen is enough to provide a good meal for the whole family. The other species, such as *L. perlatum* and *L. pyriforme,* need to be collected in far greater amounts, since each specimen seldom amounts to more than a mouthful. All the puffballs are good to eat while the flesh is firm and white, but the smaller ones need to be distinguished from the common earthball, *Scleroderma citrinum* (see opposite), which is toxic, and *Amanita phalloides* (see page 25) in the unopened-egg stage. To check the latter, cut open: in the amanita, the outline of the gills and cap will be seen, whereas the puffball is solid.

RECOGNITION

The giant puffball hasn't either cap nor gills nor stem: It is a Gasteromycete, with a subglobular fruit-body measuring up to 32 inches in diameter, its spores developing internally and "puffing" out of the top when mature. It is attached to its mycelium by a sort of fragile root that eventually breaks, leaving the puffball free to be blown about the fields by the wind, disseminating its millions of spores. It looks like a ping-pong ball at first, grows to the size of a tennis ball, and finally attains the size of a soccer ball, at least—a truly sporting life.

The outer skin, or exoperidium, is

quite firm and slightly leathery in texture, initially white and turning brown with age. The flesh—technically known as the "gleba"—is also white and firm at first, then yellow, and finally completely brown and powdery. Spores: dark yellowish-brown. The smell when fresh is wonderfully mushroomy, like a meadow mushroom; the taste is slightly stronger. The smell becomes bad as the fungus ages.

HABITAT On well-manured fields, the edge of wet meadows, along streams, in gardens. It grows singly rather than in clumps, but is very gregarious.

SEASON Summer through late autumn.

LYCOPERDON PYRIFORME

PEAR-SHAPED PUFFBALL **GOOD**

A small puffball that is edible when young. It smells slightly of latex or rubber, which tends to put collectors off eating it, and it tastes rather bland. The fruit-body is 1 1/4–2 inches in diameter. The surface can resemble coarse sandpaper, and it is beige in color, fading to a light brown. The inside flesh, or gleba, is white becoming ocher; it is porous—I think rather similar to marshmallow in texture and consistency. The spore powder is olive-brown. It is always found in large, compact groups growing on rotten trunks or buried wood, from August through November.

LYCOPERDON PERLATUM

PEARL PUFFBALL / GEM-STEMMED PUFFBALL **EDIBLE**

This small puffball is only edible if the flesh, or gleba, is still pure white when the fungus is cut in half. It becomes yellow, then olive-brown with age; if the latter color it will be unfit for eating. It is regarded as being only mediocre in taste. The fruit-body is 1 1/2–2 1/2 inches in diameter,

LYCOPERDON PERLATUM

SCLERODERMA CITRINUM

(SYN. S. AURANTIACUM / S. VULGARE)
COMMON EARTHBALL **TOXIC**

I am including this mushroom so that you will not collect it, thinking you have found a truffle or a puffball. Though it is not deadly poisonous, it can cause digestive problems and so is best avoided.

RECOGNITION

Earthballs seem to grow everywhere, either solitarily or in small groups. When young they are quite tempting, compact and fleshy. On maturity the flesh inside turns black—the color of the spores, which are released when the outer skin or peridium cracks open. It is impossible to confuse them with *Lycoperdon giganteum*, the giant puffball, which is pure white in color and far greater in size that the 4-inch maximum that *Scleroderma citrinum* attains. The small, edible puffballs mentioned above are more similar in size, but they tend to be pear- and club rather than globe shaped. Confusion with truffles should be equally impossible, since truffles are hypogeal fungi—they grow under-ground—while earthballs are epigeal and grow on the surface.

HABITAT AND SEASON They grow in dry sandy soil, from summer through autumn, associated with trees.

SCLERODERMA CITRINUM

---

club-shaped, and white, becoming brownish with age. It is covered with pyramidal spines surrounded by a ring of tiny warts that rub off to leave a mesh-like pattern. The spore print is olive-brown. It is found on the ground in woods and pastures from June through November. It is gregarious.

PICKING, CLEANING, AND COOKING

Just turn a large fungus on its base to remove, then lift gently. To tell if it is still good, tap on it. If there is a good deep and full sound, it is still edible. If it sounds hollow, the fungus is probably too old—and anyway you would see the millions of spores scattering as you

handled it. The surface may need wiping to remove grass and earth; otherwise, all the cleaning that needs to be done is to trim away the point at the base where the puffball was attached to its "root." The same applies to the smaller varieties.

In Italy, *Lycoperdon giganteum* is prepared in the same way as veal scallops and, funnily enough, the flavor is quite similar. The firm flesh is wonderful to eat when it is sliced and deep-fried or broiled, as well as in soups. It is not good for drying, but can be sliced or cubed and pickled. Do remember: only the young specimens with firm, white flesh can be eaten. The little puffballs can be sautéed together with other mushrooms.

ABOVE AND BELOW MARASMIUS OREADES

the mushrooms grew where fairies used to dance in circles! In Italy, the circles are thought to be more sinister, made by witches.

However formed, by fairies, witches, or Mother Nature, this minute mushroom is a very enjoyable one to seek and collect, provided you are able to find enough to make a meal.

Curiously, the mushroom ring is formed, and very visibly, in grass that is darker in color than that in the surrounding area. This is because the mycelium (the "root" part of the mushroom, which lies below ground and which spreads at the rate of an inch or so every year), gives the grass a darker coloring.

It is possible to confuse this mushroom with numerous other mushrooms, one of which is the poisonous *Clitocybe rivulosa* (see opposite). But the most important thing to remember is the growing pattern: in *M. oreades* you will find a perfect half or full circle, while the others are much more irregular in growth.

RECOGNITION

CAP $^1/_2$–$2^1/_2$ inches in diameter, firstly convex and bell-shaped when young, later becoming teat-shaped, with little knobs in the center. From cream to brown, darker toward the center; becomes paler when dry, darker when the weather is humid.
GILLS Concolorous with the cap, distant and free from each other, and

MARASMIUS, OR THE FAIRY RING MUSHROOM, IS IN A GROUP ALL BY ITSELF, ALTHOUGH THERE ARE MANY SIMILAR SPECIES THAT DO NOT ACTUALLY GROW IN CIRCLES, AND ARE INEDIBLE, IN SOME CASES TOXIC.

MARASMIUS OREADES

FAIRY RING MUSHROOM **GOOD**

When you come across one of these mushrooms, to find more, all you have to do is go down on your knees and trace the arc of a circle from it. For, in

the same way as the St. George's mushroom (*Tricholoma gambosum*), clouded agaric (*Clitocybe nebularis*), the meadow mushroom (*Agaricus campestris*), and a few others, this mushroom grows in circles. These are called fairy rings in ancient mythology, for people imagined that

MARASMIUS OREADES

poisonous. It is very common in Canada. But because of the different habitats, and to an extent the different seasons (*Clitocybe rivulosa* is found in late summer to autumn), the two should be fairly easy to differentiate.

RECOGNITION

CAP $1^1/_4$–$1^1/_2$ inches in diameter, elastic but not very fleshy. Flat with slight depression in the center. Dirty white, occasionally with the teat shape characteristic of *Marasmius oreades*.
GILLS Very tight, decurrent, white with slightly pinkish flecks. Spore print: white.
STEM The same height as the diameter. Fibrous, cylindric, and straight.
FLESH Pale and watery. Smells of grass; no significant taste.
HABITAT AND SEASON In sandy soil on grassy ground, also in parks and on lawns. Summer to autumn.

not regular. Spore print: white.
STEM Very thin, almost out of proportion with the size of the cap, but is full, not hollow. Mostly inedible, it measures from $1^1/_2$–$2^1/_2$ inches tall, and about $^1/_8$ inch in diameter.
FLESH Beige at first, then hazelnut or whitish. The flesh has a sweetish taste and pleasant smell.
HABITAT Grows as described above, in groups, usually circles, in grassland, fields that have not been cultivated for some time, and on lawns. It is easy to recognize.
SEASON From spring through autumn, later in milder areas.

PICKING, CLEANING, AND COOKING

Cut just underneath the cap with your sharp mushroom knife, as the stem is not good. Brush and wipe to clean. Try to avoid picking it soon after rain, as it will be full of water. And beware when buying: to increase weight they are often sprayed with water. It is an excellent mushroom to eat, and will keep for a few days in good conditions. Stewed, braised, or briefly sautéed, it is used by itself to accompany delicate dishes of meat or fish. It can also be mixed with other mushrooms for sauces. It is not recommended for preserving or freezing, although it dries very well, and rehydrates back to its original size.

CLITOCYBE RIVULOSA
DEADLY POISONOUS

It is possible to confuse *Marasmius oreades* with *Clitocybe rivulosa*, which also grows in rings (although these are irregular) and which is deadly

CLITOCYBE RIVULOSA

DRIED MUSHROOMS OF THE MORCHELLA FAMILY CAN REACH UP TO $150 PER POUND, BUT GOURMETS ARE PREPARED TO PAY THIS PRICE BECAUSE THEY ARE SO INVALUABLE IN THE PREPARATION AND FINAL FLAVORING OF SO MANY WONDERFUL DISHES.

MORCHELLA ELATA

(SYN. M. CONICA) BLACK MOREL / MOUNTAIN FISH **EXCELLENT**

This much sought-after mushroom, as well as its close relation *M. esculenta*, commands a very high price on the world's markets, and is not always readily available. Like the truffle, it belongs to the category of fungus known as the Ascomycetes, and instead of having gills or pores, the spore-bearing hymenium lines the inside of the pits or honeycomb-like depressions of the cap. It is one of the first mushrooms to appear in early spring, sometimes by late March if it is mild. Italy, France, Switzerland, the American Midwest, Tibet, and Kashmir, all with climates with a well-regulated seasonal cycle of cold/mild/hot/mild, are where morels grow best. The state of Minnesota even has its own Festival of the Morel to welcome the arrival of this valuable member of the fungus world.

This mushroom has rather fond memories for me. In the mid-1990s, a friend who was heading a charity operation not far from Katmandu, in Nepal, asked me if I might be interested in morels that were being collected and dried by local villagers, and sold to an Indian middle man for a very low price. I said yes, and that I would pay a price ten times that of the middle man for as many as they could give me. As a result I received in London about 250 pounds of dried morels packed in five specially built tin containers—and I am still using them today! The village is still waiting for me, their benefactor, to visit them, as apparently my money—about $10,500—was the most they had ever seen at one time, which led to the

mayor being re-elected, and some considerable affluence for all. I would love to go to see for myself, but shall wait for more peaceful times.

I remember as a small boy finding and collecting some morels among great stands of cane at Castelnuovo Belbo in Italy. I soon came down to earth when I got home, where my mother and brothers subjected my collection to a thorough scrutiny to make sure that what I had gathered was the true morel. It is easy for experienced eyes to distinguish it from the poisonous *Gyromitra esculenta* (false morel)—which also grows in spring—by the shape of the cap. This is fairly symmetrical in the

edible morel, and distinctly lobed and contorted in the false one.

Morchella elata and *M. esculenta* are the two very best species of morel. They differ slightly in their shape, color, and size, but their general characteristics are the same. If you cut a morel in vertical section, you will see that the cap and stem grow together, forming a single body.

RECOGNITION

CAP   Made up from many cup-like depressions or pits, giving the appearance of a rather irregularly open-pored sponge. Lining these depressions are the asci—microscopic

MORCHELLA ELATA

sacs in which the spores are produced. Conical, dark brown in color, darkening with age; the pits have a fairly regular lengthwise orientation; up to 2 inches diameter and 4 inches tall.

STEM Pale off-white; cylindrical and hollow, slightly more swollen toward the base; 1$^1/_4$ inches in diameter and up to 2 inches tall.

FLESH Both cap and stem look and feel cartilaginous and fragile, but the flesh is crisp and moist to the touch. Pale brown in the cap and white in the stem. I believe the culinary attraction of this mushroom (and *M. esculenta* below) has to be attributed more to the appearance, texture, and preparation than to its intrinsic taste and smell—which are just pleasantly and delicately perceptible.

HABITAT Prefers sandy soil with underlying chalk; given this criterion, little groups can be found in open shrubby woodland, on wood edges and banks, in pastures, orchards, wasteland—and, curiously, on burned ground. Armed with this knowledge, a few years ago some ultra-passionate morel "hunters" in Provence, France, deliberately set fire to woodland in the hope that the following spring they would see the cherished fruiting bodies popping out of the scorched earth. And they did!

SEASON Late March to June, depending on weather, which should be a cold winter followed by a nice warm spring. In mountainous regions, when the snow goes, the morels appear.

MORCHELLA ESCULENTA
(SYN. M. ROTUNDA)
YELLOW MOREL **EXCELLENT**

The cap of this mushroom has the same characteristics as *M. elata*, but is more rounded, with the pits irregularly arranged. A creamy-yellow color at first, becoming pale brown or buff with age. It is usually larger than *M. elata*, reaching up to 6 inches tall.

MORCHELLA ESCULENTA

(As with all mushrooms, the measurements vary according to location: in North America, naturally, they grow bigger!) The stem is off-white, similar to *M. elata*, but reaches 2 inches in diameter and up to 3$^3/_4$ inches tall. It looks more spongy, but is also crisp and firm; flesh color is paler than that of the surface. The flesh, habitat, and season are the same as *M. elata*.

PICKING, CLEANING, AND COOKING

Cut at the base of the stem with a sharp mushroom knife. Morels are not usually infested with any insect larvae (although slugs love them), but I would check the hollow inside, which may harbor insects or other unwanted material. Try to keep them clean when you collect them by cutting away the base, which tends to be full of sand, so that this does not find its way into the wrinkles of the caps when the specimen is placed in your basket. If sand does get into these folds (and some will probably be there anyway), then a longer and more thorough cleaning job is in store for you. Use a brush: washing is not really recommended, but may be used as a last resort.

I have already described this mushroom using many superlatives. It can be served with any type of food. I would stress, though, that it should always be cooked: when eaten raw it proves indigestible to some people, even poisonous. My best recipe is morels stuffed with foie gras (see page 128), but otherwise you can just sauté them with a little cream, and use them in egg and pasta

GYROMITRA ESCULENTA

MORCHELLA ESCULENTA

dishes, soup, and risotto. In Finland, they are served with venison. This is one of the few mushrooms that rehydrate very well from the dried state, and dried ones can be used in exactly the same way as fresh ones. (I find they taste strangely of bacon!) Although they are expensive, dried morels are becoming more readily available in stores if you are not lucky enough to pick and dry your own. They need 20 minutes' soaking in lukewarm water; you may have to cut off the stem base—and remember to filter any sand out of the soaking water. (Keep this as it will contain some of the morel flavor—but, like the morels themselves, it should be cooked.) Morels also preserve well by sterilizing in water, and by pickling and freezing. (Keep your dried morels in the freezer, as I did those from Nepal, to avoid any larvae developing.) Obviously, however, the best way to use them is fresh.

GYROMITRA ESCULENTA

FALSE MOREL / LOREL **POISONOUS**

The difference between this and the true morel is in the shape of the cap, which in *Gyromitra esculenta* consists of folded lobes and in morchella species is made up of pits or hollows, and is usually more symmetrically shaped. As the epithet "esculenta" implies, some Europeans consider these mushrooms edible and regularly eat them after boiling them thoroughly or drying them, but cases of poisoning occasionally occur among apparently seasoned consumers. In the raw state these mushrooms are certainly

very poisonous, so don't take any chances by experimenting.

RECOGNITION

CAP Made up of brain-like, meandering folds and lobes, hollow; color varying from pale tan to deep brown. Sometimes irregular in shape.

STEM Hollow; usually white; up to 3 inches high and 1 inch in diameter. Altogether the mushroom can grow to 4½ inches high in Europe, in North America up to 8–12 inches.

HABITAT AND SEASON Grows solitarily or in small groups, usually under conifers but sometimes under hardwood, in the spring.

ABOVE AND BELOW PLEUROTUS OSTREATUS

PLEUROTUS OR OYSTER
MUSHROOMS ARE FAMILIAR TO ALL
OF US BECAUSE THEY ARE WIDELY
AVAILABLE CULTIVATED. TO
FIND THEM IN THE WILD IS
A REAL TREAT, AS
THE COLONIES
ARE SO
BEAUTIFUL.

PLEUROTUS OSTREATUS
OYSTER MUSHROOM **VERY GOOD**

Named after the oyster because of its
shape and its grayish-blue color,
Pleurotus ostreatus is one of the few
mushrooms that have been found
suitable for cultivation (see page 89).
The domestic version of the oyster
mushroom can be found in supermarkets, although I still prefer the wild
version, which has a stronger taste.

Its relative, *P. cornucopiae,* takes
its name from its resemblance to a
horn of plenty. Although the two
mushrooms are different in shape and
color, I have purposely put them
together here because of their very
similar general characteristics and
culinary uses. Breaking through the

bark of fallen trees and
stumps, these typical
parasitic fungi grow
down into the structure,
absorbing the life-giving
substance, until the
wood is reduced to
worthless matter. Be
careful with identification,
however: there are similar
mushrooms growing on
stumps that are
inedible or poisonous.

RECOGNITION

CAP Flat and round;
lateral, resembling a shell or tongue.
To 6½ inches in diameter. Upper
surface varies in color from blue-gray
when small to pale brown when fully
grown; also from pale cream to noisette.
Skin quite shiny.
GILLS Pale cream, not very crowded,
decurrent. Spore print: lilac.
STEM Excentric to lateral, or almost
absent.
FLESH White and very tender in small
specimens, becoming tougher. Taste
and aroma indistinct.
HABITAT Parasitic shelves and
colonies attaching to fallen and
decaying trees, mostly beech, in parks
and countryside. Often hidden by
grass, so remember to carry a stick.
SEASON Early summer in warm
conditions to first frost (I have even
found some in December).

PLEUROTUS CORNUCOPIAE
VERY GOOD

This is distinctly funnel-shaped, and
grows more upright than lateral. It
has a more pronounced stem than in
P. ostreatus, reaching 8 inches when
several fruiting bodies are grouped
together, forming a cluster. The cap is
round and concave to the center,
forming the shape of the cornucopia.
The color of the top varies from white
to pale brown, depending on location.
The flesh is white and the spore print

PLEUROTUS
CORNUCOPIAE

pale lilac. Be careful: the cap
can appear immaculate, but open it
up to check for maggots. A close
relative, *P. sapidus*, is found in the
United States.

PICKING, CLEANING, AND COOKING

Cut off in clumps from the tree. When
cleaning, inspect the larger and older
ones carefully. Sometimes you will find
maggots in the stems: if so, simply cut
them off and enjoy the caps. And the
stems actually become a bit tough as
they age.

These are not superior mushrooms
in the culinary sense—they do not
have an outstanding flavor—but they
are versatile when cooked fresh, and
their availability in cultivation makes
them useful for adding that extra
mushroomy something to a dish. Sauté
them with garlic and butter, dip them
in egg and crumbs and deep-fry, or
use them in soups. They are worth
preserving only if you pickle them in
vinegar before bottling them in olive
oil (see page 99). Unless very small,
they become too tough when frozen,
and they lack the flavor to make them
dry well.

When buying cultivated oyster
mushrooms, choose smaller specimens,
as they are less watery.

POLYPORUS GIGANTEUS

MEMBERS OF THE POLYPORUS (OR MERIPILUS, AS MY FRIEND ROY WATLING PREFERS TO CALL THEM) FAMILY ARE ONLY EDIBLE WHEN YOUNG, AND ARE HUGE WHEN FULLY GROWN. THE PHOTOGRAPHER AND I FOUND A GIANT POLYPORE IN OCTOBER, 2002, WHICH MUST HAVE BEEN ABOUT 130 POUNDS! UNFORTUNATELY WE HAD JUST MISSED ITS EDIBLE STAGE.

POLYPORUS GIGANTEUS
(SYN. MERIPILUS GIGANTEUS)
GIANT POLYPORE **GOOD**

The word "polypore" always describes, in the mycological sense, a mushroom with millions of pores that are easily visible underneath the cap or tongue. Living up to its name, this is indeed a giant mushroom, a bracket fungus like *Fistulina hepatica* (see page 46). However, it grows on the stumps of fallen or felled trees, rather than farther up the trunks, although I have found one at the foot of a living beech tree. It grows in groups or clumps of layers or lobes of great size: one mushroom can weigh up to 175 pounds! Often I have had great difficulty in transporting it because of its size—but then I am collecting it for decorative rather than culinary purposes. This is because it is only edible when young and tender: it tends to become fibrous and inedible when older. In some mushroom books it is considered inedible, probably due to its toughness, but it is not poisonous, and I think it can be excellent.

RECOGNITION

CAP The mushroom grows in various flattish and round lobes, with a very strong stem attached to the tree. When young, the lobes exude a brown liquid, and this is when you should collect them. After this the lobes become much thinner, larger, and woodier. The caps have concentric marks of a darker brown color than the rest of the mushroom, lighter at the edges.

PORES Situated beneath the lobes. When mature you can spot a rust-colored dusting of spores on the ground beneath. Spore print: white.

STEM Tough and inedible. It attaches itself to the base of the tree.

FLESH A pale cream color. When you cut into the flesh, you can see it is fibrous, consisting of many filaments pressed together. The taste is very mushroomy. The smell is slightly sour,

POLYPORUS GIGANTEUS

but this disappears when the fungus is cooked. The surface tends to discolor to the touch, becoming streaky black (as do your fingers when you work with it).

HABITAT It grows on the stumps of dead trees like beech, oak, or other large trees, usually at the base. Many groups of clusters, but all coming from one big stem attached to the wood.

SEASON July through October.

POLYPORUS SQUAMOSUS
DRYAD'S SADDLE **EDIBLE**

The word "squamosus" derives from "squame," or "scaly," and the cuticle is formed of alternating concentric circles in different shades of brown and cream. The underside is cream, becoming brown with age. The English name of "dryad's saddle" refers to the shape of the fungus, which is said to resemble the saddle a wood nymph

might use. The fungus is also known as "scaly polypore." One day, when we were visiting the Italian Embassy in London for a reception, my wife noticed a huge specimen of this fungus hanging from a sycamore tree beside our parking space. Pity I couldn't pick it!

This polypore, like all the others, is only edible when young and tender. With age it becomes leathery and fibrously woody. The cap grows flat and round, up to 2 feet in diameter. The color is dark yellow with brown flakes growing in an irregular circular way (the "scales"). The outside of the mushroom is very thick, becoming thicker toward the center where it disappears into the stem. This is very short, black-crusted at the base, and strongly attached to the tree, from which it has to be cut to be collected. The pores are white at first and quite tight, becoming yellowish and darker with age. The tubuli are from $^1/_{16}$–$^1/_2$ inch long, becoming shorter toward the stem. Spore print: white. The flesh is fibrous and whitish, becoming tougher with age, when it becomes inedible. It smells strongly of cucumber, and the taste when

cooked is very pleasant. It attaches itself to stumps of fallen and dead trees, eventually transforming these into humus. Huge clumps or clusters, but also singly, in spring and summer, rarely autumn.

A close relative of this mushroom is now being cultivated.

PICKING, CLEANING, AND COOKING

Just cut off at the piece attaching the fungus to the tree with a sharp knife or a little pruning saw, and brush well before putting in your basket. These mushrooms will never be a first choice for gourmets, but they are extremely pleasant when young and tender. When used for culinary purposes, it is best to mix them with other mushrooms, as they do not have a lot of flavor on their own. The giant polypore turns black when handled—as do your hands, so wash them with salt and lemon juice afterward. Use in stews, or deep-fry or sauté; you can also pickle them. They don't freeze very well, but both of these polypores can be dried very successfully and reduced to a powder (see page 97), particularly when mixed with more aromatic mushrooms.

ABOVE AND BELOW POLYPORUS SQUAMOSUS

RUSSULA VIRESCENS

OF THE HUNDREDS OF RUSSULAS, I HAVE CHOSEN TO FEATURE THE MOST EDIBLE AND THE MOST POISONOUS. IN BETWEEN THESE IS AN INCREDIBLE VARIETY OF SIZES AND COLORS, MOST OF WHICH ARE INEDIBLE.

RUSSULA VIRESCENS
GREEN-CRACKED RUSSULA
EXCELLENT

This is the most delicious and sought-after of all the russulas. The Spaniards particularly value them, and in season you can find them in all the markets. I must admit to never having collected a russula in the wild, but then I have never really paid much attention to the family – until now. I think this will probably be the mycological and culinary study of my future, to find out which russula is really the best. I hope that in the process I don't make any mistakes, for there are some unpleasant and toxic ones out there as well . . .

RECOGNITION

CAP Not nice to look at. Very meaty, 2–6 inches in diameter, very solid. Slightly hemispheric then round, and flattening with a depression in the middle. Very warty. Gray-green, speckled and cracked with a white background.
GILLS Very tight, fragile, white-cream in color, and sometimes tinged brown or reddish. Spores white, as is the spore print.
STEM Full but spongy, cylindric, and irregularly white/brown; $3/4$–$3^3/4$ inches high.
FLESH White, sometimes blushing, and thick and solid. Has a very light smell and a sweet taste.
HABITAT Mixed woods, especially chestnut and oak, and in grass.
SEASON End of spring through autumn.

RUSSULA CYANOXANTHA
THE CHARCOAL BURNER
VERY GOOD

A good, edible member of the family, this is prized in Europe—but, sadly, it is also prized by maggots! The cap is 2–$4^1/2$ inches in diameter, with a large color range from green and steely blue, to violaceous or lilac, often with a mixture of all of these. The gills are soft and elastic to the touch, not brittle like most other russulas; also oily to the touch. Color varies from white to pale cream. Spore print: white. Stem pure white; 3 inches high and $1/2$ inch thick. The flesh is white and bland. Found under broad-leaved trees of all kinds from summer through late autumn.

PICKING, CLEANING, AND COOKING

Cut the stems with a sharp mushroom knife. Because russulas are quite fragile, don't transport them along with other mushrooms: they are very prone to get dirt in their gills. Never wash them, simply wipe the caps with a damp cloth. If they are big, cut in quarters or, as they do in Spain, use the cap only (and broil it). Generally just briefly sauté in butter, as they are very tender. It is best not to preserve them, but to eat them fresh.

RUSSULA CYANOXANTHA

RUSSULA EMETICA

RUSSULA OCHROLEUCA

RUSSULA EMETICA
THE SICKENER **POISONOUS**

This member of the Russula family gets its second name from the Greek, and I think its meaning is quite obvious. The "sickener" has another poisonous relative, *R. mairei*, which has the common name "beechwood sickener," because of its affinity with beech. Great care has to be taken with red mushrooms, and russulas in particular. They are mostly inedible and occasionally poisonous, as this one is. Unless they have yellow gills and stems, not white, it is best to leave them alone.

RECOGNITION

CAP $1^{1}/_{4}$–4 inches in diameter. Bright cherry red or scarlet with a shallow depression in the center. It is sticky when moist.
GILLS Fairly distant, white fading to pale cream. Spore print: whitish.
STEM 3 inches high, $^{1}/_{2}$ inch thick. White, cylindrical, and somewhat swollen at the base. Often rather soft.
FLESH White.
HABITAT AND SEASON Found typically with sphagnum moss on wet ground under conifers, from summer through late autumn.

RUSSULA OCHROLEUCA
COMMON YELLOW RUSSULA
NOT EDIBLE

This mushroom is often considered edible, but I personally think it is of very little culinary value. I have included it here primarily to show just how varied the family is. This mushroom may look fantastic, but it is inedible. Its name translates from the Greek, meaning "white to ocher yellow."

RECOGNITION

CAP 3–$4^{1}/_{2}$ inches in diameter. Color ranges from bright yellow to a dull shade of ocher, sometimes with an age-related greenish tinge.
GILLS White, contrasting with the yellow of the cap. Spore print: white to pale cream.
STEM 3 inches high, $^{1}/_{2}$ inch thick. At first white, graying with wet conditions and age.
FLESH White, with a hot taste.
HABITAT AND SEASON From late summer through autumn under broad-leaved trees and conifers.

ABOVE AND BELOW SPARASSIS CRISPA

"SPARASSIS," "BRAIN," "CAULIFLOWER," "WIG," ETC. . . . THERE ARE HUNDREDS OF NAMES FOR THIS CURIOUS FUNGUS. WHATEVER IT MIGHT BE CALLED, I KNOW FOR CERTAIN THAT IT ENJOYS A GREAT DEAL OF ROYAL APPRECIATION!

SPARASSIS CRISPA
CAULIFLOWER MUSHROOM
VERY GOOD

Whenever I am walking through pine woods during the autumn, I keep an eye on the base of the trunks, which is where this peculiar mushroom usually chooses to grow. If you find a large specimen (and they can grow very large), it will be enough to make a complete meal. It really does look like a cauliflower, and is quite as interesting in its culinary uses. You are very unlikely to find this mushroom for sale in markets—it is only of value to the connoisseur!

There is no cap in the normal sense of the word: the mushroom consists of a short, strong stem and many cartilaginous flat lobes, reminiscent of a "brain coral," hence the name "brain fungus." The fruit-body can grow in quite a short time and can envelop in its flesh anything lying nearby. Often when cutting one open I have found pine needles and even small pine cones. It is now being cultivated.

RECOGNITION

FRUIT-BODY   Usually subglobular, very variable in size: 8–20 inches in diameter. Flat, irregular lobes colored cream to pale noisette, darkening with age.

SPORES   White or pale yellow. Spore print: whitish.
FLESH   Fragile, more consistent toward center. Smell pleasant; taste sweet and nutty.
HABITAT   Singly, in coniferous woods, at tree bases and on stumps.
SEASON   Late summer through late autumn.

PICKING, CLEANING, AND COOKING

Just cut at the base with a sharp mushroom knife. Pick only specimens that are creamy-white (cauliflower color); any that have turned yellowish will be tough and indigestible. Cut into sections to check for dirt, insects, and foreign bodies. A good wash before cooking is—for once—recommended.

Sparassis crispa is very versatile to cook with. I have fried it, preserved it in oil, frozen it, and dried it (and it is one of the handful of mushrooms that rehydrates well from dried), all with excellent results. It is very good for soups, either fresh or dried, and can be used in all sorts of stews plus, of course, on its own. Used together with other mushrooms, it adds a certain sophistication to a dish through its appearance, texture, and flavor.

SUILLUS LUTEUS

THE GENUS NAME OF THESE MUSHROOMS COMES FROM THE LATIN FOR PIG, "SUILLUS." THEY ARE FOUND MOSTLY UNDER PINE OR LARCH TREES, HENCE THE ITALIAN NAME OF "LARICINO."

SUILLUS GREVILLEI
(SYN. BOLETUS ELEGANS) LARCH BOLETE / TAMARACK JACK / LARCH SLIPPERY JACK **GOOD**

SUILLUS LUTEUS
(SYN. BOLETUS LUTEUS) SLIPPERY JACK **GOOD**

The characteristics and culinary properties of these two mushrooms are so similar that I am discussing them together here, although they are distinct in appearance. Both grow under conifers of different types, and both have a slippery cuticle (hence the name "slippery jack"), so mind where you put your feet! Neither exactly reaches the high point of culinary distinction, but both are rewarding

used in soups and stews together with other mushrooms.

The powers that be have decided to classify boletes such as these with glutinous caps in the genus Suillus—though they are still listed under Boletus in many books.

RECOGNITION

SUILLUS GREVILLEI

CAP Hemispherical when young, closed underneath by a veil, later flattening to maximum 4–4½ inches in diameter. As the mushroom develops, the veil detaches itself from the cap and remains on the stem in the form of a ring or skirt. The cuticle is viscid with gluten when moist, shiny when dry. Yellow-orange when young, paler yellow later.
PORES Spongy and very absorbent. Lemon-yellow and slightly decurrent. Spore print: olive-brown.
STEM Golden-yellow above the pale yellow ring, becoming darker yellow below with a brownish patterning. Grows to a maximum 1¼ inches in diameter and 4 inches tall.
FLESH Soft and tender, lemon to

SUILLUS GREVILLEI

chrome. No distinctive aroma or taste.
HABITAT Exclusively under larch. Singly and in little groups.
SEASON Summer through late autumn.

S. LUTEUS

The cap is the same as *S. grevillei*, differing only in color: chocolate-brown when young, brown to violaceous later. The pores are spongy and very absorbent, paler yellow, and adnexed. The spore print is ocher-brown. The stem is the same height as *S. grevillei*, and is concolorous with pores above the ring (which is whitish and pale purple beneath) and yellow-brown to brown below it. The flesh is soft and tender, pale yellow to white. No distinctive aroma or taste. The habitat is usually with Scots pines, particularly near paths and banks, singly and in little groups. Season is from summer through late autumn.

A similar mushroom to *S. luteus* is *S. granulatus*. It has larger pores than *S. luteus*, and grows in the same situation, but is worthless, although not poisonous. Another is *S. bovinus*. Both appear from the end of spring to autumn.

PICKING, CLEANING, AND COOKING

Cut with a sharp mushroom knife halfway down the stem. The caps are so viscid that any grit, leaves, pine needles, etc. that come into contact with them will adhere in the basket, so I recommend removing the cuticle and ring as soon as you pick them. Both are generally relatively maggot-free.

Their lack of distinctive flavor and moist flesh puts them in the "useful" rather than the "sought-after" category. They are not good for preserving, since they freeze well only when cooked; are too moist and slight in flavor for drying; and the spongy flesh is not firm enough for pickling. Enjoy them in season, when plentiful; they are best fresh, used alone in soups and stews or added to a mixture of other mushrooms.

TRICHOLOMA AND INOCYBE ARE PUT HERE
TOGETHER TO STRESS ONCE AGAIN THAT,
ALTHOUGH THEY DO NOT GROW IN THE SAME
SITUATION, OR BELONG TO THE SAME FAMILY,
MISIDENTIFICATION CAN OCCUR.

TRICHOLOMA GAMBOSUM

(SYN. CALOCYBE GAMBOSA /
TRICHOLOMA GEORGII)
ST. GEORGE'S MUSHROOM
EXCELLENT

This excellent mushroom is one of
the first of the season. It is known as
"St. George's mushroom" in Britain,
because it usually appears around
St. George's Day, April 23rd (although
it's actually better a week or so later).
However, in Italy, it is called "marzolino,"
from "Marzo" (March), because there,
further south, it comes up earlier in
the year. The German name,
"Mairitterling," suggests that it is a

TRICHOLOMA GAMBOSUM

treat to be expected in May, but it is
around in other seasons. The mushroom, however, is most popular in Italy,
I think, as it grows so plentifully in the
lush pastures of the hilly Pre-Alps.

It's also rather popular with me.
Once, on one of my many diets in
spring, I was so hungry that I was
tempted to eat anything that came
my way. A basket of St. George's
mushrooms was what came my

way, and I ate all of them, raw—
about 8 ounces! They saved the day,
satisfying my hunger and yet not
letting me put on any weight!

It is one of those mushrooms that
likes to grow in circles, like the fairy
ring mushroom (see page 62) and
others. The mycelium, in fact, spreads
just beneath the soil in a circular
way, moving and enlarging the
circle every year by an inch or
so. The grass is darker and
often longer as well, which is
what should alert you to the
mushroom's presence.

RECOGNITION

CAP Compact, off-white in color,
sometimes split and with split edges.
Can reach 2–6 inches across.
GILLS White and crowded. Spore
print: white.
STEM One of its Latin names,
"gambosum" (like a big leg) refers to
the stem, which is bulky at the foot,
thinning toward the cap. It also thins
with age. White; $3/4$–$1^1/2$ inches high
and $1/2$–1 inch thick.
FLESH Soft, dense, and dirty white,
with a slightly mealy and cucumber
scent. A very subtle flavor.
HABITAT The best places to find
these mushrooms are fields and
grassy areas where the grass has
not been disturbed by cultivation.
Race-courses are ideal, as are parks
and roadsides. Look for greener,
lusher grass in rings.
SEASON April and May. It requires
water, and becomes slightly darker in
color when wet due to water-absorption.
Pick when the weather is dry.

PICKING, CLEANING, AND COOKING

Cut the mushroom at the base of the
stem, and brush clean of soil and
grass before putting in your basket. It
shouldn't harbor any unwanted insect
life. Trim the ends of the stems. Slice
or use whole, fried in butter or olive
oil with a little garlic and parsley or

chives. They can be included in
pasta sauces, or cooked and dressed
in a salad. They can also be pickled.

Throughout the year, this
mushroom is exported from Romania,
Hungary, Turkey, and other regions
where they grow, so a good supplier
should be able to find
you some.

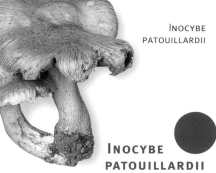

INOCYBE
PATOUILLARDII

INOCYBE PATOUILLARDII

RED-STAINING
INOCYBE **DEADLY POISONOUS**

This mushroom must be avoided
altogether, as it is extremely
poisonous. It is similar not only to
Tricholoma gambosum, but also to
small meadow mushrooms. However,
the cap becomes slightly redder in
color, longer, and more shiny with age.
There is still a possibility of confusion,
though, despite its habit of growing
with trees and in woods. It's primarily
because the seasons are so similar
that mistakes can be made. Be very
careful indeed.

RECOGNITION

CAP 1–3 inches in diameter; color
initially whitish to cream, later on
tinged reddish and shiny.
GILLS Tight, becoming freer with age.
White. Spore print: white.
STEM $1^1/2$–$2^1/2$ inches long, plum,
cylindric, quite straight, and strong
with filaments. At base bulbous white
becoming pinkish.
FLESH White, smell faintly unpleasant
and sweet when young, becoming
ranker with age.
HABITAT AND SEASON In mixed
woods, usually deciduous, alongside
paths, also in parks. May to July.

THERE ARE MANY HUNDREDS OF SIMILAR TRUFFLES OR TUBERS IN THE WORLD—IN PLACES AS FAR APART AS CALIFORNIA, NEW ZEALAND, AND CHINA—BUT ONLY THESE PRECIOUS THREE HAVE THE FLAVOR AND AROMA THAT HAVE ENSURED THEY ARE THE MOST HIGHLY PRIZED OF ALL.

TUBER MAGNATUM
WHITE ALBA TRUFFLE
EXCELLENT

TUBER MELANOSPORUM
BLACK PÉRIGORD TRUFFLE
EXCELLENT

TUBER AESTIVUM
SUMMER TRUFFLE **GOOD**

The only time a professional truffle-hunter will take someone with him is when he is absolutely certain that his location will remain a secret. As I was only seven or eight years old and incapable of divulging the route, my father's friend, Giovanin, offered to take me with him on a truffle hunt. Giovanin appeared wearing big gum boots and a real hunting jacket with a large game pocket. He had with him a stick, a funny-shaped digging tool, and a small mongrel called Fido.

I clearly remember my impression of the November woods, with the leafless branches reaching out into the fog. Something about the mysterious atmosphere fascinated me, and I have been a fanatical mushroom hunter ever since. Suddenly Fido became excited and started running up and down, his nose to the ground, sucking in the scent of the truffles like an animated vacuum cleaner. When he stopped abruptly and began clawing at the ground, Giovanin had the sign he'd been waiting for: Fido had found a truffle. Giovanin gently pushed the dog aside, dug a small hole with his special tool, and lifted out a wonderful specimen of *Tuber magnatum*. He brushed the earth from the truffle and put it gently in his pocket. Only then did Fido receive his reward of a small dog treat.

On another occasion, Giovanin gave me a truffle to take home. I was hooked and still am. I call truffles "food of gods, kings, and pigs." Some truffles contain a chemical resembling the male pig's sex hormone, and the riper the truffle the stronger and more attractive (for the female pig) the scent. The Romans used pigs to locate truffles, but it was hard to prevent the pigs from eating them; the trained dogs used nowadays are easier to handle.

A degree of mystery still attaches to truffles. Although France and Italy have increased commercial supplies by developing techniques of treating the roots of young oaks with black truffle spores, this cultivation is difficult, and requires much hands-on attention, so the prices are still high. I was once asked to appear on a television program dealing with the latest scientific innovations and use my expertise to assess the merits of a synthetic black truffle from Switzerland. After examining and tasting it I had to state that if this was man's attempt to emulate nature then he had failed dismally: the soft licorice-like substance was devoid of taste or smell, and could at best be used for decorations on pâtés.

Brillat-Savarin called the black or Périgord truffle the "black diamond," which could "make women more tender and men more agreeable." Aphrodisiac qualities have been attributed to the truffle throughout history. I personally think that the difficulties involved in finding something so rare and exquisite trigger off a demand that inflates the price to an unaffordable level, and this very process becomes a stimulation—almost a sensual experience. The fact that this delicacy sometimes reaches palates that cannot appreciate it is an old human story, applying not only to truffles but to most exotic foods.

Of the many different varieties of truffles in the world, three are the most esteemed and precious: *Tuber magnatum* (the white Alba truffle); *T. melanosporum* (the black Périgord truffle); and *T. aestivum* (the summer truffle). There are very many truffles growing in North America, but of the three here, only the black Périgord truffle and the summer truffle can be found. The aroma of the white Alba truffle is very pungent indeed. I once had a phone call from the Customs and Excise Officers at Heathrow Airport warning me that a parcel of perishable food that had arrived for me from Turin was suspected of containing "something that had spoiled." It was beyond the imagination of the poor officials that white truffles could possess such a penetrating aroma. When I collected the package even the police dogs were looking slightly disturbed by the smell.

Knowing of my obsession, a colleague of my wife's once promised to bring me back some truffles from Saudi Arabia, where apparently they grow in profusion in the desert. When they arrived my heart stopped at the sight of a big plastic bag full of large white truffles. On closer examination, however, my heart stopped again— this time with disappointment. Although these tubers are prized locally, for me there was no smell or taste at all! All that glitters is not gold. . . . And infiltrating the market now are tuber species from China, which are much less sought after.

RECOGNITION

Truffles are Ascomycetes—"spore-shooters," like the morel—with roundish fruit-bodies that develop underground in mycorrhizal association with certain trees (why they are so difficult to "cultivate"). The folded hymenium appears as a marbling of fine veins in the flesh, and the spore-producing asci are situated in the darker part of the flesh. The intense aroma of the ripe spores attracts animals to the fruit-body, which they grub up and eat, dispersing the spores by means of their droppings. Flies are important too, if a nuisance: Flies that try to deposit eggs near, on, or in truffles can disperse spores on their bodies, and larvae, once hatched, can release spores as they move on or in truffles. I have never actually seen the so-called truffle flies in clouds above a hidden truffle—one of the clues to a truffle's presence, so it is said—but they must exist, as the larvae certainly do.

T. MAGNATUM

TUBER MAGNATUM

It grows only in Italy, in symbiosis with oak, hazel, poplar, and beech; the best are in the Langhe area of Piedmont, of which the town of Alba is the center (hence "Alba truffle"). Other white truffles, which have less smell, are found in the Marches, Umbria, Emilia-Romagna, and even Calabria. An irregular potato-like tuber, it has smooth skin that is creamy yellow to pale hazel; the flesh is from pale cream to pale brown, marbled with white veins. (It occasionally has bright red spots, especially when growing with hazel or poplar, and is then highly valued by connoisseurs.) The flesh is solid, hard, and brittle—it will break in pieces if dropped on a hard floor. Specimens can reach 4 1/2 inches in diameter and weigh 1 pound, but most are 1–2 ounces.

The season is from late September, reaching the best harvest time in November. Provided the soil is not frozen, these truffles can be found until the end of January. A well-trained dog can detect the scent of a mature *T. magnatum* from 175 feet away, even if the truffle lies up to 20 inches underground. Attempts to grow *T. magnatum* commercially have failed.

Once, in the restaurant, I was standing near the door with a platter full of white truffles. A customer and his guests, leaving after a good lunch, asked what they were. "Truffles," I replied. One of the guests promptly took one, popped it in his mouth, and ate it. His face was a picture—he had expected the flavor of white chocolate! I refrained from telling him he had just devoured $120 worth.

T. MELANOSPORUM

The most famous are those of the Périgord region of France, but this black truffle is also found in Provence and in Italy, around Spoleto in Umbria and Norcia in the Marches. The French, because it is the only truffle in their country, think it the best in the world. This causes quite a degree of awkwardness between France and

TUBER MELANOSPORUM

Italy, because, as we all know, it is generally acknowledged that the white Italian truffle is the most aromatic and therefore the most valuable. *T. melanosporum* grows from mid-November to March in symbiosis with oak: the roots of young trees are treated with spores before planting, ensuring a supply for commerce in these areas of France and Italy. (Interestingly, it also grows in countries where there are vines. In New Zealand, for instance, they are commercially producing the black truffle in plantations, with good economic success.) The subterranean fruit-body is irregularly round, with a rough black skin made up of hundreds of polygonal "warts." The flesh is very solid and brittle, with a pleasant smell. It is marbled brown with white veins that disappear when the flesh turns black on cooking. It grows to a maximum diameter of 2 3/4 inches and usually weighs 1 1/2–2 ounces.

TUBER AESTIVUM

T. AESTIVUM

The "summer" truffle usually grows between June and November, but has also been found through the winter, until March. Similar in appearance to *T. melanosporum*, but with a skin covered in pyramidal black warts. The flesh is a solid brown, with white veins that disappear on cooking, and has a very delicate aroma. It is round, about 1 1/4–1 1/2 inches in diameter, and about 1 ounce in weight. Found in England on chalk soils, it usually favors beech. We don't use trained dogs in the U.K., but the keen eyes of keen humans when a fraction of the warty skin of a truffle growing just below the surface is visible above ground. The luckiest person in England is without doubt Jenny Hall, who has found some 150 examples of this tasty tuber in her own garden, beneath an oak.

PICKING, CLEANING, AND COOKING

Very rarely will any of us find a truffle to "pick." Only the summer truffle comes anywhere near the surface of the earth in order that you might identify it. The other two are hidden beneath the earth, and you will need a highly trained dog to find them. (In Italy, there is huge rivalry between truffle hunters, and I'm afraid dogs have been poisoned by their masters' competitors.) It is this dog that will smell the truffle and will probably enthusiastically dig for it. Many is the time I have received a contingent of truffles, some with claw marks on them!

During the season you can often find me at my restaurant cleaning truffles, which I do with an almost religious reverence to avoid any waste. I never wash white truffles for fear of losing some of the aroma, but use one of those little brushes with brass bristles intended for cleaning suede. Truffles can be used in cooked dishes, but are usually served raw.

Because of the high price I prefer to "shave" them with a "mandolino" over the food (pasta, risotto, salads, etc.). When you buy them, make sure they are firm and heavy, and that any holes made by insects have not been filled with earth to make up the weight, an important consideration when the price is (in 2002) $4.50 a gram!

White truffles are delicate and can be kept for a maximum of only seven days after collecting. I suggest you buy a small quantity and use right away. In the restaurant, where I need larger amounts, I keep them, wrapped singly in tissue paper, in a tightly closed plastic box in the refrigerator.

TRUFFLE HUNTING

Never leave any type of truffle in an open container in the refrigerator: the aroma will permeate all the other food around—unless, of course, you want everything to taste of truffles! (Eggs kept beside a truffle will be wonderfully flavored, even through the shell, and are magnificent scrambled for breakfast!) The best Piedmontese "fonduta"—a fondue-like mixture using fontina cheese—is finished off with shavings of white truffle.

Black truffles keep much longer than white ones—up to fourteen days when refrigerated. The tough, warty skin has to be washed and scrubbed with a brush to dislodge earth. Edible raw, shaved over foods like the white truffle, they are more often used in cooked dishes such as sauces, on pâtés, under the skin of roasted birds—all methods that retain the maximum flavor.

The summer truffle is usually used to impart the "feeling" of a truffle, mostly

in decoration. You could use it with some success, though, in combination with some truffle oil.

If you have to transport a truffle at any time, put it in an airtight container with some raw rice to absorb moisture, but don't leave it for too long, or the truffle will deteriorate. When it becomes wet and soggy, it is of no further use and must be discarded.

No truffle takes kindly to being preserved. Freezing and drying are ineffective because the aroma is lost; bottling in water retains the texture but also allows most of the aroma to disappear. A paste of white truffles is now produced commercially in tubes and jars for using in sauces or as a spread. One enterprising Italian company makes a natural essence of truffle, which I use for sauces and to flavor salad dressings. There is also an expensive truffle oil that is good for salads, but is mainly used to brush on meat before grilling.

CULTIVATED MUSHROOMS

Although mushroom cultivation is now worldwide, the name "exotic" has been applied to all those of a different shape, color, taste, and flavor to the common button mushroom. In fact, it's not too incorrect to call these mushrooms "exotic," as their cultivation started in the Far East and was then exported to the West.

Once it had been recognized that mushrooms were not only good for medicinal purposes, but also as a foodstuff, attempts were made to cultivate more crops than the brief season of nature allowed. Many mushrooms resisted—and many still do—but some very early attempts were successful. The first mushroom to be cultivated was probably *Auricularia polytricha*, as early as 600 AD. Next was *Flammulina velutipes* (enoki) in 900 AD, followed by *Lentinula edodes* (shiitake) in 1000 AD. These were all Eastern efforts, and the mushrooms are primarily used in Eastern cuisines to this day. In the West, successful cultivation of *Agaricus bisporus* started in the 1600s in France. The technique was taken to other European countries, and thence to North America.

The technology then advanced significantly, especially after World War Two. Food was scarce, so mushrooms became much sought after. Since then, ideas have been shared between East and West, and cultivated mushrooms have become an important part of our lives.

A very sophisticated technology is needed to cultivate all these mushrooms economically.

Specialized plants and factories have been created so that the growth, packing, and distribution of such fresh and perishable foods is of guaranteed quality. Each type of mushroom is grown in a different way. The major task was to recreate the ecological and biological conditions in which the mushrooms would flourish as naturally as possible. As a mushroom is a fruit-body that grows underground, or on or under the bark of trees, using the juices, which include cellulose, to gain nourishment and growth, various "food" compounds were investigated. Nowadays, straw, sawdust, manure, wood chips, and logs are first pasteurized and then injected with the relevant fungus spores. The mushrooms are then grown under controlled conditions of heat and humidity, eventually being collected by hand when mature. The technology is actually quite complicated, but it is improving all the time.

Twenty years ago I didn't regard cultivated mushrooms as proper mushrooms, but my view has now changed considerably. International gastronomy has taken this special ingredient—the cultivated mushroom—on board, recognizing that it provides wonderful food. But then I think all mushrooms are wonderful. I still maintain, though, that it is much more fun to go hunting for the wild ones. . . . In the following pages I will describe and present twelve of the most popular "exotics" with which you can create wonderful dishes.

LEFT CULTIVATING OYSTER MUSHROOMS CAN RESULT IN COLORS NOT FOUND IN NATURE

MATURE AGARICUS BISPORUS

AGARICUS BISPORUS
BUTTON MUSHROOM / CREMINI / PORTOBELLO

It was in the 1600s that French melon-growers discovered that their unused melon beds were good mediums for growing mushrooms. They later grew the mushrooms in caves, where climate, temperature, and other such considerations could be controlled. (So many mushrooms were produced in the Paris region that in the trade small mushrooms are known as "champignons de Paris" to this day.)

There were mushroom-producing quarries in England too, at the end of the nineteenth century, and the great Carême, chef to the Prince Regent, admired the English mushrooms on sale locally.

During the last 50 or so years, there has been a huge increase in production of *A. bisporus* worldwide, the total reaching millions of tons. Britain, the Netherlands, Italy, France, the United States, and China are but a few of the countries to have benefited from the latest technology. The mushrooms are usually eaten fresh, but they are also canned.

Nowadays, special mushroom "houses" are used, and trays of specially formulated compound/compost are used for the growing medium. (You can buy equipment for growing mushrooms at home!) The yield of 60 pounds per square meter of soil or compound, recorded in the Netherlands, shows how prolifically these mushrooms can grow.

However, it is in China, particularly in the south, that some 70 percent of the world supply of *A. bisporus* is produced. The cultivation there is more of a family business, while in the West we have large, technologically perfect plants in which to cultivate mushrooms.

A.bisporus can grow to the size of $^3/_4$ inch in a couple of days after appearing from under the compost, depending on the temperature and general conditions.

BUTTON Mushrooms with a stem no higher than $^3/_4$ inch and the cap $1^1/_4$–$2^1/_2$ inches in diameter. The membrane (ring) is still closed and there are no gills visible. It is white.
CAPS Mushrooms that have advanced to the next stage of growth, measuring 1 inch high, with a cap up to $2^3/_4$ inches in diameter. They are open, and the ring shows under the cap, as do gills of a pinkish color.
FLAT OR OPEN Mushrooms where the cap is totally developed, from 2–$2^3/_4$ inches in diameter, and the stem not higher than $1^1/_4$ inches. The visible gills are darkening to brown.
CREMINI AND PORTOBELLO Cremini, or crimini, are a form of *A. bisporus* with a light brown cap and richer flavor. They are similar in size and shape to button mushrooms. Portobellos, which are mature, opened creminis up to 6 inches wide, have a meaty texture and a much richer taste.

COOKING

All have a pleasant mushroomy smell and are sweet in taste. None should ever be peeled.

They are used in many different ways, starting with the button, which may be eaten raw. This can also be used in stews, fried, sautéed whole or sliced, pickled, or preserved in oil. It works well in risottos, accompanied by dried porcini to give more flavor. Creminis can be used in all of the same ways.

Caps have more flavor than buttons because they are more mature. They can be used in similar ways to buttons, but have the advantage of size, so that they can be stuffed with various ingredients. They taste better cooked than raw. They are also used finely chopped to stuff meat, or in sauces.

Flat or open mushrooms and portobellos are best sautéed (whole or sliced), brushed with oil and grilled or broiled, or baked, with or without a stuffing.

AURICULARIA POLYTRICHA
WOOD EAR / TREE EAR / KIKURAGE

According to Chang and Miles, in their masterly *The Biology and Cultivation of Edible Mushrooms* (Academic Press, New York, 1978), *Auricularia polytricha* is the first mushroom in history to have been cultivated. This was in China about 1400 years ago. Its natural wild counterpart growing in the West is *Auricularia judae* (see page 32). Like the wild counterpart, *A. polytricha* is a gelatinous fungus, ear-shaped, and ranging from a pale to dark brown color. It reaches a diameter of 6 inches and is about $3/8$ inch thick. It has a very smooth surface, almost velvety, and is very soft to the touch.

In the wild, it grows in hardwood forests on various types of trees from which it draws out the nutrients. This natural habitat has been recreated using special logs or even sawdust, with the addition of other elements.

AURICULARIA POLYTRICHA (WOOD EAR)

The Chinese, for instance, allow oak poles to rot for a year or so, then erect them into a sort of shed. The spores are introduced, and over the next two years or so the fungi grow all over them. At this point they are harvested, because the wood will have become too rotten to continue acting as host.

This mushroom is seldom sold in its fresh form in the West, but it is available in dried form from most Chinese or Japanese markets. Even in China, the mushroom is mostly sold in its dried form, which means it has become an everyday, readily available product. The dried form has the advantage of regaining its original shape and size when soaked in water and does not lose any of its proteins or vitamins. In fact, the Chinese believe this mushroom has properties that make the blood more fluid, and doctors prescribe it to counteract the effects of arteriosclerosis.

COOKING

I don't think this mushroom tastes particularly good, but its peculiar gelatinous texture is greatly appreciated in the East. I use it mainly in stews, braises, and soups, because when heated in fat, for example when fried, it tends to expand and cause an "explosion." If the fat is very hot, this could be dangerous. After poaching or braising, it could be cut into strips and used in salads.

FLAMMULINA VELUTIPES (ENOKI)

FLAMMULINA VELUTIPES
(SYN. COLLYBIA VELUTIPES)
ENOKI / ENOKITAKE / GOLDEN MUSHROOM / GOLDEN NEEDLES

In most cases, cultivated mushrooms are quite similar to their wild or natural versions, but not in the case of *Flammulina velutipes*. In the wild, this mushroom grows in clumps on deciduous logs (sometimes pine), throughout the winter until spring. It has a velvety stem (hence the English names "velvet shank" and "velvet foot") up to 4 inches tall, and a sticky yellow to orange cap that can grow to 2 inches in diameter. It is found in temperate parts of the northern hemisphere, and it is called "enoki" because in Japan (its main area of cultivation and consumption), it grows on the enoki, or Chinese hackberry, tree. However, with Japanese expertise in mushroom growing, the cultivated version has developed quite differently. It is also stunningly pretty, but much smaller and thinner. Encouraged to grow in clumps, the mushrooms resemble little bundles of short spaghetti with very small caps of $1/4$ inch, and thinner and longer stems of up to $4^{1}/_{2}$ inches tall.

The clumps of mushrooms have a deep, musty smell, and the taste is sweet and nutty. To obtain the immaculate white, almost porcelain-like color, the mushrooms are kept in the dark during cultivation. They are forced through a narrow aperture in a jar containing sterilized sawdust of various decomposing hardwoods that have been injected with the spores of the fungus. The jars often have a stiff collar to keep the tiny stems growing upright. Growth can take as little as a week from sowing to sprouting of the fruit-body. The clumps are packed in bundles of 4 ounces and wrapped in cellophane.

Western mushroom growers are experimenting with this mushroom, with some success, but there is still a time to go until major production.

COOKING

Enoki are usually eaten raw as an embellishment to salads, and I would recommend combining them with the dark purple *Laccaria amethystea* (see page 50) to have a real taste sensation. I have created recipes that lean on Japanese tradition, but I have also veered back toward the Italian, which involved enveloping a clump of enoki in prosciutto and flavoring them with olive oil and lemon juice. In Japan, enoki are mostly used in soups to make them look beautiful.

GRIFOLA FRONDOSA (MAITAKE)

GRIFOLA FRONDOSA
MAITAKE / HEN OF THE WOODS / DANCING MUSHROOM

The food industry, always in search of something that is commercially viable, has managed to isolate the spores of the wild *Grifola frondosa* (see page 47), and cultivate them on a chip and wood compound imitating its natural habitat (oak mainly). The masters in this field are the Japanese, and they have given the name "maitake" to the very success- fully cultivated variety, which has a taste and texture much loved by the Japanese. It has been cultivated for the last ten years or so, with a production of 60,000 tons a year, supplying not only the local market but also the rest of the world.

The wild variety is indisputably more valuable than the cultivated because of its better flavor. However, the disadvantages of insect infestation and other impurities in the wild *Grifola frondosa* make the cultivated variety more acceptable to the everyday consumer. Another reason for the enormous success of the cultivated mushroom, apart from its texture and taste, is that it reportedly has many beneficial health properties.

Indoor cultivation produces much smaller examples than the wild (see page 47). In indoor cultivation, glass containers with narrow openings—or plastic bags with holes—are filled with chips of wood and treated sawdust, which are impregnated with the spawn where the mycelium eventually forms. After 60–120 days the fruit-body starts to grow. In order to have a continuous output, large quantities of containers and bags have to be inoculated and rotated. The yield potential is ¹/₂–1 pound mushrooms per 5–7 pounds of sterilized, enriched hardwood sawdust.

Outdoors, cultivation is left more to nature. Logs and hardwood stumps are inoculated and buried, which is more productive than leaving them to rot naturally. How wonderful and profitable it would be if all the old stumps of pine worldwide were inooculated with maitake! Although outdoor cultivation is more vulnerable to insect infestation, in general this mushroom does not seem to be too badly affected.

COOKING

When used in Asian cooking, the maitake adds a touch of refinement and delicacy. It is excellent when fried with scrambled eggs or sautéed by itself or with garlic and chili pepper, and is ideal for adding to soups. I usually treat it as a vegetable to accompany dishes of meat or fish. I have also combined maitake with pasta, with very good results. Any of the Asian recipes that I give in this book could use maitake as their main mushroom ingredient—in fact it could be used to replace practically any mushroom.

HERICIUM ERINACEUM
POMPOM / YAMABUSHITAKE / BEAR'S HEAD MUSHROOM

This cultivated mushroom is popular in North America, and is slowly appearing in European markets as "lion's mane fungus." It is already well known in Asia, where it is highly sought after for its medicinal properties. It has been given lots of names, including "bear's head," "monkey's head," and "sheep's head," but I like "pompom" best, as it reflects its funny shape. It has also been called "hedgehog mushroom" (not to be confused with *Hydnum repandum*), because of the many white spines of which it is formed.

Completely white in color, the fruit-body—rather like a fluffy snowball or huge knitted pompom—can reach up to 16 inches in the wild once fully grown, and the color goes from white to yellow, then to pale brown. I have seen it only once in the woodlands of Britain, but it is popular and fairly common in the rest of Europe, in North America, China, and Japan. It grows on dying or dead trees, such

HERICIUM ERINACEUM (POMPOM)

as walnut, beech, maple, and other broad-leaf trees, stumps, and logs.

But the mushrooms are also cultivated indoors, in plastic bags full of treated wood chips and sawdust, which develop this mushroom from incubation to fruiting in 20 days. The mushrooms are forced through small holes in the plastic to form the desired round shape and are then easily collected and packed. It is interesting to note that 5 pounds of wood mixture produces a 1-pound cluster. They are also cultivated in narrow-topped containers in Japan.

It has been discovered in China that the pompom contains a compound able to combat cancer, and also senility. Tablets made from these mushrooms are available in China.

COOKING

Per 4 ounces of fresh mushroom, 31 grams consist of protein, 4 grams of fat, and 17 grams of carbohydrate, plus other elements and vitamins, making it nutritionally attractive.

Cultivated mushrooms need no cleaning, but this one should be quartered before use. It is very good when cooked with other mushrooms, especially shiitake, presenting a contrast in color and texture. It is said to taste of lobster or eggplant.

HYPSIZYGUS TESSULATUS

(SYN. LYOPHILLUM SHIMEJI)
BUNA-SHIMEJI / BEECH MUSHROOM /
HON-SHIMEJI

A latecomer in the cultivated mushroom market, *Hypsizygus tessulatus* is considered by the Japanese and Chinese to be a gourmet delicacy.

There has been great confusion about what to call it in the last couple of centuries, with scientists all giving it different names. A Japanese company has registered the name "Hon-shimeji." It reminds me of the first stage of *Armillaria mellea*, the honey fungus (see page 28). It grows naturally on various species of trees like beech, elm, cottonwood, willow, oak, and other hardwoods in Europe, Asia, and North America.

Cultivation takes place in containers, sometimes glass jars, which are filled with wood chips and treated sawdust. The idea is to force the growth through a small aperture, to encourage a tighter cluster of mushrooms with a longish, tapered stem and a small, hemispheric cap. The cap starts off gray, then becomes paler with age. The stem is up to 2¹/₂ inches long and is white, as are the gills. The mushrooms are excellent when the caps are still closed. I truly believe this to be one of the mushrooms of the future.

COOKING

The texture, fragrance, and taste are totally delicious and the mushroom can be prepared in many interesting ways. To use, just cut off the compressed bottom of the clustered stems. I combine the mushrooms with all sorts of ingredients. I have even pickled them in vinegar and preserved them in oil. As they are so fresh and aromatic, they may be used as an antipasto. Fried or boiled and flavored with olive oil, garlic, and chili pepper, they also make an excellent sauce for pasta.

LENTINULA EDODES

(SYN. CORTINELLUS SHIITAKE)
SHIITAKE / BLACK FOREST MUSHROOM /
GOLDEN OAK MUSHROOM

A distant relation of *Armillaria mellea* (see page 28), this mushroom must be the best-known of all the exotics. It is featured in the menus of most Chinese and Japanese restaurants, together with the wood or tree ear fungus (see page 83). Occasionally I have seen these mushrooms claimed to be porcini on Western restaurant menus, because the slices of the cap have a dark brown color and a tender, meaty texture similar to that of porcini, but without the inimitably decisive flavor. Sadly, this can happen when chefs and customers are not particularly knowledgeable about the real thing.

The cultivation of shiitake is of great importance to all of Asia, not only for its edibility, but also because it is believed to be very useful in the battle against cancer, especially in Japan where it is formally recognized as a medicine. In fact, in the West, drug companies and the medical press have started to recognize that many mushrooms, wild and cultivated,

ABOVE AND BELOW LENTINULA EDODES (SHIITAKE)

contain substances that may be beneficial to health. A great deal of money is being invested in this, as well as in the improvement of cultivation techniques.

In the wild, this winter mushroom grows on trees such as beech and oak, in temperate areas. They are known as "shii" because they commonly grow on a type of oak, the "shii" tree ("take" means mushroom). In cultivation, they use blocks of sterilized sawdust impregnated with the spores of the fungus, which are put into plastic bags with holes in to allow the clusters of mushrooms to grow. Logs are also used, and after soaking are left outside to sprout their valuable fruit-bodies, while the plastic bags are kept in humid, temperature-controlled rooms. This latter method has proved to be much more profitable for continual production, which now runs into millions of tons yearly, competing

OPPOSITE
HYPSIZYGUS
TESSULATUS
(BUNA-
SHIMEJI)

with *Agaricus bisporus* in popularity.

The cap grows up to 10 inches in diameter and is hemispheric at the beginning, expanding to convex and then flat. When small, the mushrooms are dark brown in color, becoming paler as they grow. The cap is rolled, which gives a lovely shape when cut into slices. Caps with white fissures on them are considered the best culinarily in Japan. These fissures are obtained by letting air into the growing room: as the caps dry in the air, they crack. The gills are white and quite tightly packed, becoming irregular with age, and they bruise to a light brown color when touched. The spores are white. The stems are rather tough, and not usually eaten.

The mushrooms are available fresh in most supermarkets. The Chinese actually prefer the dried version, which is also readily available. It is very flavorsome once rehydrated in water to its original size.

COOKING

I use this mushroom when an exotic flavor is required. The best marriage between shiitake and *Auricularia judae* is to be tasted in the recipe on page 188. It can be fried, stewed, stuffed, braised, or eaten in soups. There isn't a more versatile mushroom. I've even managed to pickle it with good results. Try it!

LEPISTA NUDA (WOOD BLEWIT)

LEPISTA NUDA
WOOD BLEWIT

"Wood blewit" is the name given to *Lepista nuda* in English, whether it is wild or cultivated. The wild mushroom is much darker in color than the cultivated, starting off dark violet and gradually fading to brownish-purple. The cultivated mushroom is one of the few mushrooms that is violet in color, apart from the wild *L. saeva*,

which has a brilliant violet stem.

In my restaurant we use this mushroom quite a lot. It is cultivated in Europe and North America, and is very easy to grow. Its natural habitat is in or around decomposing piles of sawdust, in conifers among the leaves — even on piles of compost. In cultivation, these conditions are imitated: treated horse manure and straw compost are inoculated and then kept in total darkness for 25–60 days. Germination occurs within two weeks. For 24–52 weeks, mushrooms

continue developing every 10–14 days.

They are gilled mushrooms, with a deformed cap. The stems are quite large at the base, with a dry texture. When fresh they are totally violet, becoming paler with age, with the stem always remaining violet.

COOKING

It is mostly sautéed, together with other mushrooms, due to its inherent lack of flavor. It is good in sauces, and can also be breaded and deep-fried.

PHOLIOTA NAMEKO
NAMEKO / GLUTINOUS PHOLIOTA

Similar to *Flammulina velutipes* (the Japanese enoki mushroom, see page 83), this mushroom is said to withstand winter temperatures. It grows naturally on logs of oak and beech in the cool, northern parts of China, Taiwan, and the islands of North Japan. It is not known in Europe or North America.

Having discovered that the nameko is an excellent decomposer of hard wood, cultivation is taking place out of doors by burying oak, beech, and poplar logs under the earth before inoculating with the spores of the fungus. It requires a high humidity but not too high a temperature. The fungus grows in clumps, and is collected when the stem is 2–3¹/₄ inches tall, and the cap 1¹/₄–4 inches thick.

The nameko is highly prized in a culinary sense in Japan, immediately after matsutake, shiitake, and enoki. It does not enjoy the same sort of popularity elsewhere—as yet— because it has a layer of slime on its cap that makes it rather sticky. This remains until maturity, and puts Westerners off it a little, although it disappears on cooking. I hope that

PHOLIOTA NAMEKO (NAMEKO)

some day we can appreciate it more in Europe and North America, as it has a good texture and taste. I certainly intend to give it a try when I can get my hands on more than the few Mr. Uchida manages to bring me back from Tokyo (which I used to make the soup on page 113).

COOKING

The Japanese use it in soups, not just for embellishment, but also for that certain "je ne sais quoi" that appeals to the Japanese palate. You can also occasionally find it preserved, packed in plastic bags, in Chinese markets. This type can be used in soups and stews.

PLEUROTUS
OYSTER MUSHROOMS

The Pleurotus family is perhaps the least exotic of the cultivated mushrooms, because it is so widely available. This is due to it being relatively easy to grow, and for this reason many people choose these mushrooms with which to start a cultivation business.

There are four types of Pleurotus mushroom, which all descend from the wild *P. ostreatus* (see page 67). All grow in the wild in small clumps, using the cellulose of hardwood trees, and other decaying woods. None of these mushrooms is very fussy about where it obtains its nutrition, and once it was discovered that it was a most prolific grower, it was then cultivated artificially. It is useful as a food for hungry populations because of its valuable protein and vitamin content.

The composts prepared for cultivation are in plastic blocks or containers, and are of wood by-products or straw, which have been previously pasteurized and tested. The mushrooms can thrive on sawdust, cereal, straw, corn and corncobs, coffee residue, banana fronds, cottonseed

husks, soy pulp, paper, and various other materials containing liquid and cellulose. One benefit is that, after the crop, the compost can be used for other purposes such as animal feed. Another is that the cultivated variety does not have to be checked for larvae and maggots, because it is produced under controlled hygienic conditions.

P. CITRINOPILEATUS
Golden Oyster / Tamogitake

This has a brilliant yellow color and is very fragile and tender. It imparts a nutty flavor when cooked. It descends from the *P. cornucopiae*, the funnel-shaped natural one, which is white with very elongated gills (see page 67). It is native to the subtropical regions of China and southern Japan. The spores are pale pink, and the fleshy cap can grow in the shape of a tongue up to 4 inches in diameter.

P. DJAMOR
Pink Oyster / Takiiro Hiratake

Also known as "salmon oyster," "strawberry oyster," and "flamingo mushroom." The brilliant pink color fades as the mushroom grows, but it is still very attractive. It grows in a similar way to the yellow variety, although its evolution is still being studied by mycologists. The wild variety is collected in Thailand, Singapore, Sri Lanka, Malaysia, and other nearby countries. It is cultivated in plastic bags filled with sterilized compound—as listed above—which is impregnated with the mycelium.

P. OSTREATUS
Oyster Mushroom / Hiratake

According to Salvatore Terracina, a Sicilian farmer, the largest *P. ostreatus* he managed to collect weighed nearly 42 pounds. It sounds unbelievable, but it's true!

The cultivation of this mushroom takes place in controlled rooms, in plastic bags full of treated straw and

PLEUROTUS CITRINOPILEATUS (GOLDEN OYSTER MUSHROOM)

wood chippings. The display of these clusters growing out of the bags is no less impressive than in nature (if you forget the plastic containers). The taste and flavor of the cultivated variety is slightly different from the wild, but is still very attractive and produces good dishes. The mushrooms bought in supermarkets are usually cut at the base of the lateral stem, showing the white gills. They are rather delicate, and therefore don't have a long shelf life, so don't delay in using them.

P. ERYNGII
King Oyster

This mushroom grows mainly in Europe, is easy to cultivate, and, because of its impressive size and solidity, is called the king oyster. It fully deserves this name because it is the most substantial of them all, as well as the most tasty. In the south of Italy, it is called "cardoncello," and grows in late summer through autumn on hardwood trees.

Cultivation is easy—on hardwood sawdust and chips or straw—and the results are stunning. The cap ranges in diameter from $1^1/_4-4^1/_2$ inches, and is very solid, as is the large stem. It grows in impressive clusters, becoming a broad funnel-shape first, then getting flat. It has a grayish color, and white, firm, thick flesh.

COOKING

Culinarily, all pleurotus mushrooms are similar despite the differences in color: once cooked the colors fade. None of them needs washing or peeling, just slicing, or they can be left whole if small. All in all they are good mushrooms, full of vitamins and proteins. They can be eaten raw in salads, or cooked in most ways (stir-fried and served as a vegetable, breaded and deep-fried, in quiche fillings). Large, flat ones can be sautéed, stewed, or braised; the eryngii can be cut into slices and broiled.

STROPHARIA RUGOSOANNULATA (KING STROPHARIA)

STROPHARIA RUGOSOANNULATA
KING STROPHARIA / BURGUNDY MUSHROOM

This massive and excellent mushroom is grown in Europe, North America, and other parts of the world with equal enthusiasm. Its size has led to another name: "Godzilla mushroom"!

It is mostly cultivated out-of-doors, using hardwood chips, straw, or sawdust. This method of cultivation was discovered by pure chance, when somebody in the U.S. transplanted the mycelium off a tree stump into a private garden where wood chips and sawdust were being stored (perhaps the only mushroom that can be successfully transplanted!). It has a good yield, and the clusters are beautiful to look at, but it grows very slowly, over 8–10 weeks.

The stem is white, with a meaty, reddish-brown cap measuring 1 1/2–5 inches in diameter. The gills are also white, becoming gray with age.

COOKING

The king stropharia can be used in all the recipes in this book, either as a substitute or as the main mushroom. The cleaning is simple: just cut off the stem at the base. They don't have maggots or insects. It is wonderful just sautéed in butter or as part of a mixed stew. Bigger examples can be cut in half, brushed with oil, and broiled.

TRICHOLOMA MATSUTAKE
MATSUTAKE

For the Japanese this is the finest of all mushrooms. It is so greatly appreciated that 2 pounds of good wild specimens can fetch up to $1,200. (This is still quite a way from the white truffle, which—in late 2002—was priced at $4,500 for the same weight!) I have never seen this mushroom growing wild, as it does not occur in Europe or North America, but I have had the pleasure of tasting one or two examples brought to me by an enthusiastic Japanese customer. The husband of a Japanese friend of mine, Miho Uchida, recently brought some back from Tokyo, so I could have the photographs taken for this book.

This mushroom, together with the truffle and others, belongs to the mycorrhizal type, which requires a symbiosis with the roots of certain trees. These types of mushroom are much more difficult to cultivate than the saprophytic or parasitic ones, which grow from dead matter, or attach themselves to living trees and organisms. The difficulty in growing matsutake and similar fungi is being continually researched, because it concerns the most highly prized mushrooms in the culinary world. As a result, cultivation is limited, and prices are very high!

The matsutake grows in a similar way to the fairy ring mushroom: in circles around certain types of pine, usually the Japanese red pine ("matsu" means pine, and "take" means mushroom). The size of the circle increases every year by 4–6 inches. The mushroom itself grows up to 4 1/2 inches high in the wild, with a very strong stem. The hemispherical cap is 2–8 inches in diameter when open, initially cream on the outside edges, red-brown with streaks in the center. In cultivation, the cap is red-brown, a little flaky, and still closed. It is always collected as soon as its head pops out of the earth, because this is the best time to enjoy it—tender and sweet, rather than open and tougher.

A North American counterpart is called *Tricholoma magnivelare*; that in Europe is *T. caligatum*. It grows in coniferous woods in a similar way, but is slightly bitter compared to the superb flavor of true *T. matsutake*.

COOKING

The matsutake has a nutty, sweet taste, and the delicate fiber of the stem makes it ideal for grilling when cut in half. It is also good in soups and other delicate dishes.

TRICHOLOMA MATSUTAKE (MATSUTAKE)

THE RECIPES

Wild mushrooms are vitally important in the food chain. You only have to look at the histories of medicine and cooking in the East to realize how valued these little miracles of nature are. They have been a source of food and health in China and Japan, for instance, for thousands of years. In the West, Alexander Fleming was the first to scientifically appreciate the health potential of fungi when he discovered penicillin, but since then huge efforts have been made, and are still being made, to isolate and extract other useful compounds believed to exist in many fungi.

But it is as food that fungi are most appreciated. The definition of "edibility" is, of course, something of a moveable feast. A handful of mushrooms is universally acknowledged to be gastronomically superb in flavor; a lot more are praised or dismissed according to the opinion of the person who is passing judgment. This is partly a question of taste in the most literal sense, and partly, perhaps, a cultural matter. In Italy, for instance, people will ignore delicious mushrooms in their single-minded quest for porcini, even regarding with suspicion the agarics. These, which include the meadow and horse mushrooms, are probably the only ones many British people will actually recognize and eat.

Local markets all over Europe sell wild mushrooms in season—gathered by professional collectors whose supply is systematically checked before appearing on the stalls and in the stores. Many European governments appoint specially trained officers to inspect mushrooms before they are sold. There is also an industry collecting desirable species such as porcini for the busy commercial concerns that dry and preserve wild mushrooms.

Mushroom appreciation is full of contrasts and contradictions. On the one hand, wild mushrooms are often considered as peasant food, to be eaten by more sophisticated people only when they need to supplement dietary shortages during wartime. On the other, city people pay dearly now for the privilege of eating this same "peasant" food in restaurants. In some communities, the autumn hunting season involves the whole family in the gathering of sufficient mushrooms to preserve for the winter, and people go to some lengths to render edible mushrooms that others would consider toxic. And, of course, alongside all the delicious mushrooms, there are those that are unpleasant to eat, are toxic, or are downright poisonous. The Field Guide (see pages 10–79 should help you with identification of these.

LEFT Honey fungus ready for the kitchen, as is Antonio wearing his apron, a birthday present from his great friends, Valérie and Fabrice Moireau

A SUCCESSFUL DAY'S HARVEST READY TO BE CLEANED

THE FOOD VALUE OF MUSHROOMS

Most mushrooms consist of approximately 90 percent water, but also contain important minerals—potassium salts and phosphates—plus varying quantities of vitamins B1, B2, D, and E. In nutritional terms, the key qualities of a mushroom are its low calorie content (only 42 per 100 grams/3 ^{1}/$_2$ ounces), its low fat (1–2 percent), and its protein (3–9 percent, comparable with meat and milk). But it is texture and flavor (and, in certain cases, a unique aromatic quality) that make mushrooms generally so indispensable in cooking.

The most sensible way to approach eating wild mushrooms is with caution, and this doesn't only refer to the need to identify them accurately. Even those acknowledged to be edible can cause gastric upsets since their micro-structure makes them less digestible than many other plants. Also, their mycosine content affects the stomach juices, making the juices take longer to break food down. So never over-indulge with mushroom-eating: it is best to limit portions to 4–5 ounces. Even good edible mushrooms can become indigestible if not treated or prepared properly. The rule is to eat them as fresh as possible and to choose only the best specimens. Deterioration that results in the production of damaging toxins can take place when mushrooms are badly stored (and that includes transporting them from the gathering site to the kitchen in a plastic bag). And they can deteriorate after cooking as well, so eat immediately and do not reheat more than once.

Some mushrooms are inedible unless cooked or blanched before cooking; the Field Guide indicates which these are. And, finally, many mushrooms react badly with alcohol, so limit alcohol consumption when eating most wild mushrooms.

DEALING WITH YOUR MUSHROOM HARVEST

A common autumn spectacle in Italy is a group of people sitting around a table piled high with mushrooms, sorting and cleaning them. Mushrooms don't improve once they have been gathered, and even if you have picked

The mushroom world may be full of contrasts, but it is also full of changes. Wild mushrooms are now becoming much more popular in countries where once they were considered virtually inedible. And the science of mushroom cultivation has grown enormously in the last decade or so. In the East, they have been cultivating selected species for hundreds of years (see page 81), but now many more fungi are being grown commercially. With truly wild mushrooms, we are subject to location, season, and weather vagaries, while their cultivated cousins can be grown in suitable conditions almost anywhere in the world, and throughout the whole year. This avoids expensive transport costs (although I will always have to import my precious white truffles from Italy!), and guarantees fresh quality. I truly believe that fungi are becoming more and more important in our lives, and that they can be regarded as the food of the future.

only a few handfuls, you should perform this
ritual as soon as you get home to avoid the
disappointment of finding that they have gone
soggy overnight, or that the maggots have had
a feast in your stead.

The ritual involves having someone
knowledgeable check the identity and edibility
of each specimen. Then there is the cleaning,
inspecting, and sorting into size and type. (See
the Field Guide for more detail.) And finally,
there is the challenge of assessing the best way
to make the culinary most of each mushroom.
Sometimes a special find calls for a particular
accompaniment and you must buy a piece of
prime fish or meat to make a meal. Sometimes
a tiny amount of a good mushroom needs
ekeing out. Sometimes (perhaps most often),
you have a miscellaneous assortment that,
while not gourmet material, is at least versatile.
Sometimes there is enough to have some for
preserving. So what do you choose?

Imagine you have come back from the
woods with a small basketful of mixed fungi.
If they are extremely fresh and tender you might
make a *fritto misto* or eat them in a salad, but
if they look a bit tired, then soups and stews
are a better idea. For more elderly specimens,
drying is the best bet. You might have found a
nice big cauliflower mushroom or a cluster of
honey fungus. After you have put aside enough
for a sauce to accompany a plate of pasta and
perhaps cooked some for a stew, cook the rest
in vinegar to preserve as an antipasto.

Imagine your basket contains a substantial
number of a single species—porcini if you are
very lucky. Sort them out according to whether
they are small and firm (incidentally, the most
expensive to buy), medium, big, and young or
big but old. Do your cleaning and maggot-
excising. Once you can see how much good
mushroom material you have, you can explore
the options for eating them.

● Small ones in prime condition: slice raw for
salads
● Small and medium: sauté for immediate use
or for freezing; or freeze, sliced or whole; or
slice and preserve in oil
● Big and young (pores still creamy): grill or
broil whole, or slice and use as above
● Big but elderly: slice for drying, or for
immediate cooking
● Bits and pieces, old and young: dry for
powdering, or cook into duxelles or extract.

MIXED SAUTÉED MUSHROOMS

COOKING METHODS

Although my recipes specify *how* to cook the
mushroom ingredients in all cases, I include
these notes to help explain *why*, as well as to
offer a summary of processes for you to draw
on to develop your own recipes.

FRYING I do this in oil, or butter, or a mixture
of both. A mixture helps prevent the butter
from turning brown. Or, I use oil first and add
butter later to give sauces a nice taste and a
shiny, creamy look. When you sauté mushrooms briefly in very hot fat, add seasoning at
the end: salt will make the mushrooms exude
water and alter their taste. Garlic should on no
account be allowed to brown. The purpose of
frying is to cook the outside of the mushroom
so it is nice and crisp, sealing in the flavor,
and it is a good thing to do so right away,
since it is the first stage of any number of

recipes. Mushrooms treated like this will keep for a few hours or can be frozen.

SAUTÉING This uses a lower heat than frying and is good for combinations of fresh and dried mushrooms. Flavor is exuded with the juices, making a delicious sauce.

GRILLING AND BROILING These are good for substantial mushrooms—big caps of porcini, parasols, agarics, slices of giant puffball, and chunks of blanched cauliflower mushroom.

BLANCHING This is sometimes a useful precaution for preserving young ink caps in their closed stage, for example, but is also a necessary measure to remove the toxins present in some raw mushrooms.

DEEP-FRYING This is a favorite of mine. Dip mushrooms in beaten egg and then into bread crumbs, then deep-fry. This seals in flavor and gives an appetizingly crisp texture to the outside.

MICROWAVING I do not recommend this for cooking mushrooms, although it can be useful for reheating dishes—but once only.

PRESERVING METHODS

The art of preserving food is as old as humanity itself. Prehistoric hunters dried and salted their foodstuffs, and these early methods are still used today, particularly with wild mushrooms. Later, pickling and bottling or canning offered additional methods of preservation, and most recently freezing has opened up new possibilities. Different mushrooms call for different approaches. The various methods maintain, enhance, or even transform the natural qualities of the original, and your choice depends both on the means available and on how you want to use your preserves.

Speaking personally, no matter which way I preserve mushrooms, I always enjoy them and continually find new ways of using them. From the anonymity of the convenient frozen blocks of mushrooms in the freezer to the rows of glass jars packed with dried and pickled delights, which turn my pantry into a mycophagist's Aladdin's cave, preserving enables me to serve and enjoy wild mushrooms all year.

DRYING

Until recently, anyone entering our house in autumn was assailed by an intense smell of wild mushrooms, and confronted in every room by sheets of newspaper spread with thin slices of drying porcini. Then, in Switzerland, I came across a machine specially made for drying quantities of mushrooms, and now I can dry over 6 pounds of mushrooms in about 2 hours.

Drying captures and preserves the taste, aroma, and texture of mushrooms, but very few retain their shape after they have been rehydrated by soaking in water—morels, cauliflower mushrooms, and shiitake are exceptions.

WHAT TO DRY
Not all mushrooms are suitable: the fibrous texture makes some stringy and tough, while others lose their aroma. The best results come from the following.

BOLETUS EDULIS (PORCINI) This has the perfect texture for slicing and drying, intensifies in taste when dried, and rehydrates quite well. Considering the price of the fresh mushrooms, it is no wonder that just a little of bought dried porcini is expensive.

BOLETUS BADIUS (BAY BOLETE) Although the flavor is less intense than that of the porcini, the texture is similar and it dries equally well. Since it is a common mushroom, I dry large quantities and find it very useful.

MORCHELLA ELATA AND M. ESCULENTA (MORELS) Probably the most expensive to buy dried and much sought after. Haute cuisine—especially French and Swiss—makes abundant use of morels. The dried rehydrate well, with a good taste and texture, but relatively little aroma. They can be dried whole. Look out for dirt at the stem base in bought ones.

CRATERELLUS CORNUCOPIOIDES (HORN OF PLENTY) Ideal for drying because of the absence of watery flesh and the increase in aroma when dry. They rehydrate well, and are also extremely easy to reduce to powder.

SPARASSIS CRISPA (CAULIFLOWER MUSHROOM) Ideal for drying (it needs slicing) because of its good texture and slight aroma. When rehydrated, it regains the cartilaginous quality

ABOVE PICKLED BUNA-SHIMEJI IN OIL

TOP PICKLED PORCINI IN OIL

of the fresh fungus, so is ideal for soups and dishes requiring some texture.

Suitable but not so highly recommended are *Agaricus campestris* (meadow mushroom), *Auricularia judae* (jew's ear), *Hydnum repandum* (hedgehog mushroom), *Marasmius oreades* (fairy ring mushroom), the polypores, and shiitake. Sadly, the least successful of all is *Cantharellus cibarius* (chanterelle), which becomes tough and tasteless. The only thing it retains is its charming color.

How to dry

● Never wash the mushrooms. Brush or cut away parts that are dirty or sandy.

● Use only mature but not overripe specimens. The odd insect larva doesn't matter—it will vacate its habitat once the mushroom is sliced.

● Small mushrooms can be threaded whole on string (with space between for air to circulate) and hung up to dry. For larger, fleshy mushrooms, cut cap and stem into $^1/_4$-inch slices.

● In warm climates, lay mushroom slices on gauze-covered mats and place in an airy spot in the sun—they should dry in a day. Where colder and more humid, dry indoors, on clean newspaper covered by a clean cloth. Leave in a well ventilated room, on top of a radiator or in an airing cupboard, turning occasionally. They can be dried in a convection oven at a very low temperature with the door slightly open. If using a conventional oven, keep the door open and put a fan in front to ensure air circulation.

● Store the perfectly dried mushrooms in airtight jars or plastic bags.

● Make mushroom powder from dried mushrooms using a mortar and pestle or a food processor. Keep in an airtight jar and add to soups, sauces, and omelets, or incorporate in savory butters and fresh pasta dough.

● If buying dried mushrooms, inspect to make sure they contain whole slices, not scrappy bits. Keep in the refrigerator or freezer.

To rehydrate Soak in lukewarm water for 15 to 20 minutes before preparing as directed in the recipe. Dried shiitake take about 30 minutes: discard the stem, which is usually tough and dirty. Use the soaking water—after straining through a fine sieve—for added flavor or as stock. Dried mushrooms can be added as they are when cooking soups and some sauces; they revive during the long, slow cooking.

PORCINI THREADED ON A STRING FOR DRYING

Salting

Salting is still widely used to preserve food in Poland and Russia, not only for meat and fish, but also for vegetables, including mushrooms. The process simply consists of embedding the mushrooms in plenty of salt, which gradually dissolves into a preservative brine. Saffron milk caps and porcini are two that are traditionally salted, but any young, firm mushrooms are ideal. Once you have cleaned the mushrooms thoroughly (without, of course, washing them), remove any grit, check for maggots, and cut in slices if large. Allow $^1/_3$ cup kosher salt to each 2 pounds of mushrooms. Alternate layers of salt and mushrooms in non-corrosive containers

A HARVEST OF FRESH MORELS

FREEZING FROM RAW Good to freeze raw are:
● The agarics (though I wouldn't bother, as the cultivated ones are sold year round).
● All the boletes (Boletus and Leccinum, of which the porcini and bay bolete are the best).
● Chanterelles and horn of plenty. The latter, however, are very fragile after freezing.
● Hedgehog mushroom, after its spikes are removed.
● Morels.
● St. George's mushroom.
● Giant polypores and sulfur shelf.
● Wood and field blewits.

Saffron milk caps freeze perfectly after blanching. Other mushrooms need cooking before they freeze successfully.

Choose only small and maggot-free specimens, and clean thoroughly. If necessary, blanch in boiling salted water for 30 seconds or so, then drain well and let cool completely on a clean cloth. Put 8 or 10 at a time in a clear plastic bag and seal, extracting as much air as possible. Put into the freezer. Or, spread the mushrooms on a tray and freeze, then bag them up and return to the freezer. Remember to date and label the bags.

Thaw either by deep-frying in hot oil or by boiling in water. To deep-fry, drop the frozen mushrooms into hot oil and leave for just a few seconds (this seals the outside and thaws the inside, but be careful not to let the oil bubble over). Alternatively, plunge them into boiling salted water for a few minutes until they are soft. Drain, slice, and use as if fresh.

with lids; start and finish with salt. You can add more layers of salt and mushrooms later, as you gather them. Press the contents down with a weight, such as a can of food, and cover closely. Check occasionally that the mushrooms are covered with salt solution. To use, rinse well and cook without additional salt.

FREEZING

Since they may be up to 90 percent water, mushrooms are not difficult to freeze. The problems arise when you come to thaw them. Experiments over the years have taught me which mushrooms can be frozen raw without becoming tough, or "frostbitten," and which need blanching before freezing. I have also developed reliable ways of thawing.

FREEZING IN BUTTER My own favorite way of freezing boletes in particular is to cook them in butter, which helps protect them against "frostbite." Use plenty of butter—1 cup (2 sticks) unsalted butter to each 2 pounds mushrooms. Gently sauté $^2/_3$ cup minced onions in $^1/_2$ cup of the butter until golden, then add the sliced mushrooms and cook for 2 to 4 minutes. (If the mushrooms are wanted later for sautéing or frying, omit the onions.) Take the pan off the heat, add the remaining butter, and let it melt. Cool, then put into plastic freezer boxes with lids, labeled with the date and type of mushrooms, and freeze.

To thaw, leave the block at room temperature for an hour. The mushrooms and butter can be used together to provide the basis for soups and sauces, or can be used separately, after the mushrooms have been drained from the thawed butter. Mushrooms frozen in this way are ideal for risottos. You won't be able to tell the difference from fresh.

FREEZING DUXELLES I give a recipe for this mushroom basic on page 105. Duxelles is the standard way of beginning sauces and soups, and in itself is a superb filling for stuffed pasta. I freeze the mixture in an icecube tray, then put the cubes in a plastic bag in the freezer. (The amazing advantage is that you don't have to thaw the whole block of mushrooms when you only want a little to flavor a sauce—exactly as I recommend for stock.)

PICKLING

Whether the mushrooms are to be kept in brine or olive oil (brine is cheaper), they must first be boiled in a vinegar solution so they retain their texture and appearance. But since a traditional Italian antipasto must include something piquant and vinegary to tease the appetite, these delicacies are just what are needed. Commercially, you will usually only find pickled porcini, but almost all the edible mushrooms in this book are suitable for pickling. I like to serve a mixture.

Choose only the most tender specimens, because they are likely to be maggot-free, and clean them thoroughly. For once you can use water to rinse the mushrooms. They reduce in volume by about half when pickled. Store them in sterilized canning jars, using smaller jars in preference to larger ones because, once opened, the contents need to be consumed quickly. See page 102 for the recipes.

MUSHROOM EXTRACT

A useful way of coping with either a mixture of small quantities of different mushrooms or a glut of any one kind is to make this concentrate.

Clean and mince the mushrooms, then just cover with water and simmer until they have exuded as much as possible of their natural juices. Strain off the liquor. The mushrooms themselves will now be pretty tasteless, but could be used to make up a quantity for pickling. Add to the liquor a sprig of rosemary, some sage leaves, a few bay leaves, some black pepper, and a lot of salt. (I further reinforce the mushroom flavor by adding some dried mushrooms and garlic.) Boil until the liquid starts to thicken, then strain into a clean bottle and store in the refrigerator. Use a drop here and a

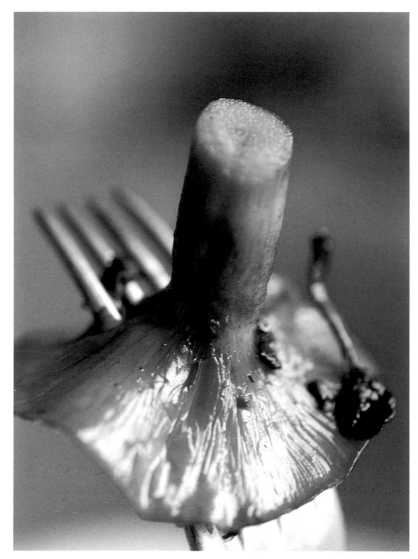

A JUICY MORSEL OF WOOD BLEWIT

drop there to flavor all sorts of dishes, and it will disappear in no time! Alternatively, you can freeze it in cubes.

THE RECIPES

I hope you enjoy cooking my recipes. As with everything in cooking, nothing is set in stone. You may decide that you need more salt here or more chili there, or you may want to make more substantial changes. Alternatively, you may use my ideas as a starting point for your own experiments. I leave it to your imagination and, I hope, pleasure. But please remember my warning, one that you will find everywhere in this book: do not experiment with mushrooms about which you are unsure. *Buon appetito!*

CHAPTER ONE
SOUPS, SAUCES, AND PRESERVES

In this chapter, I give you recipes for soups, sauces, preserves, and other basic preparations necessary for producing delicacies based on mushrooms. Soups are very much to the fore, and all are very interesting and delicious. They use mostly cultivated mushrooms, which are highly sought after and many of which are produced in the Far East. They are increasingly to be found in Asian markets and good supermarkets. In the West, we use mushrooms in soups as well, but mainly in sauces and stews. The sauces here are basic, but do not forget about those hidden within recipes for pasta, fish, and meat throughout the rest of the book. These are just as good, and may be used in many contexts. In fact, by combining various of my ideas or suggestions, you will probably be able to develop excellent new recipes. And, last but not least, here you will find many ways of preserving your wild mushrooms.

LEFT HONEY FUNGUS IS SLIGHTLY POISONOUS WHEN RAW, BUT DELICIOUS COOKED

PICKLED MUSHROOMS IN BRINE

Mushrooms pickled in brine have to be mixed with some oil before serving to make them more palatable and to reduce the sharpness (although the taste of the vinegar can be softened by adding extra herbs).

FILLS A 1-QUART JAR

4^1/$_2$ LB FRESH MUSHROOMS
SALT TO TASTE

BRINE
5 CUPS GOOD WHITE WINE
    VINEGAR
2^1/$_2$ CUPS WATER
1 TBSP SALT
1 SMALL SPRIG ROSEMARY
A FEW BLACK PEPPERCORNS
5–6 BAY LEAVES
1 MEDIUM ONION, QUARTERED
2 GARLIC CLOVES

Clean the mushrooms, then slice or chop according to size.
Combine the brine ingredients in a large, non-corrosive pan and boil for 15 minutes. Meanwhile, cook the mushrooms separately in salted water for 8 minutes. Drain the mushrooms, then add to the vinegar mixture and boil 5 minutes longer. Remove the mushrooms with a sterilized spoon and fill your jars with them, leaving some space for the vinegar liquor. Let the liquor cook 10 minutes longer, then strain and set aside to cool. When completely cold, cover the mushrooms with the strained vinegar liquor. Cover the jars tightly. They will keep for a few months in a cool place.
To serve, drain the mushrooms well, and toss with a few drops of olive oil.

PICKLED MUSHROOMS IN OIL

This second method of pickling, the usual one in Italy, is slightly more expensive, since after pickling in vinegar, the mushrooms are packed in good olive oil (but never extra virgin, as that is too strong). However, the results are so delicious that it is well worth it.

FILLS TWO 1-QUART JARS

4^1/$_2$ LB FRESH MUSHROOMS
OLIVE OIL
2 MEDIUM-SIZED, DRIED HOT RED
    CHILI PEPPERS (OPTIONAL)

BRINE
5 CUPS GOOD WHITE WINE
    VINEGAR
2^1/$_2$ CUPS WATER
2 TBSP SALT
5 BAY LEAVES
10 WHOLE CLOVES

Clean the mushrooms, then slice or chop according to size.
Combine the brine ingredients in a large, non-corrosive pan and bring to a boil. Add the mushrooms and boil until cooked through to the center: allow 5 minutes for small mushrooms, 10 to 12 minutes for large ones. Drain and, without using your hands (because the mushrooms are now sterilized), spread them out on a very clean cloth to cool and dry for a few hours. Put a few mushrooms into a sterilized jar, pour in a little oil to cover them, and (using the same spoon) toss gently so that the oil reaches all parts of the mushrooms. Add more mushrooms and more oil in the same way until the jar is full. If you wish, you can add a couple of red chili peppers for added flavor. Close the lid tightly and keep for at least a month before use (and for up to a couple of months thereafter). Once opened, however, a jar should be used up fairly rapidly. Occasionally I find a few pinpoints of mold on the mushrooms after some months. If I catch them early enough, the situation can be retrieved. I discard the oil, boil the mushrooms in pure vinegar for a minute or so, then store in fresh olive oil as before.

RIGHT PICKLED MUSHROOMS IN OIL

BASIC STOCK

Homemade stocks immeasurably improve many dishes, do not cost much, and only require a little patience. For chicken stock, use a whole chicken or pieces (thighs and drumsticks are good). For beef stock, use the same weight of a stewing cut (not the best filet mignon!). Grinding the meat or poultry makes for greater flavor. For fish stock, the preparation is similar, but replace the meaty ingredients with white fish pieces, bones, and heads, and cook for 1 hour only (but see also page 184). For vegetable stock, simply omit the meat. You can use chicken, meat, game, fish, or vegetable stocks freshly made, or after a day if kept in the refrigerator. You can also freeze them in a suitable container, or in an icecube tray, then pack the cubes in a plastic bag.

MAKES 8 CUPS

3 LB MEAT/FISH PIECES AND BONES
1 LARGE ONION, QUARTERED
4 MEDIUM CARROTS, DICED
2 CELERY STALKS, DICED
3 GARLIC CLOVES, LEFT WHOLE
10 BLACK PEPPERCORNS
2 BAY LEAVES
1 SMALL BUNCH PARSLEY
3 CUPS SLICED BUTTON MUSHROOMS,
    DRIED FOR 15 MINUTES IN
    A 350°F OVEN
1 SPRIG MARJORAM

Put the meat or fish pieces and bones into a large pan and cover with 12 cups cold water. Bring to a boil quickly and boil for a few minutes. Skim off the foam and reduce the heat to simmering point. Add the remaining ingredients and cook for 1½ hours.

Strain the liquid through a fine sieve and, if further reduction is needed to intensify the flavors, cook a little longer to allow evaporation. Store when cool.

MUSHROOM SAUCE

This Italian sauce can be used in many ways and is utterly delicious. It is good for flavoring pasta, rice, and polenta, but can also top crostini or flavor meat or fish dishes. It is best when made with fresh and dried porcini, but you can also use giant polypore or sulfur shelf. The sauce can be frozen.

MAKES 2 CUPS

10 OZ SMALL, FRESH PORCINI
½ OZ DRIED PORCINI,
    SOAKED IN WARM WATER FOR
    20 MINUTES
2 GARLIC CLOVES, MINCED
4 TBSP OLIVE OIL
SALT AND PEPPER TO TASTE
2 TBSP MINCED PARSLEY
2 MINT LEAVES, MINCED
1 TBSP TOMATO PASTE
SALT AND PEPPER TO TASTE

Clean the fresh porcini, then cut into small cubes. Drain and mince the dried porcini, reserving the soaking liquid.

Sauté the garlic in the oil until translucent, then add the fresh and soaked, dried mushrooms. Sauté for about 10 minutes over medium heat. Season with salt and pepper to taste.

Add the parsley, mint, tomato paste, and 4 tablespoons of the reserved soaking liquid. Warm through, and the sauce is ready.

If you use this sauce for pasta, sprinkle with a little grated Parmesan before serving.

DRIED MOREL AND TRUFFLE SAUCE

This is one of the best sauces for roasted meat or game, or even to flavor risottos and pasta dishes. In this recipe of Italian origin I used the dried morels that I got from Nepal (see page 64), as I still had some left from the original purchase!

When reduced in a sauce, the morels have a full, smoky flavor. My favorite way of serving this sauce is to pair it with handkerchief pasta (see page 160). The sauce can be frozen.

SERVES 6

2 OZ DRIED MORELS, SOAKED IN
   WARM WATER FOR 20 MINUTES
4 TBSP (¹/₂ STICK) BUTTER
2 SMALL SHALLOTS, MINCED
1³/₄ CUPS CHICKEN STOCK (SEE
   OPPOSITE)
¹/₂ CUP HEAVY OR WHIPPING CREAM
SALT AND PEPPER TO TASTE
10 DROPS TRUFFLE OIL
2 OZ FRESH SUMMER TRUFFLE

Drain the morels, then trim off the base of the stems, and mince the mushrooms.

Melt the butter in a casserole, add the shallots, and sauté until soft. Add the morels and the stock, and cook for 8 to 10 minutes. Let cool, then add the cream, and salt and pepper. Process in a blender. Clean the summer truffle; cut it into ¹/₈-inch slices, then dice. Stir in the truffle oil and truffle dice. Warm gently before using.

WILD MUSHROOM DUXELLES

This is actually nothing more than minced and flavored mushrooms that have been deprived of most of their moisture. The resulting duxelles can be used as a filling for many dishes, such as ravioli, stuffed mushrooms, squid, or pockets of puff or other pastry, or they can be added to sauces, stews, and soups. You could also use this tasty treat on toast or bruschetta. Of French origin, it is now used all over the world. Duxelles can be frozen.

MAKES ABOUT 6 OZ

8 OZ FRESH WILD MUSHROOMS
   (PORCINI, MORELS, CHANTERELLES,
   BAY BOLETES) OR 7 OZ CREMINI
   MUSHROOMS PLUS ¹/₂ OZ EACH OF
   DRIED PORCINI, MORELS, AND
   SHIITAKE
4 TBSP (¹/₂ STICK) BUTTER
3 TBSP MINCED GREEN ONION
1 GARLIC CLOVE, MINCED
1 TBSP FRESH BREAD CRUMBS
2 TBSP COARSELY CHOPPED PARSLEY
SALT AND PEPPER TO TASTE

Clean and trim the fresh mushrooms. Chop the cremini coarsely, if using. Soak the dried mushrooms in warm water for 30 minutes, then squeeze and mince. (Save the soaking liquid for a later use.)

Melt the butter in a pan over low heat and sauté the green onion and garlic for a few minutes to soften. Add the mushrooms and bread crumbs, and sauté for a few more minutes. When the moisture has almost evaporated, add the parsley and some salt and pepper, then cook for a little longer.

Cool, then refrigerate for up to 5 days. (Although I usually advise not to eat reheated mushrooms, cooked and flavored in this way they are quite useful.) The duxelles can also be frozen.

MUSHROOM MINESTRONE

The famous Italian thick soup, or minestrone, uses all sorts of mixed vegetables, so I used mixed mushrooms for this collection of flavors, textures, and colors— a celebration of nature. This recipe is useful for when you have only a few specimens of each mushroom. Some dried mushrooms can always come to the rescue if needed. For vegetarians, simply omit the prosciutto, and use vegetable stock.

SERVES 6

2 LB MIXED FRESH WILD MUSHROOMS
1 ONION, MINCED
7 OZ PROSCIUTTO, CHOPPED
6 TBSP OLIVE OIL
2 GARLIC CLOVES, MINCED
5 FRESH BAY LEAVES
1 SMALL SPRIG ROSEMARY
3 TBSP CHOPPED PARSLEY
2 CUPS VEGETABLE OR CHICKEN STOCK
   (SEE PAGE 104)
2 CUPS COOKED BORLOTTI OR
   CRANBERRY BEANS (THEY COULD
   BE FROM A JAR OR CAN)
6 SLICES GOOD ITALIAN BREAD,
   TOASTED (OPTIONAL)
FRESHLY GRATED PARMESAN
   (OPTIONAL)
SALT AND PEPPER TO TASTE

Clean and prepare the mushrooms. You could use sulfur shelf, wood blewits, hedgehog mushroom, chanterelles, or porcini.

Sauté the onion and prosciutto in the oil until the prosciutto has taken on some color, then add the garlic and herbs. Add the cleaned mushrooms and the stock, and cook for 10 minutes. Add the cooked beans. Bring to a boil again, then cook for 3 to 4 minutes. Remove the bay leaves and rosemary, and season the soup.

Put a slice of toasted bread in each soup bowl, if using, and pour the soup on top. Sprinkle with Parmesan, if desired. Buon appetito!

MUSHROOM AND PEARL BARLEY SOUP

This soup from the Slavic countries used to be a delicacy for poor people and gypsies. I like the idea of these humble ingredients being brought together to produce a simple dish. The original recipe called for heavy or whipping cream, but I have substituted thick sour cream to give another dimension. You could also use thick heavy or whipping cream soured with a little lemon juice. Serve with toasted bread.

SERVES 4

$1/4$ CUP PEARL BARLEY
$1^1/_2$ OZ DRIED PORCINI
3 GARLIC CLOVES, CRUSHED
2 TBSP MINCED SHALLOT
SALT AND PEPPER TO TASTE
A PINCH OF FRESHLY GRATED NUTMEG
6 TBSP SOUR CREAM

Soak the pearl barley in water to cover for a few hours. Soak the porcini in warm water for 20 minutes. Drain both well (reserve the mushroom soaking liquid), and coarsely chop the mushrooms.

Put the barley, mushrooms, garlic, and shallot into a pan. Season with salt, pepper, and nutmeg. Cover with water, add the mushroom soaking liquid, and cook until the barley is tender, about 10 to 15 minutes.

Just before serving, taste for seasoning, then stir in the sour cream.

Tuscan Soup with Saffron Milk Caps

The original Tuscan dish is made with porcini, but the addition of the saffron milk caps, with their nuttiness and interesting color, makes it new. Both mushrooms are freshly available in autumn, but should you have only the saffron milk caps, then you can add the ubiquitous dried porcini for flavoring. In that case, increase the amount of saffron milk caps to 1 1/4 lb.

Serves 4

1 LB FRESH SAFFRON MILK CAPS
7 OZ FRESH PORCINI, OR
   1 1/2 OZ DRIED PORCINI, SOAKED IN
   WARM WATER FOR 30 MINUTES
4 GARLIC CLOVES
4 TBSP EXTRA VIRGIN OLIVE OIL
2 CUPS TOMATO PULP (FRESH
   OR CANNED)
2 1/2 CUPS CHICKEN OR VEGETABLE
   STOCK (SEE PAGE 104), HOT
SALT AND PEPPER TO TASTE
4 SLICES BREAD (PREFERABLY
   TUSCAN), TOASTED
6 BASIL LEAVES, TORN
1/2 CUP FRESHLY GRATED PARMESAN
   OR PECORINO CHEESE

Clean the fresh mushrooms thoroughly, and thinly slice them. Rinse the dried porcini, if using, and reserve the soaking liquid.

Chop 3 of the garlic cloves and sauté in 2 tablespoons of the olive oil. When they start to color (but not too much), add the tomato pulp and, if fresh, cook for 10 to 15 minutes (less for canned). Add the mushrooms, stock, and soaking liquid, and cook until the mushrooms are tender, about 8 to 10 minutes. Season with salt and pepper.

Rub the remaining garlic clove gently over each slice of toast and brush with the remaining olive oil. Add the basil to the soup and cook for 1 minute.

Place the toasts in 4 deep soup plates and divide the soup among the plates. Add the grated cheese and serve.

PUMPKIN AND PORCINI SOUP

Pumpkins and fresh porcini both arrive in autumn, and this is the ideal time to make this warming, sustaining soup. Should you not be able to find fresh porcini, you could use dried porcini with fresh cultivated varieties such as blewits. The porcini recreate that inimitable "wild" flavor. The pumpkin gives color and a floury texture to the soup, as well as flavor, and I recommend that you serve it in the pumpkin shells for maximum effect. Scoop out the flesh to use in the soup, discarding the seeds. Keep the "lids," and cut a sliver off the base of the pumpkins so they stand upright without wobbling.

SERVES 6

10 OZ FRESH PORCINI, OR
  2 OZ DRIED PORCINI PLUS 10 OZ
  CULTIVATED BLEWITS
6 SMALL PUMPKINS, HOLLOWED OUT
  (YOU WANT 6^1/$_2$ CUPS DICED FLESH)
1 MEDIUM ONION, MINCED
6 TBSP BUTTER
2 TBSP OLIVE OIL
ALL-PURPOSE FLOUR FOR DUSTING
^{2}/$_3$ CUP DRY WHITE WINE
CHICKEN OR VEGETABLE STOCK (SEE
  PAGE 104), AS REQUIRED
2 TBSP MINCED ROSEMARY
1 TSP MARJORAM LEAVES
SALT AND PEPPER TO TASTE

Clean the fresh porcini or blewits, and slice. If using dried porcini, soak in warm water for 20 minutes, then drain, and save the soaking liquid for use another time. Cut the soaked porcini into strips. Cut the pumpkin flesh into dice.
Sauté the onion in the butter and olive oil until soft. Dust the cubes of pumpkin with flour and sauté in the same fat until golden. Add the wine and cook a little to evaporate the alcohol, then cover with stock and bring to a boil. If using dried porcini, add them now and cook for 25 minutes; add the fresh variety after 15 minutes cooking. Crush some of the cubes of pumpkin to obtain a thick soup. Add half of the herbs and some salt and pepper.
Serve in the pumpkin shells with their lids on (standing in soup plates for safety) and sprinkle with the remaining herbs.

HOLSTEIN MUSHROOM SOUP

I lived in this part of Germany for a while and I had the impression that almost every dish contained either butter, cream, or both. The following thick soup is no exception, and I admit it is not a light dish, but as with German tradition, lightness is replaced with "Schmackhaft"—which means it is very tasty indeed.

SERVES 4

2 LB FRESH BAY BOLETES
4 TBSP (^{1}/$_2$ STICK) BUTTER
2 TBSP MINCED GREEN ONION
^{1}/$_2$ CUP CHICKEN OR VEGETABLE STOCK
  (SEE PAGE 104)
1 TBSP MARJORAM OR THYME
  LEAVES
1 TBSP MINCED PARSLEY
4 TBSP HEAVY OR WHIPPING CREAM
JUICE OF ^{1}/$_2$ LEMON
SALT AND PEPPER TO TASTE

Clean and chop the mushrooms.
Put the butter in a pan with the green onion and let sweat over low heat. Add the mushrooms and continue to sweat for 10 minutes. Add the stock and cook for 5 minutes longer.
Add the herbs and cream and warm gently. Transfer to a blender or food processor and process to a coarse texture (add more stock if you want the soup to be more liquid). Add the lemon juice and season to taste. Serve with toasted bread.

MUSHROOM AND BEAN SOUP

Some of my most interesting recipes evolve when I experiment with ingredients. One sunny, late-autumn day, I was picking some mature runner beans, which were almost shriveled, but the beans inside the pods were so large and such a wonderful color that I wanted to cook them straightaway. They would be delicious in a soup, I thought, so my companions and I collected some wild mushrooms as well. The result was very tasty, and was swiftly devoured by all of us. You can use any other type of bean, and in an emergency you could even use frozen ones. Serve with slices of toasted Pugliese bread rubbed with garlic and drizzled with extra virgin olive oil.

SERVES 4

1 LB MIXED LATE-SUMMER SHELL
  BEANS, SHELLED
7 OZ MIXED FRESH MUSHROOMS
³/₄ OZ DRIED PORCINI
1 LARGE ONION, MINCED
6 TBSP OLIVE OIL
1 FRESH, HOT CHILI PEPPER, SLICED
6 CUPS CHICKEN OR VEGETABLE
  STOCK (SEE PAGE 104)
SALT AND PEPPER TO TASTE

Wash the beans, and clean the fresh mushrooms as appropriate. Soak the dried mushrooms in warm water for about 20 minutes. Drain well, reserving the soaking liquid.

Sauté the onion in the olive oil until translucent, then add the chili and drained, dried porcini. Add the beans and cover with stock. Bring to a boil, reduce the heat down, then simmer for about 20 minutes or until the beans are soft. Add the fresh mushrooms, either sliced or whole, and cook for 10 minutes longer. Add salt and pepper and serve immediately.

HOT THAI SOUP OF OYSTER MUSHROOMS AND SHRIMP

The herbs and aromas of Thailand are very intense indeed. At home I like to accompany this soup with a dish of plain boiled rice; lightly dip a spoonful of rice into the soup to collect just enough of the wonderful liquid to flavor the rice. This may be not what Thai etiquette requires, but it gives me great satisfaction!

SERVES 4

7 OZ FRESH CULTIVATED YELLOW OYSTER MUSHROOMS
20 MEDIUM-SIZED RAW SHRIMP
2 TBSP CORN OIL
3¼ CUPS WATER
4 LIME LEAVES
2 LEMONGRASS STALKS
A FEW LEAVES THAI BASIL
1 GARLIC CLOVE
1 TBSP CHILI OIL
4 FRESH, HOT RED CHILI PEPPERS
SALT TO TASTE

Trim the oyster mushrooms and cut into small pieces. Peel the shrimp, keeping the shells, and set the shrimp aside.

Sauté the shrimp shells in a casserole in the corn oil until crisp, then add a little of the water. With a pestle, crush the shells to release all the juices. Add the rest of the water and the lime leaves, lemongrass, basil, and garlic. Bring to a boil, reduce the heat, cover and simmer for about 10 minutes. Strain the broth into a pan, and discard the solids.

Add the mushrooms, peeled shrimp, and chili oil to the broth. Season with salt. Bring to a boil and cook for 3 to 4 minutes. Serve in bowls with a whole red chili pepper for a garnish.

NAMEKO AND MISO SOUP

Probably the best-known Japanese soup in the West, miso can be found ready-made in Asian markets and wholefood stores. This, according to Miho, my Japanese friend, is nonsense because the subtlety of miso can be tasted only if you add it at the end. Such bastardization of ethnic food takes place in the West and East to the same degree, in the name of business, unfortunately diluting the culture. The nameko mushroom is essential to this soup, but don't worry—it is available cultivated.

SERVES 4

4 OZ FRESH NAMEKO MUSHROOMS
3¼ CUPS JAPANESE STOCK OR DASHI (SEE PAGE 115)
4 OZ FIRM TOFU, CUT INTO SMALL CUBES
2 OZ RED MISO (A THICK BEAN OR CEREAL PASTE)
A LITTLE MITSUBA (A GREEN STEM, RATHER LIKE FLAT-LEAF PARSLEY), OR ANY FRESH GREEN HERB CUT INTO MATCHSTICKS

Clean the mushrooms. Bring the stock or dashi to a boil. Add the mushrooms and tofu, and cook for 1 to 2 minutes.

Meanwhile, in a small bowl dissolve the miso in a small amount of the hot stock. Add the dissolved miso to the soup, and serve garnished with mitsuba.

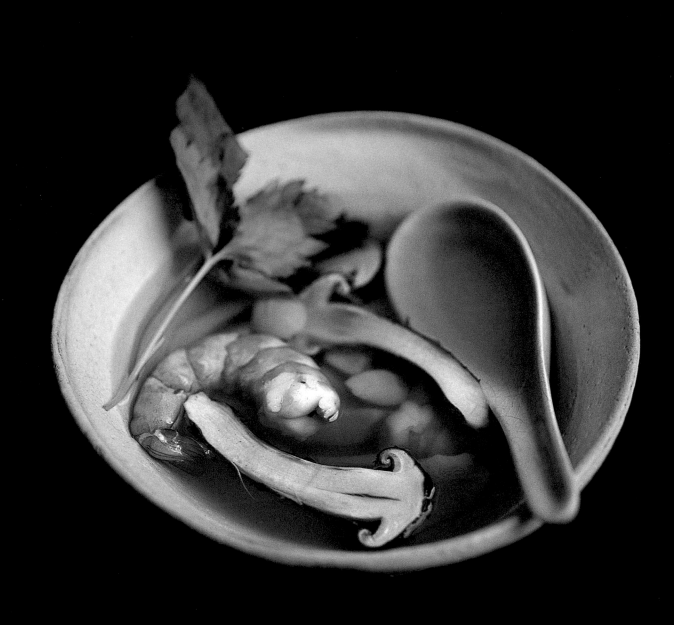

MATSUTAKE SOUP

For this recipe I had the vital help of Miho Uchida and her husband, Michiya, a Japanese couple living in London. Miho helped me get to know a great deal more about Japanese food, my knowledge previously being limited to sushi, sashimi, and tempura. (I find it fascinating to discover details of other food cultures, which have been enjoyed for centuries.) They helped me even more when Michiya came back from Japan. He had been instructed to bring back some fresh matsutake, which were used in this recipe and can be seen in the photograph. You can get all the ingredients from a Japanese market.

SERVES 4

4–6 FRESH MATSUTAKE
  MUSHROOMS
$^{1}/_{2}$ TSP SOY SAUCE
1 TSP SAKÉ (RICE WINE)
A FEW DROPS OF LIME JUICE (OR
  JAPANESE CITRON)
SALT
4 OZ SKINNED CHICKEN BREAST MEAT,
  CUT INTO SLIVERS
4 MEDIUM-SIZED RAW SHRIMP,
  PEELED
12 GINGKO NUTS, SHELLED
SOME FRESH MITSUBA (A GREEN
  STEM, RATHER LIKE FLAT-LEAF
  PARSLEY), OR SMALL SLIVERS
  OF CELERY

JAPANESE STOCK (DASHI)
4 CUPS WATER
6-INCH PIECE OF KOMBU (DRIED
  SEAWEED)
1 OZ DRIED BONITO (KATSUOBUSHI),
  FLAKED

Clean the mushrooms as needed, and cut off and discard the hard stem tip. Cut into slivers lengthwise and set aside.

For the stock or dashi, heat the water in a pan over low heat and add the kombu. When you see bubbles, add the bonito flakes. Just before the water boils, take the kombu out. Boil for 2 minutes, then remove from the heat. Wait for the bonito to sink to the bottom of the pan, then strain and discard the solids. This is a basic Japanese stock.

Add the soy sauce, saké, lime juice, and a pinch of salt to the stock. Add the chicken, mushrooms, and shrimp, and cook for 5 minutes.

Serve the soup in earthenware bowls. Add 3 gingko nuts to each bowl, and garnish with mitsuba or celery.

GAME CONSOMMÉ WITH MORELS

When morels are in season in springtime, you should be able to find game birds, such as pheasant, partridge, and pigeon and squab, to make this richly flavored soup. In the autumn and winter, when fresh morels are not available, you can use dried morels.

SERVES 4

7 OZ FRESH MORELS, OR 2 OZ DRIED
1 SMALL PHEASANT
1 BOUQUET GARNI (BAY, PARSLEY, THYME)
1 CELERY STALK, MINCED
1 SHALLOT, FINELY SLICED
1 CARROT, MINCED
SALT AND PEPPER TO TASTE
CHICKEN STOCK (SEE PAGE 104) OR WATER
1/3 CUP PORT
4 TBSP CRÈME FRAÎCHE
1 TBSP MINCED CHIVES

Clean the fresh morels carefully, or soak the dried morels in warm water for 20 minutes, then drain.

Put the pheasant into a pan with the bouquet garni, celery, shallot, carrot, and some salt and pepper. Cover the pheasant with stock (or water), put the lid on, and simmer for 1 hour.

After an hour, add the soaked dried morels or the fresh morels, and simmer for 30 minutes longer.

Strain the consommé through a fine strainer set over a bowl. Reserve the morels and discard the other solids. Season the consommé and add the port. Warm through.

Add the crème fraîche and chives, then serve immediately, with a portion of morels in each bowl.

CREAM OF PORCINI SOUP

It may seem extravagant to use such treasures as porcini in a soup, but this is undeniably one of the most delicious soups I have ever made. You can use them fresh—the best are the mature ones, which have a fuller flavor—or you can use them after freezing. They actually keep so well with freezing that they can be sautéed when required, but you can also just add the frozen slices to the boiling stock. If you can't find porcini, use cultivated button mushrooms as a base and for texture, with dried porcini to enhance the flavor.

SERVES 4

1 LB FRESH PORCINI, OR 1 LB BUTTON MUSHROOMS PLUS 1 OZ DRIED PORCINI
1 MEDIUM ONION, MINCED
4 TBSP OLIVE OIL
5 CUPS BEEF STOCK (SEE PAGE 104)
4 TBSP HEAVY OR WHIPPING CREAM
SALT AND PEPPER TO TASTE

CROÛTONS
2 SLICES WHITE BREAD
2 TBSP BUTTER

If you are using fresh porcini, clean them and cut into pieces. Sauté the onion in the oil for 3 to 4 minutes, then add the porcini and sauté them for 6 to 7 minutes. Add the stock, bring to a boil, and simmer for 20 minutes.

If you are using a combination of cultivated and dried mushrooms, soak the dried porcini in warm water for 10 minutes. Meanwhile, sauté the button mushrooms with the onion in the oil. Add the soaked porcini with their water and the stock. Simmer for about 30 minutes.

To finish either method, take the pan off the heat and process the contents in a food processor or blender. Return the soup to the pan, add the cream and some salt and pepper, and reheat slowly.

To make the croûtons, simply cut the bread into little cubes and sauté in the butter until they are golden and crisp. Scatter the croûtons over the top of each helping.

RIGHT GAME CONSOMMÉ WITH MORELS

CHAPTER TWO
LIGHT DISHES

From canapés to snacks, from antipasti to breakfasts or first courses, all are united in this chapter. On the whole they are easy-to-prepare dishes that can be enjoyed as a light meal by themselves, or as part of a meal. A couple of recipes served together would make a good lunch or supper, or you could offer a selection as a buffet, say, or as antipasti in the Italian style. The selection of light dishes also includes salads, which are increasingly in demand for their ease of preparation and healthfulness. The essence of most salads is rawness—and indeed some fungi can be eaten and enjoyed raw—but you will find an interesting selection here, both raw and cooked. By increasing the quantities of many of these dishes, they can also be eaten as a main course—especially useful for vegetarians. And, of course, you can increase or decrease the quantity of any of the ingredients to suit your palate. I am not offended at such a thought, so please, let me know about any major improvements!

THE BIG MUSHROOM SALAD

Anything can go into this salad, meaning any and all of the mushrooms you managed to collect when out picking. If you don't have enough, then you can always add some cultivated ones. The difference between this and a normal salad is that the "vinaigrette" is cooked and the mushrooms are slightly pickled by boiling with salt and vinegar. (Some, like the honey fungus, have to be cooked before eating anyway.) The salad can also be served cold.

SERVES 4

2^1/$_4$ LB MIXED FRESH WILD
    MUSHROOMS (CLEANED WEIGHT)
6 CUPS WATER
3 TBSP SALT
2 CUPS WHITE WINE VINEGAR
^{1}/$_2$ CUP OLIVE OIL
2 GARLIC CLOVES, SLICED
2 SLICES FRESH, HOT RED CHILI
    PEPPER
SALT AND PEPPER TO TASTE
1 TBSP EACH MINCED PARSLEY
    AND CILANTRO
1 LEMON

Clean the mushrooms as appropriate, and cut to roughly the same size.
Bring the water to a boil and add 3 tablespoons salt and the vinegar. Add the mushrooms and cook for 10 minutes. Drain well and cool.
In a pan, heat the oil and sauté the garlic and chili to soften. Add the mushrooms, heat through, and taste for seasoning. Stir in the herbs and serve immediately, sprinkled with lemon juice.

BEEFSTEAK FUNGUS AND BEET SALAD

I have experimented with beefsteak fungus for a long time, but a decent result had always eluded me. However, during the creating and testing of new recipes for this book, I came across a new way to use the "poor man's meat," as they call it in Italy. It is actually one of the few wild mushrooms that can be eaten raw, and the combination of its acidity with the sweetness of beets makes, I think, for compulsive eating.

SERVES 4

7 OZ FRESH BEEFSTEAK FUNGUS
12 OZ SMALL, TENDER BEETS,
    FRESHLY BOILED
EXTRA VIRGIN OLIVE OIL
2 TBSP BALSAMIC VINEGAR
2 TBSP MINCED CILANTRO
SALT AND PEPPER TO TASTE

FOR SERVING
4 LARGE SLICES RUSTIC BREAD,
    FOR BRUSCHETTA
1 GARLIC CLOVE

Clean the fungus, then cut into slices the same size as the beet slices will be. Skin the beets and slice as well.
Toss the fungus and beets together in a bowl with 4 tablespoons olive oil, the vinegar, cilantro, and some salt and pepper.
Toast the bread on both sides, then rub the garlic over each slice and brush with olive oil.
Arrange a little of the salad on each bruschetta, or serve the salad on a plate with the bruschetta to the side.

MUSHROOM, SPINACH, AND PROSCIUTTO SALAD

The mushroom used in this Italian recipe, Amanita caesarea, *is undoubtedly one of the prettiest and most delicate mushrooms, and it would be a sin to cook with it.* A. caesarea *belongs to the nastiest family, the Amanitas, which includes many of the most poisonous mushrooms. But identify it well, or buy it in season from a reliable vendor, and you will enjoy a real delight.*

SERVES 4

10 OZ FRESH AMANITA CAESAREA
8 OZ BABY SPINACH LEAVES
4 TBSP EXTRA VIRGIN OLIVE OIL
1 TBSP MILD, PREPARED MUSTARD
2 TBSP BALSAMIC VINEGAR
SALT AND PEPPER TO TASTE
2 OZ PROSCIUTTO, VERY THINLY SLICED, THEN CUT INTO STRIPS

Clean the mushrooms thoroughly, then cut them into ¼-inch-thick slices. Wash the spinach well and pat it dry.

Make a vinaigrette by combining the oil, mustard, and vinegar, and season with salt and pepper.

Toss the spinach in the vinaigrette, then divide among 4 plates. Garnish with the mushroom slices and strips of prosciutto. Serve accompanied by good toasted bread.

TUNA, MUSHROOMS, AND BEANS

This recipe comes from the old-fashioned repertoire of many Italian restaurants over the last 30 years or so. "Tonno e fagioli"—tuna and beans—is mostly made with canned tuna with some canned beans included. Adding some chopped onions is usually one way of reviving the basic mixture, but I thought some mushrooms would also add flavor, especially if pickled. I would use "ventresca di tonno," the belly, which is the most tender and best canned tuna available. The dish is very simple to prepare.

SERVES 4 AS A FIRST COURSE OR 2 AS A LIGHT MEAL

1 CUP PICKLED MUSHROOMS IN OIL (SEE PAGE 102)
14 OZ CANNED BORLOTTI BEANS (CRANBERRY BEANS)
14 OZ CANNED "VENTRESCA DI TONNO"
4 GREEN ONIONS, MINCED, STEM INCLUDED
3 TBSP EXTRA VIRGIN OLIVE OIL
2 TBSP BALSAMIC VINEGAR
SALT AND PEPPER TO TASTE

Drain the mushrooms from their liquid and dry slightly on a paper towel. Drain the beans and rinse them, and drain and flake the tuna.

Simply stir everything together, season with a little salt and plenty of freshly ground black pepper, and allow the flavors to meld for about 1 hour before serving. Serve with grissini (breadsticks).

SALAD OF CAESAR'S MUSHROOMS AND WHITE TRUFFLE

This is a marriage of wild food ingredients at the very highest level. The supreme reputation of both fungi is undisputed—they are two of the most delicate and delicious foods in the world. I always say that this Italian dish is for gourmets and kings—and (truffle-hunting) pigs.

SERVES 4

14 OZ FRESH AMANITA CAESAREA,
   PREFERABLY YOUNG AND STILL
   CLOSED
1 OZ FRESH WHITE TRUFFLE
4 TBSP EXTRA VIRGIN OLIVE OIL
2 TBSP LEMON JUICE
1 TBSP MINCED PARSLEY
1$^{1}/_{2}$ OZ PARMESAN, FRESHLY SHAVED
SALT AND PEPPER TO TASTE

Clean and finely slice the mushrooms. Clean the truffle carefully.
Mix the oil with the lemon juice, parsley, and some salt and pepper.
Arrange the mushroom slices on a large, flat plate. Sprinkle with Parmesan shavings first, then add the vinaigrette. Shave a little of the truffle over all. Serve with toasted bread.

SHELLFISH AND HEN OF THE WOODS SALAD

In summer you want to eat just a small amount of delicate food to combat the heat. This salad is perfect for that purpose, accompanied by some toasted bread and shared with a friend or two, perhaps in the garden, with a glass of crisp, chilled white wine. You could also use sulfur shelf or beefsteak fungus instead of the hen of the woods.

SERVES 4

1 LB FRESH HEN OF THE WOODS
   MUSHROOMS
$^{1}/_{2}$ CUP WHITE WINE VINEGAR
$^{1}/_{2}$ CUP WATER
5 OZ RAW SHRIMP, NOT TOO LARGE
5 OZ FRESH SEA SCALLOPS
1 CUP COOKED CRABMEAT, PICKED
   OVER FOR CARTILAGE
6 TBSP EXTRA VIRGIN OLIVE OIL
1 TBSP EACH COARSELY CHOPPED
   CILANTRO, PARSLEY, AND DILL WEED
JUICE OF 1 LEMON
SALT AND PEPPER TO TASTE

Clean the mushrooms and separate into lobes, then cook in the vinegar and water with some salt for 2 to 3 minutes. Drain and cool. Peel the shrimp, then cook briefly in fresh boiling water, about 4 to 5 minutes. Cut the scallops into slices.
Make the vinaigrette by whisking together the olive oil, herbs, and lemon juice, and season with salt and pepper. Marinate the scallops in the vinaigrette for 10 minutes.
Mix the mushrooms with the shrimp and crabmeat. Add the scallops with their marinade and combine gently. Adjust the seasoning, and serve the salad at room temperature.

Saint George's Mushrooms with Scrambled Egg and Wild Garlic

April 23rd, St. George's Day in Britain, usually marks the start of the mushroom season, and this is when this dirty white mushroom normally appears. It is deliciously delicate in flavor. Wild garlic appears in the same season (but if you can't get hold of it, use another soft herb generously).

SERVES 4

14 OZ FRESH ST. GEORGE'S MUSHROOMS (CLEANED WEIGHT)
4 TBSP ($^{1}/_{2}$ STICK) BUTTER
SALT AND PEPPER TO TASTE
12 FREE-RANGE EGGS, BEATEN
$^{1}/_{2}$ CUP FRESHLY GRATED PARMESAN
2 TBSP COARSELY CHOPPED WILD GARLIC

If the mushrooms are large, then cut in two. Sauté them in half the butter until they start to brown at the edges. Season to taste, then set them aside, keeping them warm.

In a nonstick pan, melt the remaining butter and, when hot, add the beaten eggs mixed with the Parmesan. Stir gently with a wooden spoon to scramble; but keep the eggs soft.

Mix the wild garlic with the warm mushrooms and arrange on a plate. Place the scrambled eggs on the other side of the plate. Eat with good Italian toasted bread.

Mushroom Tortilla

Eggs "carry" many dishes, either as a component, or as a main ingredient. The entire world has specialties using eggs, because they are so nutritious and extremely easy to handle. Frittata, tortilla, and omelet, all with a multitude of flavorings, have one thing in common: "solidified" eggs. Naturally, I had to use mushrooms in this recipe, and this Spanish version contains the Spaniards' favorite, one of the russulas.

Serves 4

10 oz fresh green-cracked
  russula mushrooms
12 eggs, beaten
1 tbsp chopped parsley
¼ cup grated Manchego cheese
salt and pepper to taste
4 tbsp extra virgin olive oil
1 large onion, minced

Clean the mushrooms and quarter them if large. Combine the eggs, parsley, cheese, and some salt and pepper together in a large bowl.
Heat the oil in a 10-inch nonstick frying pan and sauté the onion for 5 or so minutes, until softened. Add the mushrooms and sauté for 7 to 8 minutes. Add the egg mixture to the pan and, with a wooden spatula, stir from time to time until the egg begins to solidify. When you notice that the egg is not liquid on the top any more, leave it to build a brown crust underneath. Take a large plate and, taking care not to burn yourself, cover the pan with the plate and turn it upside down. Slide the tortilla back into the pan on its soft side and cook for a few more minutes until solid.
The tortilla may be eaten cold, but I prefer it hot with good fresh bread.

Truffle-Hunter's Breakfast

Truffle hunters are a breed of their own, having to get up very early in the morning or even when it is still dark, to avoid being seen by competitors! Their patches of ground are contested very fiercely, because the truffles command an extremely high price. If the hunters have to go far from their homes, they take with them a gas burner, a pan, a little butter, eggs, and fresh bread. They can then have breakfast in the woods with some of their bounty.

The ingredients here are for one person only, as truffle hunters are loners, but you can multiply this amount by as many as you want to feed.

Serves 1

as much fresh truffle as you
  can afford
1½ tbsp butter
2 to 3 eggs
fresh crusty bread
salt and pepper to taste

Clean the truffle well before cutting or shaving.
Melt the butter in a pan, add the eggs, and stir gently with a wooden spoon to scramble. While the eggs are still soft, add salt and pepper to taste. Next, add shavings of black truffle or, if you are very lucky, white truffle, and eat with the bread.
Nothing could be more delicious, especially when you are hungry after several hours' hunting. The truffle dog gets to eat the last piece of bread with which the pan is cleaned!

MORELS STUFFED WITH FOIE GRAS

This French dish is for grand occasions and is extremely opulent—just don't think about how many calories it contains! Morels are one of the few hollow mushrooms destined to be stuffed. The recipe inevitably works much better with large, fresh morels, but it is possible to use large dried ones.

I dedicate this recipe to the composer Rossini, who, I'm sure, would have loved this rich dish.

SERVES 4

12 VERY LARGE, FRESH MORELS, CLEANED
4 TBSP (¹/₂ STICK) BUTTER
4 TBSP GOOD CHICKEN STOCK (SEE PAGE 104)
2 TBSP COGNAC OR BRANDY
4 TBSP HEAVY OR WHIPPING CREAM
1 TBSP FINELY SNIPPED CHIVES
SALT AND PEPPER TO TASTE

STUFFING
2 EGGS, BEATEN
3 CUPS FRESH BREAD CRUMBS
1 TBSP MINCED FLAT-LEAF PARSLEY
3 OZ PÂTÉ DE FOIE GRAS, CUT INTO CUBES

Cut the stem of the morels almost at the base, just leaving the hole to be stuffed. For the stuffing, mix the eggs with the bread crumbs, parsley, and some salt and pepper to obtain a smooth paste. Fill the mushroom cavities with small cubes of foie gras, then add a little of the bread crumb mixture, remembering to leave some space as the filling will expand during cooking.

Melt the butter in a frying pan and sauté the stuffed morels gently, stuffed side first, then the other side, for 3 to 4 minutes. Add the stock and Cognac, and cook for 5 minutes longer. Stir in the cream and some salt and pepper, and cook for a minute more before adding the chives. Serve the morels hot with the sauce, accompanied by freshly toasted baguette slices.

ENOKI BUNDLES

This very nice idea—worked out with my Japanese friend, Miho—uses one of the prettiest cultivated mushrooms, the enoki. The recipe is very simple and can be made anywhere because of the general availability of the ingredients.

SERVES 4

14 OZ FRESH ENOKI MUSHROOMS, DIVIDED INTO 8 BUNCHES
8 THICK SLICES PROSCIUTTO (OR SMOKED SALMON)
SALT AND PEPPER TO TASTE
4 TBSP OLIVE OIL
JUICE OF 2 LIMES

Trim the base of the tight little mushroom bunches.
Wrap a slice of prosciutto (or smoked salmon) around each bunch, and fix with a wooden toothpick. Sprinkle the enoki with a little salt and abundant pepper, followed by the olive oil and lime juice, and serve.

GRILLED MATSUTAKE

This is another recipe worked out with my Japanese friend Miho. When I asked her about the principles of Japanese food, she said the most important aspect was the freshness of the ingredients (although various dried items are used, mainly for flavor), followed by presentation and the look of the dish, followed by taste, flavor, and, but no less important, texture.

This is possibly the simplest of all the recipes, although it has a great deal of sophistication. Naturally you start by getting hold of the matsutake, the wild variety of which costs about $350 per pound! (Even the cultivated are quite expensive.) But the rest of the ingredients are very cheap!

SERVES 4

8 OR MORE FRESH MATSUTAKE MUSHROOMS, DEPENDING ON SIZE
2 TBSP SOY SAUCE
JUICE OF 1 LEMON

Prepare a charcoal grill or preheat the broiler. Wipe any dust off the matsutake. Clean with paper towel. (Do not use water because this washes away aroma and flavor.) Cut the hard tip off the stem. Tear each mushroom into 2 to 4 pieces, depending on size, starting from the stem, which will split up to the cap, leaving a sort of network of tender filaments.
Grill or broil on each side for 1 to 2 minutes. Either sprinkle with a "vinaigrette" made from the soy sauce and lemon juice, or dip the mushrooms into a bowl containing the liquid mixture. It's that simple.

NOTE I have tried preparing other mushrooms in a similar way, but it seems that this is the only one to have this special filament structure.

ASIAN MUSHROOMS IN ASPIC

This recipe from Miho, my Japanese friend, is excellent. I laughed a lot when she insisted on using "Western stock"—chicken bouillon cubes! Mushrooms in aspic look attractive, are practical to serve, and delicious to eat.

SERVES 4

1¼ LB MIXED FRESH MUSHROOMS
(MAITAKE, BUNA-SHIMEJI, ENOKI,
SHIITAKE, AND BUTTON)
1 GARLIC CLOVE, MINCED
1 TSP CORN OIL OR OLIVE OIL
SALT AND PEPPER TO TASTE
1 TBSP WHITE WINE
½ TSP LEMON JUICE
2 TBSP UNFLAVORED GELATIN,
DISSOLVED IN ½ CUP "WESTERN
STOCK"

FOR SERVING
A HANDFUL OF SALAD LEAVES
8 CHERRY TOMATOES, HALVED
VINAIGRETTE (MADE OF 1 TBSP RICE
VINEGAR, 3 TBSP SUNFLOWER OIL,
AND 1 TSP DIJON MUSTARD)

Trim and wipe the mushrooms as appropriate, then slice the maitake, shiitake, and button mushrooms.

Sauté the minced garlic in the oil in a pan, then add the sliced maitake, shiitake, and button mushrooms, and the trimmed buna-shimeji and enoki. Sauté over high heat for a minute or two, then add some salt and pepper. Add the white wine and lemon juice, and bring to a brisk boil, then remove from the heat. Add the dissolved gelatin mixture and combine well.

Pour into a 5-cup-capacity terrine mold or similar container and let cool. Put in the refrigerator and let set for a couple of hours. Turn the mold upside down and unmold onto a platter. Cut into even slices with a very sharp knife. Serve with the salad leaves and halved tomatoes sprinkled with the vinaigrette.

STUFFED SHIITAKE

This Japanese recipe also suggests Chinese cooking because the shiitake mushroom, so popular now and available in every supermarket, is very commonly used in both countries (and indeed, increasingly, in the rest of the world). The recipe was suggested by my Japanese friend, Miho.

SERVES 4

12 MEDIUM-SIZED FRESH SHIITAKE
MUSHROOMS
A LITTLE ALL-PURPOSE FLOUR
1¼ CUPS GROUND CHICKEN
⅔ CUP GROUND RAW SHRIMP
3 GREEN ONIONS, MINCED
1 TSP MINCED FRESH GINGER
2 TBSP SAKÉ (RICE WINE)
1 TBSP SOY SAUCE
SALT TO TASTE
OLIVE OIL

SAUCE
4 TBSP SOY SAUCE
2 TBSP MIRIN (SWEETENED RICE WINE)
1 TBSP SUGAR
1 TBSP SAKÉ (RICE WINE)

Clean the shiitake well and discard the stems.

Dust the inner part of the shiitake with the flour. Mix together the chicken, shrimp, green onion, ginger, saké, soy sauce, and a pinch of salt. Use a little to fill the cavity of each mushroom. Sauté the stuffed mushrooms gently for 5 minutes on each side in a little olive oil, covered. Uncover and add the ingredients for the sauce. Let them heat through and evaporate a little. Serve 3 mushrooms per person, with a little sauce on each one.

East–West Bruschetta

With great reluctance I accept the idea of "fusing" ingredients from totally alien culinary cultures for the purposes of research. Very often these fusions are made for fashion or food snobbism, without complying to the rules of good taste and flavor. But here the combination of two totally different fungi, one from the East, the other from the West, makes for a light and simple, but sophisticated dish. I used the cheaper summer truffle to limit the cost, but if money is no object then you can use either Périgord or Alba truffles.

SERVES 4

2 FRESH SUMMER TRUFFLES, ABOUT
  1 OZ EACH
7 OZ FRESH ENOKI MUSHROOMS
4 SLICES GOOD ITALIAN BREAD FOR
  BRUSCHETTA
1 GARLIC CLOVE
JUICE OF 1 LIME
EXTRA VIRGIN OLIVE OIL
1 TSP MINCED PARSLEY
SALT AND PEPPER TO TASTE

Clean the truffles very well and cut into thin slices, but not too thin. Cut the bases off the stems of the enoki mushrooms.

Toast the bread until it is brown and crisp on both sides, then rub very gently with the garlic. Brush with oil and divide among 4 plates.

In a bowl, mix the lime juice and 2 tablespoons of olive oil with the parsely and some salt and pepper. Combine well with the mushrooms, then divide among the slices of toast. Serve as a salad or first course.

BAKED MUSHROOM BRUSCHETTA OR TOAST

Bruschetta or toast? That is the question! Whichever, this dish is a welcome snack when you feel peckish. You will need large slices of rustic Italian bread, toasted, or if you want to call it toast, then use sliced bread. Either way, it is delicious. You can use any mushrooms you have on hand, but a good mixture would be hedgehog mushroom, giant polypore, parasols, and larch boletes.

MAKES 4

10 OZ FRESH MUSHROOMS
4 TBSP (¹/₂ STICK) BUTTER
4 TBSP OLIVE OIL
1 GARLIC CLOVE, MINCED
1 SMALL, FRESH, HOT RED CHILI
  PEPPER, MINCED
JUICE OF ¹/₂ LEMON
1 TBSP MINCED PARSLEY
6 TBSP HEAVY OR WHIPPING CREAM
4 LARGE SLICES RUSTIC ITALIAN
  BREAD, TOASTED
4 OZ TALEGGIO OR MOZZARELLA
  CHEESE, CUT INTO CHUNKS
1¹/₂ CUPS FRESH BREAD CRUMBS
SALT AND PEPPER TO TASTE

Preheat the oven to 450°F, or preheat the broiler. Clean and trim the mushrooms as appropriate, and cut the larger ones into pieces if necessary.

Sauté the mushrooms in the butter and oil, with the garlic and chili, until slightly softened. Add the lemon juice and parsley, and stir briefly. Add the cream and cook for about 10 minutes, or until the mushrooms are tender. Season to taste. Top each slice of toast with some of the mixture and dot with cheese. Sprinkle with the bread crumbs and bake for 5 minutes in the preheated oven, or put under the broiler, until the cheese is bubbling. Serve immediately.

MINI BRIOCHES WITH TRUFFLE

I ate these mini brioches at a bar in Florence, Italy, where they were filled with truffle butter and a slice of fresh truffle. They make very elegant and sophisticated "stuzzichini" (appetizers), especially when served before dinner with a glass of good Champagne.

SERVES 4

12 MINI BRIOCHES
3 TBSP SOFT BUTTER, MIXED WITH
  1 TBSP TRUFFLE OIL
1 SMALL, FRESH ALBA TRUFFLE, CUT
  INTO 12 THIN SLICES
SALT AND PEPPER TO TASTE

Slice the mini brioches in half, and spread one half of each with the truffle-flavored butter. Place a truffle slice on top of the butter. Sprinkle with salt and pepper, then replace the top. Enjoy.

WILD MUSHROOM CROSTINI

This Italian dish is extremely popular because of its versatility: it can be served as a snack or antipasto, or with drinks. Crostini can be topped with chicken liver pâté, a mixture of tomato, mozzarella, and basil, or with grilled vegetables. This version using wild mushrooms is exceptionally good—even if you can't get hold of any wild mushrooms and have to use cultivated instead. For the photograph we used sulfur shelf, horn of plenty, wild Agaricus bisporus, *and oyster mushrooms.*

SERVES 4

14 OZ MIXED WILD MUSHROOMS (WHATEVER YOU CAN GET)
2 GARLIC CLOVES, 1 MINCED AND 1 WHOLE (PEELED)
1 SMALL, FRESH, HOT RED CHILI PEPPER, MINCED
8 TBSP OLIVE OIL
1 TBSP COARSELY CHOPPED PARSLEY
1 TBSP MARJORAM LEAVES (TO REPLACE THE NEPITELLA OR WILD MINT USED IN TUSCANY)
SALT AND PEPPER TO TASTE
4 LARGE SLICES PUGLIESE BREAD

Clean the mushrooms thoroughly and cut them all into cubes.
Sauté the minced garlic and chili in 6 tablespoons of the olive oil. Before the garlic starts to color, add the mushrooms. Sauté them for a few minutes only so that they retain their crisp texture. Add the parsley, marjoram, and some salt and pepper.
Meanwhile, toast the slices of bread on both sides, then rub them very lightly with the whole garlic clove. Brush with the remaining olive oil and top with the mushroom mixture. Serve immediately.

FRIED PARASOL MUSHROOMS

Some wild mushrooms can grow so huge that one cap alone can be a meal in itself, or sometimes can even feed two or three people. The parasol is one such mushroom. The cap and the thick but tender gills underneath form a round, flat, and substantial whole, just asking to be dipped in beaten egg and bread crumbs, then fried until golden. The finished result—an Italian idea— looks like an omelet, and can easily cover your plate. Good fresh bread and a fresh green salad are all that you need for a delicious late-summer snack.

SERVES 4

4 FRESH PARASOL MUSHROOM CAPS, ABOUT 6 INCHES IN DIAMETER
3 EGGS
2 TBSP MINCED PARSLEY
2 TBSP FRESHLY GRATED PARMESAN
SALT AND PEPPER TO TASTE
FRESH WHITE BREAD CRUMBS FOR COATING
OLIVE OIL FOR FRYING

Clean the parasol caps, using a damp cloth to remove any dust from the top, but without washing them. Inspect the gills to check that no "tenants" are present.
Beat the eggs and mix in the parsley, Parmesan, and some salt and pepper. Dip the parasol caps in this mixture first and then into the bread crumbs, making sure the whole of the cap is covered. Chill to let the coating "set." Heat the oil to medium heat and add the mushrooms (you'll probably have to do one at a time, if they are really large). Sauté each cap until golden on both sides.

RÖSTI WITH KING STROPHARIA

The idea for this recipe came to me in India, where I saw a woman carrying a flat wicker basket on her head, full of freshly fried food. Using my highly developed culinary imagination (!), I substituted a Swiss potato rösti for the basket and covered this with sautéed fresh mushrooms. It is a wonderful "piatto unico," a complete dish, based on potatoes and fungi. Other mushrooms you could use are honey fungus, buna-shimeji, or hen of the woods.

SERVES 4

1¼ LB FRESH KING STROPHARIA
  MUSHROOMS
6 TBSP OLIVE OIL
2 GARLIC CLOVES, MINCED
2 TBSP MINCED GREEN ONION
1 SMALL, FRESH, MEDIUM-HOT RED
  CHILI PEPPER, MINCED
2 TBSP CHOPPED CILANTRO LEAVES
SALT AND PEPPER TO TASTE

RÖSTI BASKETS
2¼ LB WAXY POTATOES, PEELED AND
  CUT INTO MATCHSTICKS
2 OZ FRESH GINGER, CUT INTO
  MATCHSTICKS
VEGETABLE OIL FOR FRYING
2 TBSP LEMON JUICE

Clean the mushrooms, and cut in half if large.

For the rösti, combine the potato and ginger sticks well, and divide the mixture into 4 piles. Heat some of the oil in an 8-inch pan, and add one pile of the rösti mixture. Pat down to make a round just slightly smaller than the diameter of the pan, and fry until the potatoes stick together and are cooked and brown on one side. Turn over by covering the pan with a plate, inverting the rösti onto it, and sliding back into the pan to cook the other side. Repeat to make 4 röstis. Keep them warm.

Meanwhile, in another frying pan, sauté the mushrooms in the olive oil for 5 minutes. Add the garlic, green onion, chili, and half the cilantro. Sauté for a few more minutes, then season to taste.

Sprinkle the lemon juice over the röstis just before topping with the mushrooms and the remaining cilantro.

POTATOES AND PORCINI

An excellent combination of two natural ingredients, which seem made for each other. As with many things in life, here simplicity approaches perfection. In this Italian recipe, texture, flavor, and looks blend superbly. To enhance the porcini flavor, I didn't even add any garlic or onion.

SERVES 4

7 OZ FRESH PORCINI
1¼ LB WAXY, FIRM POTATOES
6 TBSP BUTTER
6 TBSP OLIVE OIL
12 SAGE LEAVES
SALT AND PEPPER TO TASTE

Clean, trim, and finely slice the porcini. Peel the potatoes. Boil the potatoes in salted water until tender. Drain and let them cool, then slice thickly.

Sauté the porcini slices in half the butter and half the oil until brown, then set aside. Sauté the potatoes and two-thirds of the sage leaves in the rest of the butter and oil.

Mix the porcini and potatoes together in a large dish and season to taste. Scatter the remaining sage leaves over. Serve either as a first course or a side dish with meat or fish.

Mushroom Dumplings

During the years I lived in Austria and Germany, I had many opportunities to appreciate the Germanic take on gnocchi. Dumplings there come in all shapes and sizes, from "Klösse" up to "Knödel"—and smaller ones, as here, known by the diminutive, "Klösschen." These little mushroom dumplings could be served by themselves, or accompanied by a tomato sauce. Saffron milk caps give the dish a good crunchiness, but you could use other firm-textured mushrooms. I once used sulfur shelf, and that worked well.

SERVES 4

DUMPLINGS
6 OZ FRESH WILD MUSHROOMS
2 TBSP OLIVE OIL
$1/2$ CUP (1 STICK) BUTTER
3 EGGS
3 TBSP ARROWROOT OR CORNSTARCH
1 TBSP MINCED PARSLEY
ABOUT 4 CUPS FRESH WHITE BREAD CRUMBS
SALT AND PEPPER TO TASTE

TOMATO SAUCE (optional)
14 OZ CANNED PEELED PLUM TOMATOES
4 TBSP ($1/2$ STICK) BUTTER
1 GARLIC CLOVE, SLICED
2 FRESH BASIL LEAVES, TORN

If you are using saffron milk caps, first clean them, then blanch them and drain well. Clean and trim other mushrooms as appropriate.

Sauté the mushrooms in the olive oil until tender when pierced with the tip of a sharp knife, then let cool and reserve.

In a clean pan, melt the butter and let it cool. In a medium bowl, beat the eggs and butter until foamy. Beat in the arrowroot, parsley, mushrooms, and some salt and pepper to taste, then add as much of the bread crumbs as you need to obtain a stiff dough that is easily shaped with your hands. Cover the dough and let it rest for 30 minutes.

Take a little of the mixture at a time and form walnut-sized dumplings with your hands. Cook in simmering, lightly salted water: they are ready when they rise to the surface, usually in 2 to 3 minutes. Serve as they are, or with the following tomato sauce.

For the tomato sauce, strain the tomatoes to remove the seeds, then purée them in a food processor. Put the butter and garlic in a small pan and cook until the garlic just starts to turn golden. Stir in the tomato purée and the basil, add salt and pepper to taste, and simmer for 10 to 15 minutes. Serve the dumplings with a little tomato sauce on the side.

CLAMS WITH MUSHROOMS

This recipe comes from Galicia, one of the most important culinary regions of Spain. Spaniards eat seafood with gusto and are equally enthusiastic about meat, but mushrooms are not as popular there as they are in France or Italy. This curious but very tasty recipe is one I ate in a restaurant and then managed to recreate from memory.

SERVES 4

1 LB FRESH PORCINI OR ORANGE
   BIRCH BOLETES
2¼ LB SMALL HARD-SHELL CLAMS
1 MEDIUM ONION, MINCED
1 RED BELL PEPPER, SEEDED AND
   CUBED
2 GARLIC CLOVES, CRUSHED
2 TBSP MINCED PARSLEY
4 TBSP OLIVE OIL
²/3 CUP DRY WHITE WINE
SALT AND PEPPER TO TASTE
1 PINCH POWDERED SAFFRON

Clean the mushrooms, then coarsely chop. Clean the clams and discard any that are broken or that gape open.

Sauté the onion, bell pepper, garlic, and parsley in the oil in a large pan for 5 minutes over low heat. Add the chopped mushrooms and continue to cook until soft. Add the wine and continue cooking for a minute to let the alcohol evaporate. Add some salt and pepper and the saffron, and stir well. Finally, add the clams. Cover the pan and cook over high heat until the clams open. Discard any that remain closed.

This can be eaten as a first course with bread.

MUSHROOM VOL-AU-VENTS

In recipes like this, I use mushrooms that I have frozen from the year before. The main reason for this is that the mushrooms have to be coarsely chopped anyway for freezing. The second reason is that you can bring back to mind the wonderful flavor of summer and autumn mushrooms at any time of the year. You can, of course, use fresh or dried wild mushrooms, if you prefer.

I put the mushroom mixture into the little puff pastry cases called vol-au-vents, which in Germany and Austria are usually filled with a ragù of veal.

**MAKES 16 SMALL
VOL-AU-VENTS**

10 OZ FROZEN PORCINI OR SAFFRON
   MILK CAPS
3 TBSP BUTTER
1 GARLIC CLOVE, MINCED
1 TSP ALL-PURPOSE FLOUR
1 TBSP SHERRY VINEGAR
2 TBSP MINCED PARSLEY
6 TBSP HEAVY OR WHIPPING CREAM
SALT AND PEPPER TO TASTE
16 SMALL PUFF PASTRY CASES
   (VOL-AU-VENTS OR PATTY SHELLS)

Preheat the oven to 350°F. Blanch the frozen mushrooms in lightly salted boiling water for 3 to 4 minutes. Drain and pat dry, then mince.

Melt the butter in a pan, add the garlic, and cook briefly without letting the garlic brown. Add the mushrooms and sauté for 5 minutes. Stir in thoroughly the flour and then the sherry vinegar, then add the parsley, cream, and salt and pepper to taste.

Meanwhile, heat the pastry cases in the preheated oven.

Fill each case with the warm mushroom mixture and serve as a first course.

MUSHROOM STRUDEL

Having lived for a couple of years in Vienna, I knew strudel only as an excellent dessert, filled with apples, pears, or sour cherries, or with a paste of poppy seeds. The idea of making it savory, with a mushroom filling, is new for me, and here it is. When feeling lazy, I use bought phyllo pastry, but if you are a skillful maker of the original strudel pastry, feel free!

SERVES 4

7 OZ PHYLLO PASTRY (12 SHEETS)
4 TBSP (1/2 STICK) BUTTER, MELTED
1 EGG, BEATEN

FILLING
1 LB MIXED, FRESH WILD AND CULTIVATED MUSHROOMS (CLEANED WEIGHT)
1 MEDIUM ONION, MINCED
3 TBSP BUTTER
LOTS OF FRESHLY GRATED NUTMEG
1 TBSP DRY SHERRY
1 TBSP ALL-PURPOSE FLOUR
LEAVES FROM 1 SPRIG MARJORAM
4 TBSP FRESHLY GRATED PARMESAN
SALT AND PEPPER TO TASTE

Preheat the oven to 400°F. Take 3 sheets of phyllo from their package at a time; keep the remaining sheets tightly wrapped. Brush 1 sheet on both sides with melted butter, then place it on top of another sheet, and cover with a third. Repeat 3 times, to make 4 stacks of triple-layer phyllo. Cover with a damp cloth while you prepare the filling.

Make sure the mushrooms are dust- and sand-free, wash if necessary (it rarely is), and trim if need be. Cook the onion in the butter and, when soft, add the mushrooms with the nutmeg. Sauté for 3 to 4 minutes. Add the sherry and evaporate the alcohol by cooking over low heat for 2 to 3 minutes. Stir in the flour, marjoram, and some salt and pepper, and let cool. The mixture will be moist. Grease a baking sheet with butter and lay one of the 4 stacks of phyllo on it. Brush the edges with beaten egg. Put one-fourth of the mushroom mixture on the center of the phyllo and add 1 tablespoon Parmesan. Fold in the sides, then fold over and over into a neat parcel. Brush with beaten egg, turn over so that the seam is on the bottom, and brush with egg again. Repeat to make 3 more strudels. Bake in the preheated oven for 15 minutes. Serve warm.

MUSHROOM "CAVIAR"

Alaskan cuisine is rich in ingredients like squirrel and moose, but the more easily accessible wild mushrooms are also much loved. Giving you this recipe proves that wherever you are in the world, mushrooms are used in cooking to prepare interesting and wonderful dishes.

SERVES 4

10 OZ MIXED, FRESH WILD MUSHROOMS (PUFFBALLS, SHAGGY INK CAPS, SAFFRON MILK CAPS, SULFUR SHELF)
1 ONION, MINCED
3 TBSP OLIVE OIL
2 TBSP MINCED CHIVES
JUICE OF 1/2 LEMON
1 TBSP SOUR CREAM
SALT AND PEPPER TO TASTE

Clean and trim the mushrooms as appropriate, then mince them.

Sauté the onion in the oil until soft, then add the mushrooms and cook until tender, about 5 to 10 minutes. Stir in the chives, lemon juice, sour cream, and some salt and pepper.

Serve hot or cold on toasted bread, sliced tomatoes, or potatoes, or with whatever you fancy.

GRILLED MUSHROOMS

Italians are very fond of grilling wild mushrooms, especially the caps of porcini and slices of puffball. Don't throw away the stems—use them for a duxelles (see page 105). Large puffballs look and taste like steak—ideal for vegetarians. Eat as a first course, or as a side dish for a grilled steak. In Tuscany, they would use nepitella, a wild mint, instead of the parsley and thyme.

SERVES 4

4 YOUNG, LARGE FRESH PORCINI CAPS (PORES STILL CREAMY)
4 SLICES FRESH PUFFBALL MUSHROOM, ABOUT $^3/_4$-INCH THICK
4 TBSP OLIVE OIL
1 TBSP MINCED PARSLEY
1 TSP THYME LEAVES
1 LARGE GARLIC CLOVE, MINCED
JUICE OF $^1/_2$ LEMON
SALT AND PEPPER TO TASTE

Clean the mushrooms well and slice. Prepare a charcoal grill, or heat a ridged grill pan on the stovetop. Combine the oil, parsley, thyme, garlic, and lemon juice, and brush this all over the mushroom caps and puffball slices. Grill for a minute or so on each side. Season with salt and pepper, and serve immediately. You can also use parasol, *Amanita caesarea*, or sulfur shelf for this recipe.

MUSHROOMS AND SAUERKRAUT

The recipes I create or recreate usually come to me through someone explaining them to me, or from ideas picked up when I am eating out. A Russian friend was telling me about this typical combination of mushrooms and cabbage, and that's what inspired my recipe. Meaty mushrooms are best for this dish, especially boletes. Serve with boiled potatoes.

SERVES 4–6

7 OZ FRESH PORCINI
7 OZ FRESH ORANGE BIRCH BOLETES
BUTTER
3 TBSP OLIVE OIL
1 ONION, SLICED
2 MEDIUM SWEET-SOUR PICKLED CUCUMBERS, SLICED
SALT AND PEPPER TO TASTE
$3^1/_2$ CUPS SAUERKRAUT, DRAINED
1 TSP SUGAR
2 TBSP TOMATO PASTE
1 TSP JUNIPER BERRIES
$^1/_2$ TSP BLACK PEPPERCORNS
2 TBSP FRESH BREAD CRUMBS

Clean the mushrooms as appropriate, then slice. Heat 3 tablespoons butter in a heavy pan with the oil. Add the onion and cook until soft. Add the mushrooms and sauté gently for 8 to 10 minutes. Let cool, then add the pickles and season.

Put the sauerkraut in a separate pan with $1^1/_2$ tablespoons butter and a little water, and cook for 40 to 50 minutes. Add the sugar, tomato paste, juniper berries, and peppercorns, and cook for 10 more minutes.

Meanwhile, heat the oven to 400°F.

Spread half of the sauerkraut on the bottom of a medium baking dish, then put the cooked mushrooms on top. Cover with the rest of the sauerkraut and dot with a little butter. Sprinkle with the bread crumbs and dot with some more butter. Bake for 15 minutes.

As an option, you could also add some bacon or ham to the sauerkraut. And if you would like it richer, then add 6 tablespoons heavy or whipping cream before baking.

RIGHT YOU CAN USE A "BRUSH" MADE FROM A BUNDLE OF THYME TO BASTE MUSHROOMS WITH THE OIL MIXTURE BEFORE GRILLING

SMOKED BREAST OF DUCK WITH PRESERVED MUSHROOMS

This isn't exactly a recipe, but rather an assemblage of preserved fungi and meats that in Italy works very well as an antipasto. The task of an appetizer is to titillate the stomach, possibly with something vinegary—which preserved mushrooms are, even though they're kept under oil. The exercise is also to offer to the guests the very best of the autumn harvest, particularly when the harvest was abundant (for it is always wonderful to eat later in the year what you preserved). You might offer pickled porcini or honey fungus, or some cultivated mushrooms, or a mixture. And you can use smoked goose, smoked wild boar, or simply ham instead of the duck.

SERVES 4

12 OZ SMOKED DUCK BREAST, THINLY SLICED
1¹/₂–2 CUPS PICKLED MUSHROOMS IN OIL (SEE PAGE 102)
4–8 SPRIGS PARSLEY

Arrange the duck in the middle of a large platter. Surround it with the mushrooms, draining off most of the oil in which they have been kept. Garnish with parsley and serve as an antipasto, either with grissini (breadsticks) or good toasted bread.

DUCK LIVER PÂTÉ

I proudly claim this recipe as mine, but it owes a great deal to the inspiration of Santiago Gonzales, who was chef at my restaurant for some 16 years, and a master in the preparation of foie gras. This is easy to make, and quite delicious—especially if you use the truffle.

SERVES 4

A 1-OZ FRESH BLACK TRUFFLE (SUMMER OR WINTER)
3 OZ PORK FATBACK, CHOPPED
1 SMALL ONION, CHOPPED
4 GARLIC CLOVES, CHOPPED
1 LB CLEANED DUCK LIVERS, COARSELY CHOPPED
2 BAY LEAVES
1 SPRIG ROSEMARY
SALT AND PEPPER TO TASTE
5 TBSP EACH BRANDY AND DRY SHERRY
4 TBSP (¹/₂ STICK) BUTTER
A LITTLE ASPIC FOR GARNISH (OPTIONAL)

Preheat the oven to 350°F. Clean the truffle carefully.

Put the fatback in a pan and sauté for 3 to 4 minutes. Add the onion and sauté until it is translucent. Add the garlic, livers, bay leaves, and rosemary, and continue cooking for 5 minutes over a moderate heat. Add some salt and pepper and the spirits. Let the alcohol evaporate for a minute, then stir in the butter and set aside to cool a little.

Remove and discard the bay leaves and rosemary. Purée the mixture in a blender if you want it a little smoother, but it should still have some texture. Transfer the mixture to a 5-cup-capacity pâté mold and press the truffle into the mixture so that it is just under the surface. Put the mold in a bain-marie (a large pan containing 1 inch of water), cover tightly, and bake for 1 hour. Let cool.

To serve, cut into slices. If you want to decorate it for a cold buffet, you could garnish the slices with some aspic cut into little cubes.

CHAPTER THREE
PASTA, RICE, AND POLENTA

Inevitably, the food in this chapter is almost entirely Italian, because it is very traditional to combine pasta, rice, and polenta with mushrooms—and few pizzas lack sliced mushrooms! I have tried to give some variety by using different types of fungi, but, to be honest, when Italians talk about mushrooms they really mean only porcini, which is what they use and appreciate most. (And, in fact, to improve the taste of various recipes, we often add dried porcini to sauces.) Pasta is the "carrier" par excellence for wild mushrooms, both fresh and dried: Their succulent textures complement each other perfectly, and the savory juices exuded by cooked mushrooms provide just the right amount of moisture. The association may be traditional, but a word of advice: Mushroom sauces are used almost exclusively to accompany long pasta shapes such as spaghetti and tagliatelle—rarely short pasta. Different regions in Italy favor their own types of homemade pasta and of gnocchi, while in the north, polenta and rice make equally delicious vehicles for mushrooms. Here, rice and fungi are often seen together in risottos, and in rice salads and soups, and polenta with fungi is used as an accompaniment to meat, usually with tomato-based sauces. The sauces and mushrooms in my recipes are interchangeable, so feel free to experiment and create your own specialties.

Tagliolini with Black Truffle

Depending on the season, this dish can be prepared with white Alba truffle, or simply with a black truffle. To give more flavor to the dish when using summer or Périgord truffle, add a few drops of truffle oil. This is a classic first course for an elegant meal.

SERVES 4

FRESHLY MADE TAGLIOLINI (SEE PAGE 160 FOR BASIC PASTA DOUGH)
6 TBSP (³/₄ STICK) BUTTER
2 OZ FRESH BLACK TRUFFLE, CLEANED AND THINLY SLICED
A FEW DROPS OF TRUFFLE OIL (OPTIONAL)
¹/₂ CUP FRESHLY GRATED PARMESAN
SALT AND PEPPER TO TASTE

If you've made your own pasta, you need only its cooking time—3 to 4 minutes—to cook the sauce! Is this the ultimate in fast food?

While the pasta is boiling in plenty of salted water (2 tsp salt to each 4 cups of water), melt the butter in a pan, then add the truffle with a few drops of truffle oil. (If using Alba truffle, the oil is not necessary.)

When the pasta is al dente, drain, reserving a few tablespoons of water, and add it to the pan with the butter and truffle. Add the Parmesan and some salt and pepper. Toss well, using a little of the reserved cooking water to moisten, then serve immediately, with more truffle and/or more Parmesan, if you like.

Pasta with Caesar's Mushrooms

In Italy, the different regions develop their own shape of pasta. Umbria and Marche have ciriole, and the smaller cirioline, which are like tagliatelle with a square profile. A similar pasta from other regions is called "spaghetti alla chitarra," because it is made by hand with a tool consisting of steel strings just like a guitar. This pasta is usually made with eggs and has a delicious flavor.

SERVES 4

14 OZ CIRIOLE PASTA, OR TAGLIOLINI
  OR TAGLIATELLINI
1/2 CUP FRESHLY GRATED PARMESAN
SALT AND PEPPER TO TASTE

SAUCE
10 OZ VERY FRESH AMANITA
  CAESAREA
1 GARLIC CLOVE, HALVED
4 TBSP (1/2 STICK) BUTTER
4 TBSP OLIVE OIL
A PINCH OF FRESHLY GRATED NUTMEG
1 SPRIG ROSEMARY

Clean the mushrooms carefully, then cut into chunks.

Cook the pasta for 4 to 6 minutes, depending on thickness, in boiling salted water. Drain, reserving some of the cooking water.

Rub a frying pan with the garlic halves, then discard the garlic. Melt the butter in the pan, then add the oil, nutmeg, some pepper, and the rosemary. Let the rosemary cook for a few minutes, then remove and discard. Sauté the mushrooms briefly in the aromatic butter and oil mixture.

Toss the drained pasta with the mushroom mixture, and add the Parmesan. Sauté gently to combine the flavors. If necessary, add a little of the cooking water for moisture. Serve with a sprinkling of extra Parmesan and a few thin slices of raw mushroom if you have them.

Spaghetti with Honey Fungus

It is always around October 15th that, seemingly out of nowhere, the honey fungus suddenly appears in the woods. I am always very excited at the sight of a colony, still with closed caps, very tightly packed in bunches at the foot of the trees, or sometimes just shooting out of the grass. When raw they have a strange smell, but once cooked they are delicious, and also lose any toxicity.

SERVES 4

1 LB MEDIUM SPAGHETTI
$1/2$ CUP COARSELY GRATED PARMESAN
SALT AND PEPPER TO TASTE

SAUCE
$1^3/4$ LB FRESH AND TIGHT HONEY
   FUNGUS MUSHROOMS
$1/2$ CUP OLIVE OIL
2 GARLIC CLOVES, SLICED
1 FRESH, HOT RED CHILI PEPPER,
   SLICED
2 TBSP COARSELY CHOPPED PARSLEY

Clean the honey fungus, and remove the toughest part of its stem. Boil for 3 to 4 minutes in lightly salted water, then drain well.
Cook the pasta in plenty of boiling salted water for 6 to 7 minutes until al dente.
Meanwhile, heat the oil in a large pan and add the garlic and chili. Before the garlic browns, add the mushrooms and the parsley. Cook for a few minutes only. Drain the pasta well, then mix it with the mushroom sauce. Add the Parmesan and enjoy!

Spaghetti with Mushroom and Lamb Sauce

The Neapolitans love thin spaghetti (also called vermicelli), which resembles little strings ("spago" means "string"). Ordinarily they normally eat it with just a tomato and basil sauce, but on special occasions they add a meat sauce. The seasonal fungi in this slowly cooked sauce makes the dish even more succulent.

SERVES 4

1 LB THIN SPAGHETTI
PARMESAN OR PECORINO CHEESE,
   FRESHLY GRATED

SAUCE
10 OZ FRESH HONEY FUNGUS
   MUSHROOMS
$1/2$ OZ DRIED PORCINI, SOAKED IN
   WARM WATER FOR 20 MINUTES
$1/2$ CUP OLIVE OIL
1 LARGE ONION, FINELY SLICED
14 OZ BONED LAMB, NOT TOO
   FATTY, COARSELY GROUND
1 FRESH, HOT CHILI PEPPER, CHOPPED
$2/3$ CUP DRY RED WINE
2 CUPS TOMATO PULP (CANNED OR
   FRESH)
SALT AND PEPPER TO TASTE

Clean the honey fungus and remove the toughest part of its stem. Boil for 3 to 4 minutes in lightly salted water, then drain well and set aside. Drain the dried porcini, reserving the soaking liquid, and chop. Put the olive oil in a pan and sauté the onion in it until soft. Add the meat and brown thoroughly. Stir in the chili and wine, and let simmer briefly. Add the chopped dried porcini, along with their strained soaking liquid, and the tomato pulp. Cook over low heat for $1^1/2$ hours.
When ready to serve, cook the spaghetti in boiling salted water until al dente. Add the fresh mushrooms to the sauce, season and cook for a couple of minutes. Drain the spaghetti and divide among warm dishes. Top with the sauce and sprinkle with Parmesan.

PAPPARDELLE WITH PORCINI

This type of pasta—like large tagliatelle—is usually combined with meat ragùs or sauces containing wild boar, game, and other meats. It is very popular in my restaurant, because the large size of the pasta really satisfies the palate and gives a sense of pleasure. An even larger pappardelle was known in Ancient Roman times; this "laganum" was eaten with an anchovy-based sauce.

SERVES 4

14 OZ PAPPARDELLE
$^3/_4$ CUP FRESHLY GRATED PARMESAN
2 TBSP MINCED PARSLEY
SALT AND PEPPER TO TASTE

SAUCE
14 OZ FRESH, FIRM PORCINI
$^3/_4$ OZ DRIED PORCINI, SOAKED IN
    WARM WATER FOR 20 MINUTES
1 MEDIUM ONION, MINCED
6 TBSP OLIVE OIL
3 TBSP BUTTER
1 GARLIC CLOVE, MINCED
4 TBSP DRY WHITE WINE

To start the sauce, clean and finely slice the fresh porcini. Drain the dried porcini, reserving the soaking liquid, then chop them.

Sauté the onion in the oil and butter until soft, then add the garlic. Add the chopped porcini and then the wine, and simmer until the alcohol evaporates. Add the fresh porcini and cook gently for 10 minutes, adding the reserved soaking liquid. Stir well, then reduce the sauce for a few minutes. Season to taste.

Cook the pasta in plenty of boiling salted water until al dente, about 8 to 10 minutes. Drain well, then add some of the sauce. Divide this among warm plates. Pour more of the sauce over each serving and sprinkle with Parmesan and parsley.

CART DRIVER'S SPAGHETTI

I wanted to include this recipe, despite it being in one of my previous books, as it is an example of something rather alien to me—virtually none of the ingredients in the dish is fresh! It is said to have been made by the cart drivers transporting goods from the provinces to Rome: hungry on the long journey, they would want to make themselves something that would not spoil, that was quite undemanding, and that would still be delicious.

SERVES 4

1 OZ DRIED PORCINI, SOAKED IN
    WARM WATER FOR 20 MINUTES
4 TBSP OLIVE OIL
1 GARLIC CLOVE, CRUSHED
2 OZ PANCETTA, MINCED
7 OZ CANNED TUNA IN OIL, DRAINED
    AND FLAKED
$1^1/_4$ LB SWEET CHERRY TOMATOES,
    CHOPPED, OR 2 CUPS TOMATO PULP
    (FRESH OR CANNED)
14 OZ SPAGHETTI
SALT AND PEPPER TO TASTE
FRESHLY GRATED PECORINO CHEESE
    FOR SERVING

Drain the porcini, reserving the soaking liquid, and chop them.

Heat the olive oil in a frying pan, add the garlic, and sauté gently until soft. Add the pancetta and let it brown a little. Stir in the porcini and tuna, and cook for a few minutes, then add the tomatoes and some salt and pepper. Simmer for 20 minutes. Stir in a few spoonfuls of the soaking liquid just to flavor the sauce. Cook for about 5 minutes longer.

Meanwhile, cook the spaghetti in a large pan of boiling salted water until al dente. Drain the spaghetti and toss with the sauce. Season with black pepper and sprinkle with cheese.

SARDINIAN RAVIOLI WITH FAIRY RING MUSHROOMS

It is interesting that two Italian regions as far apart as Sardinia and the Veneto have a very similar way of shaping their homemade ravioli. Although the fillings are different, they both taste wonderful. You need a little patience to make these "culurzones," but the result is very rewarding. The great soccer player, Gianfranco Zola, was delighted when I made this dish from his home town of Oriena, in Sardinia, as a surprise for him. The setting was less traditional—the grounds of Chelsea Football Club in London.

SERVES 6–7

1 RECIPE BASIC PASTA DOUGH
(SEE PAGE 160)
SALT AND PEPPER TO TASTE
FRESHLY GRATED PARMESAN OR
PECORINO CHEESE

FILLING
1³/₄ LB POTATOES, BOILED AND
MASHED (ABOUT 4 CUPS)
2 CUPS GRATED FRESH (DOLCE)
PECORINO CHEESE
¹/₂ CUP GRATED AGED PECORINO
CHEESE
1¹/₄ CUPS FRESHLY GRATED
PARMESAN
2 ¹/₂ TBSP EXTRA VIRGIN OLIVE OIL
2 ¹/₂ TBSP MINCED MINT

SAUCE
7 OZ FRESH FAIRY RING MUSHROOMS
¹/₂ OZ DRIED PORCINI, SOAKED IN
WARM WATER FOR 30 MINUTES
1 SMALL SHALLOT, MINCED
4 TBSP (¹/₂ STICK) BUTTER
ABOUT 4 TBSP CHICKEN OR
VEGETABLE STOCK (SEE PAGE 104)
4 TBSP DRY WHITE WINE
1 TBSP MINCED PARSLEY

To make the filling, combine the potatoes, three cheeses, oil, and mint, then set aside. Roll out the pasta, either by hand or with a pasta machine, until it is very thin—about ¹/₁₆ inch. Cut out 4-inch rounds. Knead the trimmings together, re-roll, and cut out more rounds. To shape the culurzones, take a pasta round in one hand and put a teaspoon of the filling mixture off-center on it. Turn up the bottom of the dough over the filling, then pinch a fold of dough over the right and then the left side to give a pleated effect. Pinch the top together to seal. You should end up with a money-bag shape. To prevent the pasta from drying out, it is important to work quickly and to keep the remaining pasta rounds covered.

For the sauce, clean the fairy ring mushrooms. Drain the porcini, reserving the soaking liquid, then mince. Sauté the shallot in the butter for 5 minutes, then add the mushrooms, fresh and dried, and sauté for a few more minutes. Add the stock and wine, and continue to cook to reduce the liquid a little before adding the parsley.

Meanwhile, cook the culurzones in plenty of lightly salted boiling water until al dente, or 6 to 7 minutes if you like them really soft. Drain and combine with the sauce, stirring to coat well. Serve with more grated pecorino or Parmesan—whichever you prefer.

RAVIOLO WITH SULFUR SHELF AND CAULIFLOWER MUSHROOMS

I call this an "extrovert" raviolo, because the filling is partly visible, resting between two large, square sheets of pasta. It is possible to use a variety of filling, from meat to fish or vegetable. This is a vegetarian version, an elegant dish to be offered as a first course.

The minimal bother of making your own pasta dough is justified by the result, and with the addition of a little chicken or veal, it could become a dish for everybody.

SERVES 4

²/₃ QUANTITY BASIC PASTA DOUGH
   (SEE PAGE 160)
OLIVE OIL
1¹/₂ TBSP BUTTER, MELTED
¹/₂ CUP FRESHLY GRATED PARMESAN
SALT AND PEPPER TO TASTE

FILLING
   10 OZ MIXED FRESH SULFUR SHELF
   AND CAULIFLOWER MUSHROOMS
   (CLEANED WEIGHT)
¹/₂ OZ DRIED PORCINI, SOAKED IN
   LUKEWARM WATER FOR
   20 MINUTES
¹/₂ CUP OLIVE OIL
2 GARLIC CLOVES, MINCED
A LITTLE FRESH, HOT RED CHILI
   PEPPER, MINCED
²/₃ CUP DRY WHITE WINE
¹/₄ CUP MINCED PARSLEY
4 TBSP HEAVY OR WHIPPING CREAM

Slice the fresh wild mushrooms. Drain and squeeze any excess water from the dried porcini, then mince them. Reserve the soaking liquid. Heat the oil in a pan and sauté the garlic, chili, and porcini briefly. Add the sliced fresh mushrooms and sauté for a few more minutes. Add the white wine and a little of the soaking liquid, and continue to cook for 2 to 3 minutes. Set aside. Roll out the pasta dough to make sheets ¹/₁₆ inch thick. Cut into 5¹/₂-inch squares. Put the pasta squares, one by one, into lightly salted boiling water (to which, exceptionally, you will have added a few drops of oil to prevent them from sticking together) and cook for 3 to 4 minutes, carefully stirring with a wooden spoon a couple of times. When the pasta is al dente, add cold water to the pan so you will be able to handle the pasta without burning yourself. Drain all very well.

Just before serving add some salt and pepper, the parsley, and cream to the mushrooms, and combine well. Put a square of pasta on each plate and put 2 or 3 spoonfuls of the filling in the center. Cover with another sheet of pasta. Brush melted butter on top of each raviolo and sprinkle with Parmesan. Serve immediately.

Handkerchief Pasta with Morel and Truffle Sauce

This recipe gives instructions to make the basic pasta dough, as this shape of pasta represents what freshly made pasta is all about—silkiness and fine texture, with developing flavors that provide enormous pleasure to the palate. Once you have made your fresh sheets of pasta, any use is possible thereafter. According to its thinness, it may be used for lasagne, rolled up and cut into ribbons for tagliatelle or tagliolini, or used to make ravioli, tortellini, and any other fresh pasta shapes. This same sauce can be used with ravioli, other pasta shapes, rice, meat, and game.

Serves 6

BASIC PASTA DOUGH
2¹/₂ cups Italian type-00 flour,
   or 2 cups all-purpose flour
   plus ¹/₄ cup cake flour
large pinch of salt
3 large eggs

TO SERVE
dried morel and truffle sauce
   (see page 105)
a little stock if necessary
   (see page 104)
3 tbsp butter
¹/₂ cup freshly grated Parmesan

Mound the flour and salt on a work surface (marble if possible), and make a well in the middle. Break the eggs into the well and, using a fork, gradually mix the flour into the center. The first stage will be very crumbly and not at all workable. Now use your hands to pull the dough together, and make it as homogeneous as possible. Work it with the palms of your hands, push with alternate hands, and use the weight of your body to press down, in a movement away from you. After 10 minutes of kneading, the dough should start to be smooth and silky. If you have time, wrap it in plastic wrap and let it rest for about 30 minutes.

Take a rolling pin and flatten the dough in a circular motion away from you, always starting from the center and working outward. Once you have rolled the dough to a thickness of ¹/₁₆ inch (as thin as you can), it is ready. Cut it into whatever shapes you want (see the introduction above). Here we need large squares of about 3 inches. Let rest on clean dish towels, covered.

Prepare and warm up the sauce, adding a little stock (or water) if necessary, and the butter.

Meanwhile, bring 4 quarts water and 2¹/₂ tablespoons salt to a boil in a large pan. When it is boiling, immerse the pasta sheets, one by one, and cook for 1 to 2 minutes. Drain these well, put in a ceramic bowl with some of the sauce, and mix. Divide among warm plates with more of the sauce poured over, and sprinkle with the Parmesan. Wonderful!

INDIVIDUAL MUSHROOM LASAGNE

There are limitless types of lasagne. This recipe is from the area where I grew up and is extremely simple, but with a maximum of flavor.

To make the special green pasta dough for these individual lasagne, follow the basic recipe, but replace one of the eggs with $1/3$ cup boiled spinach (very well drained and squeezed dry). The green pasta dough can then be rolled out and cut into squares.

SERVES 4

12 OZ FRESH, YOUNG PORCINI
1 RECIPE BASIC PASTA DOUGH
   (SEE OPPOSITE), BUT MADE AS
   NOTED IN RECIPE INTRODUCTION
4 TBSP OLIVE OIL
1 GARLIC CLOVE, MINCED
$1^1/4$ CUPS HEAVY OR WHIPPING
CREAM
2 GRATES OF NUTMEG
SALT AND PEPPER TO TASTE
2 TBSP MINCED PARSLEY
1 TBSP BUTTER
10 OZ FONTINA CHEESE, CUT INTO
   THIN SLICES
$1/2$ CUP FRESHLY GRATED
   PARMESAN

Clean the porcini well and cut into thin slices. Make the pasta dough and let rest. Preheat the oven to 425°F. Roll out the pasta dough as thin as you can, as in the basic recipe, then cut into 4-inch squares. Cover with a cloth.

Put the oil, garlic, and mushrooms into a pan and sauté for 3 minutes. Add the cream, nutmeg, and salt and pepper, and bring to a boil. Simmer to reduce a little. Remove from the heat and stir in the parsley.

Cook the pasta squares in plenty of boiling salted water for 3 minutes. Drain and dry on a cloth. Butter 4 individual oven-to-table dishes with sides. Lay a sheet or two of pasta in each one. Top with some of the mushroom mixture and cover with a few of the Fontina cheese slices. Repeat this layering of pasta, mushroom, and cheese twice, finishing with the mushroom mixture. Sprinkle Parmesan on top and bake for 15 minutes.

PELMENI WITH PORCINI

This recipe is usually reserved for grand occasions, because wild mushrooms—collected in the autumn—are thought of as a luxury by the Russians. At other times of the year, the filling would normally be meat. Pelmeni resemble huge ravioli or dumplings, and are made with fresh pasta. Polish pierogi are similar.

SERVES 4

1 RECIPE BASIC PASTA DOUGH
   (SEE PAGE 160)
6 TBSP (³/₄ STICK) BUTTER
¹/₂ CUP FRESHLY GRATED PARMESAN
A FEW DILL WEED SPRIGS

FILLING
7 OZ FRESH PORCINI
³/₄ OZ DRIED PORCINI, SOAKED IN
   WARM WATER FOR 20 MINUTES
3 TBSP BUTTER
2 GARLIC CLOVES, MINCED
SALT AND PEPPER TO TASTE
2 TBSP COARSELY CHOPPED PARSLEY
1 TBSP MINCED DILL WEED
¹/₃ CUP CRÈME FRAÎCHE

For the filling, clean and finely slice the fresh porcini. Drain the dried porcini, reserving the soaking liquid, and chop them. Sauté the fresh porcini in the butter. After a few minutes add the garlic and sauté gently for 2 minutes longer. Add the chopped porcini to the pan and sauté for 2 more minutes. Season with salt and pepper, and stir in the parsley and dill weed. Let cool, then add the crème fraîche. Mix everything together well.

Roll out the fresh pasta thinly and cut into twelve 5-inch squares. Line up on a work surface and divide the filling among the squares. Moisten the edges of the pelmeni with water and fold each over to obtain a large filled triangle. Press the edges with the prongs of a fork to seal. Boil in lightly salted water for 4 to 5 minutes. Drain well, then put into a large, flat pan in which 6 tablespoons butter has been melted. Heat through briefly, then sprinkle with Parmesan (the Italian influence!) and garnish with the sprigs of dill weed.

RIGHT FRESHLY GRATED PARMESAN

STICKY RICE WITH MUSHROOMS AND GINGKO NUTS

For this Asian-inspired recipe, which is not a risotto, you could use sulfur shelf, hen of the woods, orange birch boletes, or whatever was the result of a not-very-successful fungus foray. Cultivated mushrooms could be used too: buna-shimeji would be good. I like rice in my combination and this one should be the Japanese or Chinese sticky rice (which I find has a slight scent of bacon or pork). The dish sounds Asian, but you can make it to your liking by simply changing the seasoning.

SERVES 4

$1^1/_2$ CUPS JAPANESE STICKY RICE, RINSED UNTIL THE WATER RUNS CLEAR
4 OZ PROSCIUTTO, FINELY DICED
1 SMALL ONION, MINCED
A LITTLE OIL
SALT TO TASTE

RAGÙ
$1^3/_4$ LB MIXED FRESH MUSHROOMS
$^3/_4$ OZ DRIED PORCINI, SOAKED IN WARM WATER FOR 20 MINUTES
1 GARLIC CLOVE, MINCED
4 GREEN ONIONS, MINCED
4 TBSP OLIVE OIL
1 FRESH, HOT RED CHILI PEPPER, MINCED
1 TBSP MINCED FRESH GINGER
3 TBSP SOY SAUCE
JUICE OF $^1/_2$ LEMON
12 SHELLED GINGKO NUTS
A HANDFUL OF BASIL LEAVES, COARSELY CHOPPED
2 TBSP COARSELY CHOPPED CILANTRO

Make the ragù of mushrooms first. Clean the mushrooms thoroughly and, if big, quarter them. Drain and chop the porcini, reserving the soaking liquid. Sauté the garlic and green onion in the olive oil until soft. Add the chili, ginger, chopped porcini, and the fresh mushrooms, the liquid from the porcini, the soy sauce, lemon juice, and gingko nuts. Bring to a boil, reduce the heat, then simmer for 10 to 15 minutes. Stir a few times, adjust the salt and, just before serving, add the herbs.

Meanwhile, sauté the prosciutto and onion in a pan with a little oil. Add the rinsed rice with 2 cups cold water and some salt. Bring to a boil and simmer for 2 minutes. Cover with a lid, then simmer very gently for 6 minutes. Remove the pan from the heat and let stand for 10 minutes, covered. Serve the rice with the mushroom ragù.

MOREL AND PORCINI RISOTTO

According to Italian tradition, a porcini risotto is a must in the autumn, and in my opinion is one of the best dishes, only beaten by a risotto containing white truffles! However, when experimenting one day, I found I was short of porcini, and so used some dried morels. The result was rather impressive! (You can, of course, make it with only porcini.)

SERVES 4

10 OZ FRESH PORCINI (CLEANED WEIGHT), SLICED
2 OZ DRIED MORELS, SOAKED IN WARM WATER FOR 30 MINUTES
6 CUPS CHICKEN OR VEGETABLE STOCK (SEE PAGE 104)
2 TBSP OLIVE OIL
1 1/2 TBSP BUTTER
1 MEDIUM ONION, FINELY SLICED
1 1/2 CUPS CARNAROLI, VIALONE NANO, OR ARBORIO RICE
SALT AND PEPPER TO TASTE

TO FINISH
4 TBSP (1/2 STICK) BUTTER
1/2 CUP FRESHLY GRATED PARMESAN

Prepare the mushrooms, reserving the morel soaking liquid for use at another time. Trim off the end of the morel stems at the base and discard. Heat the stock to a gentle simmer.

Heat the oil and butter in a large pan, then fry the onion gently until soft. Add the morels and sauté briefly. Add the rice and stir it thoroughly so that each grain is coated with oil and lightly toasted. Now start to add the hot stock, ladle by ladle, to the pan. Each time you add a ladleful, make sure that it is fully absorbed before adding the next. Stir the mixture constantly to prevent it from sticking to the bottom of the pan, and also to create a creaminess when the starch is exuded from the grains of rice. After 10 minutes' cooking, add the sliced porcini. Continue to cook and stir until the rice is al dente. The result should be a quite moist, but not brothy dish: this should take about 18 minutes to achieve. To finish the dish, remove from the heat, season, and stir in the butter and Parmesan. Serve immediately.

RISOTTO WITH CAESAR'S MUSHROOMS

When we were taking the photographs for this book, I had to import the fresh Caesar's mushrooms (Amanita caesarea) from Italy, because, unfortunately, they don't grow in Britain. It was lunchtime, and the recipe I created there and then for our break was stunning!

SERVES 4

7 OZ FRESH AMANITA CAESAREA
6 CUPS CHICKEN OR VEGETABLE STOCK (SEE PAGE 104)
1 MEDIUM ONION, MINCED
1/2 CUP (1 STICK) BUTTER
1 3/4 CUPS CARNAROLI RICE
1/2 CUP FRESHLY GRATED PARMESAN
SALT AND PEPPER TO TASTE

Clean and trim the mushrooms, then cut them into small chunks. Have the stock at a steady simmer next to where you will cook the risotto.

Sauté the onion in half of the butter until soft, then add the rice and stir to coat the grains with fat. Now add a ladleful of the hot stock and stir until it is absorbed. Continue in this way, stirring continuously, until all the stock has been added and the stock has been absorbed each time. After about 15 minutes, test a grain of rice, which should be al dente, then stir in the mushrooms. You don't really want to "cook" them. The texture should be moist but not soupy.

Add the remaining butter, the Parmesan, and salt and pepper to taste, and stir vigorously. Serve immediately.

FRIED PIZZA WITH MIXED MUSHROOMS AND TOMATOES

I used to believe that what my mother used to cook could not be improved upon. I believe that, if she were still alive, she would agree that the addition of mushrooms to her fried pizza, which we grew up with, would be desirable.

SERVES 6

PIZZA DOUGH
2¹/₂ CUPS ITALIAN TYPE-00 FLOUR OR ALL-PURPOSE FLOUR
1 CAKE (0.6 OZ) FRESH YEAST, OR 1 ENVELOPE ACTIVE DRY YEAST, PROOFED IN A LITTLE LUKEWARM WATER
A PINCH OF SALT
WATER AS REQUIRED

TOPPING
14 OZ MIXED WILD AND CULTIVATED MUSHROOMS (CHANTERELLES, BLEWITS, HORNS OF PLENTY, ETC.)
3 GARLIC CLOVES, MINCED
EXTRA VIRGIN OLIVE OIL
1 FRESH, MILD RED CHILI PEPPER, SLICED
1¹/₄ CUPS TOMATO PULP (FRESH OR CANNED)
10 BASIL LEAVES, TORN
SALT AND PEPPER TO TASTE

For the pizza dough, mix together the flour, yeast, and salt. Add enough water to make a soft dough. Let it rise for 1–2 hours, covered with a cloth, in a warm but not drafty place.

Meanwhile, for the topping, clean the mushrooms as appropriate and coarsely chop them. Sauté two-thirds of the garlic in 4 tablespoons of oil. Just before they brown, add the mushrooms and chili. Sauté for 7 to 8 minutes. To make the tomato sauce, sauté the remaining garlic in 2 tablespoons of oil, then add the tomato, half the basil, and some salt and pepper. Keep warm.

Take one-sixth of the dough and flatten it to make a disk about 8 inches in diameter. Do the same with the rest of the dough.

Heat enough oil in a frying pan to come 1 inch up the sides. For each pizza, carefully put one disk of dough in the oil and fry until brown and crisp on one side. Turn with tongs and fry on the other side until crisp and brown. (Interestingly, for the health-conscious, this pizza doesn't absorb the oil. Instead, it becomes crisp on the outside but not oily inside.) Place the fried pizza disk on a plate and top with some of the tomato sauce. Place the mixed mushrooms on top and garnish with the remaining basil. Eat while hot.

Polenta with a Mushroom, Tomato, and Sausage Sauce

One of the classic dishes of the valleys of the Italian Alps is polenta, a cornmeal mush. Many people don't like its simplicity, but cooked this way you won't have any complaints at all. The tomato and sausage ragù (or even tomato and chicken) makes a good combination with fungi.

Serves 6

6 cups water
2¹/₂ cups italian polenta meal or yellow cornmeal
6 tbsp (³/₄ stick) butter
2 oz fontina or Taleggio cheese, finely diced
1 cup freshly grated Parmesan
salt and pepper to taste

SAUCE
7 oz button mushrooms
1 oz dried porcini, soaked in warm water for 20 minutes
7 oz luganiga or other fresh spicy sausage
1 medium onion, minced
6 tbsp olive oil
1 bay leaf
2 cups tomato pulp (fresh or canned)

For the polenta, salt the water, then bring it to a boil. Slowly add the polenta meal, stirring with a wooden spoon all the time to avoid lumps. Be careful: when all the meal is in the water it will start to bubble and may burn your skin, so use a long wooden spoon. Cook, stirring occasionally, for about 40 minutes. If using "instant" polenta or cornmeal, just follow the package directions. When cooked, add the butter, the diced cheese, and half the Parmesan, and combine thoroughly.

Meanwhile, for the sauce, clean the fresh mushrooms and slice finely. Drain and chop the dried porcini, reserving the soaking liquid for another use. Remove the sausage meat from its skin and chop into small chunks. Sauté the onion in the oil until soft, then add the sausage meat and cook for 10 minutes, stirring from time to time. Add the sliced mushrooms, the soaked porcini, and the bay leaf, and cook for 5 minutes longer. Add the tomato pulp and cook for 20 minutes. Adjust the seasoning. Serve the sauce over or next to the polenta. Sprinkle with the remaining Parmesan before serving.

GNOCCHI WITH HORN OF PLENTY AND SULFUR SHELF MUSHROOMS

Many types of dumplings exist in the world, but none equals the very simple Italian version, typical of 20 regions, which is made with flour and potatoes. Their lightness, when freshly made, is the major characteristic, but when the gnocchi are combined with an appropriate sauce they become irresistible and very nourishing. They are very good simply with butter and Parmesan, exquisite with tomato and basil, excellent with pesto, a bolognese sauce, or even with a Gorgonzola sauce, but—and this is the first time I have done this—they are wonderful combined with mushrooms.

SERVES 6

GNOCCHI
1³/₄ LB BAKING POTATOES, PEELED AND QUARTERED
1¹/₃ CUPS ALL-PURPOSE FLOUR
1 EGG, BEATEN
SALT AND PEPPER TO TASTE

SAUCE
10 OZ FRESH HORN OF PLENTY MUSHROOMS (CLEANED WEIGHT)
7 OZ SULFUR SHELF MUSHROOMS (CLEANED WEIGHT), OR USE FRESH OPEN CAP OR CREMINI MUSHROOMS
³/₄ OZ DRIED PORCINI, SOAKED IN WARM WATER FOR 20 MINUTES
4 TBSP OLIVE OIL
4 TBSP (¹/₂ STICK) BUTTER
1 MEDIUM ONION, MINCED
²/₃ CUP DRY WHITE WINE
3 TBSP MINCED PARSLEY
¹/₂ CUP FRESHLY GRATED PARMESAN

Cook the potatoes in lightly salted water. When soft, drain them thoroughly. Put them back into the empty pan and stir over a gentle heat for a few seconds to get rid of any lingering moisture. Mash them finely, then mix gently with the flour on a work surface, together with the egg, to make a soft dough. Keeping your hands well floured, take part of the dough and roll it with your hands into a soft sausage, about ³/₄ inch in diameter. Cut into chunks about 1 inch long. With the help of a fork and more flour, press each chunk against the prongs of the fork with a downward movement, to mark and shape the gnocchi. Let rest on a clean cloth.

For the sauce, clean the fresh mushrooms and cut into thin strips. Drain and mince the porcini, reserving their soaking liquid. Heat the oil and butter in a pan and sauté the onion in the mixture until soft, then add all the mushrooms. Cook very slowly for 15 minutes to reduce them. Add some of the porcini soaking liquid and the wine, and cook for 5 to 10 minutes longer. Add the parsley, some salt, and lots of black pepper.

To cook the gnocchi, plunge them all at once into a large pan of lightly salted boiling water. They will be cooked when they float to the surface. Scoop them out with a slotted spoon and add to the sauce. Combine well, then divide among warm plates and sprinkle with Parmesan.

RIGHT GNOCCHI WITH HORN OF PLENTY AND SULFUR SHELF MUSHROOMS

EEL FILLETS WITH BEEFSTEAK FUNGUS

If there is a fish that can match, in flavor and texture, the beefsteak fungus, it's the eel. The fungus has an acidity that compensates for the fattiness of the eel. The fish itself is actually cooked so that it loses a great deal of its natural fat: pan-grilling not only melts and burns off most of the fat, but the heat also gives the fish a desirable smokiness. The marinade is important too. I also tried this recipe using conger eel, and the result was equally good. In this case you need to marinate only for 30 minutes.

SERVES 4

14 OZ FRESH BEEFSTEAK FUNGUS
1 LB FRESH EEL FILLETS, WITH SKIN
2 TBSP OLIVE OIL
2 TBSP HEAVY OR WHIPPING CREAM
2 TBSP CHOPPED DILL WEED
SALT AND PEPPER TO TASTE

MARINADE
JUICE OF 2 LEMONS
4 TBSP OLIVE OIL
1 GARLIC CLOVE, MINCED
ABOUT 6 MINT LEAVES

Clean the fungus thoroughly and cut into thin slices. Cut the eel into 3-inch chunks. Some 3 to 4 hours before cooking, mix the marinade ingredients together, adding a little salt, and pour this over the eel in a nonreactive dish. Heat the oil in a pan, then add the fungus slices and sauté for 5 minutes. Add the cream, dill weed, and some salt and pepper.
Heat a ridged grill pan. Drain the eel. Pan-grill the eel, about 5 minutes each side, then stir it thoroughly into the mushroom mixture. The color will be a bit reddish; this is because the fungus exudes a reddish moisture during cooking. Accompany with bread or plain polenta (see page 169).

DOVER SOLE WITH FAIRY RING MUSHROOMS

The Dover sole, caught on the European side of the Atlantic, is to me the height of marine deliciousness, with its firm flesh and delicate flavor. Whichever way you cook a fresh Dover sole, it is always wonderful, but combined with the delicate fairy ring mushroom, it becomes a dish worthy of serving at the most demanding table. To retain the fullest flavor I prefer to cook the fish on the bone, then fillet it before serving.

SERVES 4

4 MEDIUM-SIZED DOVER SOLE
ALL-PURPOSE FLOUR FOR DUSTING
4 TBSP (¹/₂ STICK) BUTTER

SAUCE
14 OZ FRESH FAIRY RING MUSHROOMS
1 SHALLOT, MINCED
3 TBSP BUTTER
5 TBSP DRY WHITE WINE
JUICE OF 1 LEMON
2 TBSP MINCED PARSLEY
2 TBSP DILL WEED (OPTIONAL)
SALT AND PEPPER TO TASTE

Clean the mushrooms well. Clean and skin the fish (or ask the fishmonger to do this for you), then dust with flour. Fry the fish on each side in the butter until crisp. You may have to use two large frying pans because Dover soles are always quite sizeable. While you are preparing the sauce, keep the soles warm in a low oven.

Sauté the shallot in the butter until soft. Add the mushrooms and sauté for a few minutes. Add the wine and lemon juice, and stir for another minute. Add the herbs—saving a little of the dill for garnish—and finally some salt and pepper. Combine well and set aside.

Fillet the sole carefully by making an incision in the middle of the spine lengthwise. Then cut off and discard the edges, fins, tail, and head. Carefully lift one of the upper fillets, starting from the center. If the sole is well cooked, this should come off the bone easily. Do the same with the other. When both upper fillets are off, remove the main bone, leaving the lower part of the sole intact. Repeat with all four fish. To serve, put the lower fillet on a hot plate, arrange some of the mushroom mixture lengthwise along this, and put the two upper fillets on top. Decorate with a little dill weed, if using and serve with plain boiled potatoes.

MONKFISH WITH BUNA-SHIMEJI

This recipe uses one of the "exotic" mushrooms, so-called because of its Eastern origins. Because it is cultivated, it is available most of the year. It has a delicate flavor, and is very easy to cook with.

SERVES 4

$1\frac{1}{4}$ LB MONKFISH FILLET, IN 4 PIECES
10 OZ FRESH BUNA-SHIMEJI
   MUSHROOMS, CUT AT THE BASE
ALL-PURPOSE FLOUR FOR DUSTING
6 TBSP OLIVE OIL
2 GARLIC CLOVES, FINELY SLICED
1 SMALL, FRESH, HOT CHILI PEPPER,
   MINCED
4 TBSP ($\frac{1}{2}$ STICK) BUTTER
JUICE OF 1 LIME
2 TBSP CHOPPED CILANTRO
SALT AND PEPPER TO TASTE

In this recipe, the monkfish is plainly cooked to safeguard its delicacy, as well as that of the mushrooms. Dust the fish with flour and shake off any excess. Heat the oil in a frying pan and sauté the mushrooms for 2 minutes. Add the garlic and chili, and sauté for 2 to 3 minutes longer, stirring from time to time. Sauté the fish in the butter for a couple of minutes on each side. Season with salt and pepper and the lime juice.

Finish the mushrooms by stirring in the cilantro and some salt and pepper. Serve the fish and mushrooms together.

SWORDFISH OLIVES WITH HONEY FUNGUS

This is an excellent combination of fish and fungi. A little patience is required to make the "olives," but you will certainly be rewarded for your work. If you can't find honey fungus, then use cultivated buna-shimeji instead.

SERVES 4

12 SWORDFISH SLICES, $\frac{1}{2}$-INCH THICK
   (ABOUT $1\frac{1}{2}$ LB TOTAL WEIGHT)
$\frac{3}{4}$ CUP FRESH WHITE BREAD CRUMBS
1 TBSP MINCED DILL WEED
2 TBSP PINE NUTS
2 GHERKINS, CUT INTO SMALL DICE
2 EGGS, BEATEN
ALL-PURPOSE FLOUR FOR DUSTING
OLIVE OIL FOR FRYING
SALT AND PEPPER TO TASTE

MUSHROOM SAUCE
10 OZ FRESH HONEY FUNGUS
   MUSHROOMS
6 TBSP OLIVE OIL
2 GARLIC CLOVES, MINCED
1 SMALL, FRESH, HOT RED CHILI
   PEPPER, MINCED
$\frac{1}{4}$ CUP FRESH WHITE BREAD CRUMBS
7 TBSP VEGETABLE STOCK (SEE PAGE 104)
2 TBSP MINCED PARSLEY
JUICE OF 1 LEMON

Clean the honey fungus thoroughly, then blanch in boiling salted water for 5 minutes. Drain well.

Make the stuffing for the swordfish olives by combining the bread crumbs, dill weed, pine nuts, gherkin, and eggs, seasoning well with salt and pepper.

Lay the fish slices out on a work surface and place 1 tablespoon of the stuffing in the center of each one. Roll up and secure with a wooden toothpick. Dust with flour, then fry in hot oil until brown on all sides. Keep warm.

In another pan, heat the olive oil, then add the garlic and chili, and sauté briefly before adding the honey fungus. Cook for 5 minutes. Add the bread crumbs, stock, parsley, and lemon juice, and mix well, seasoning with salt and pepper. When the honey fungus is cooked, add the swordfish olives, coat them with the sauce, and serve warm.

RED MULLET WITH CHANTERELLES

For me, there is nothing more delicious than freshly caught red mullet fried in olive oil until crisp. For you, however, the easier option might be to find a fishmonger who has already filleted some fish for you. Here, I have combined the red mullet with lovely little chanterelles.

SERVES 4

8 OZ FRESH CHANTERELLES
4 RED MULLET FILLETS (ABOUT
    14 OZ TOTAL WEIGHT)
6 TBSP OLIVE OIL
JUICE OF 1 LIME
1 SHALLOT, MINCED
1 TBSP BRANDY
4 TBSP HEAVY OR WHIPPING CREAM
SALT AND PEPPER TO TASTE
1 TBSP MINCED PARSLEY

Clean and trim the mushrooms. Marinate the fish fillets in 2 tablespoons of the oil with the lime juice and some salt and pepper for 2 hours.

In a pan, heat the rest of the oil and sauté the shallot gently to soften. Add the mushrooms and sauté gently for 5 minutes. Add the brandy and, when the alcohol has evaporated, the cream, salt, pepper, and parsley.

In a nonstick pan, fry the fish fillets, skin-side down, until the skin is crisp and the flesh is cooked. This should take about 5 to 8 minutes. Add any remaining marinade to the pan and heat gently.

Serve the fish immediately on hot plates with the mushrooms on the side. Eat with bread.

TUNA STEAK WITH WILD MUSHROOMS

The Italians love tuna and swordfish, and like to grill them in steak form, a superb and simple way of enjoying these meaty fish. However, the delicacy of a slice of fresh tuna, just grilled or fried in olive oil and accompanied by some mixed wild mushrooms, has to be tasted to be believed! This recipe is particularly delicious with bay boletes, honey fungus, and wood or field blewits, but you can use any mushrooms, even cultivated ones.

SERVES 4

1 LB MIXED FRESH WILD
    MUSHROOMS, OR FRESH SHIITAKE
    MUSHROOMS
4 SLICES TUNA OR SWORDFISH,
    ABOUT 5 OZ EACH
SALT AND PEPPER TO TASTE
4 TBSP OLIVE OIL
4 TBSP (1/2 STICK) BUTTER
1 GARLIC CLOVE, MINCED
A PINCH OF MARJORAM LEAVES
A FEW NEEDLES OF ROSEMARY

Clean the mushrooms well, then cut into even-sized pieces.

Season the fish with salt and pepper, then sauté it in the oil for 5 minutes on each side. Remove from the pan and set aside. Add the butter, mushrooms, and garlic to the pan, and sauté for 10 minutes. Add the herbs and salt and pepper to taste.

Return the cooked fish to the pan and stir in 1 tablespoon of water to help combine the ingredients. Warm through gently, then serve.

CONSTANZA'S SALT COD WITH POTATO AND MUSHROOMS

Constanza Guimares is our invaluable housekeeper. When I asked her how the Portuguese would use mushrooms, she came up with the idea of combining them with what is probably the most used and best-loved ingredient in Portugal – bacalau, the salt cod from Norway. The recipe sounded so homely and comforting that I had to have a go, and here it is, using the very large brown cultivated Portobello mushroom.

SERVES 4–6

800 G SALT COD, CUT INTO CHUNKS AND SOAKED FOR 2 DAYS IN WATER, CHANGING THE WATER EVERY FEW HOURS
300 G PORTOBELLO MUSHROOMS
6 TBSP OLIVE OIL
1 GARLIC CLOVE, FINELY CHOPPED
3 TBSP FINELY CHOPPED PARSLEY
400 G POTATOES, COOKED, PEELED AND SLICED
200 G MATURE CHEDDAR CHEESE, GRATED
SALT AND PEPPER TO TASTE

WHITE SAUCE
30 G PLAIN FLOUR
60 G BUTTER
400 ML VERY HOT MILK
A PINCH OF FRESHLY GRATED NUTMEG

Rinse the cod and cook in boiling water for 30 minutes until tender. Leave to cool in the cooking water, then drain well. Discard all the bones and skin and flake the flesh.

Preheat the oven to 200°C/Gas 6. Clean the mushrooms thoroughly, then slice them thickly.

Meanwhile, prepare the white sauce. Fry the flour in the butter for a few minutes, stirring, then add the hot milk and whisk energetically to avoid lumps. Add some salt and pepper and the nutmeg. Cook, stirring, for 10 minutes.

Fry the mushrooms briefly in the oil, adding the garlic and most of the parsley towards the end. Take care to save the best-looking and largest mushroom slices to decorate the top of the dish.

Now assemble everything in an earthenware container, starting with a couple of spoonfuls of white sauce in the bottom. Cover this with a layer of cod flakes, then add some of the mushrooms with some potatoes and more white sauce. Sprinkle with a generous layer of Cheddar cheese, then start again with the cod, mushrooms, potatoes and white sauce, then distribute the cheese and the last layer of cod. Decorate with the reserved mushroom slices and the remaining parsley, and grind over some black pepper. Bake in the preheated oven for 25–30 minutes, then serve hot.

Poached Seafood with Mushrooms

This is a recipe that you can vary infinitely. I first introduced it to my restaurant during the winter months, using dried mushrooms, as I thought the light, summery feel of the poached fish would cheer people up! But of course you can cook it at any time of year, using fresh or dried mushrooms only, or a mixture of the two. You can vary the seafood as well; you just need a selection of at least three firm-textured fish. Buy the dried shiitake mushrooms in Chinese markets.

Serves 4

16 dried shiitake mushrooms
    plus $^3/_4$ oz dried porcini, or
    10 oz fresh shiitake
10 oz raw jumbo shrimp, peeled
    (reserve the shells)
10 oz monkfish fillet
4 sole or flounder fillets (have
    your fishmonger fillet a 1-lb
    fish, and give you the skin and
    bones)
4 tbsp ($^1/_2$ stick) butter
salt and pepper to taste

FISH STOCK
fish scraps (see page 104)
4 cups water
1 carrot, sliced lengthwise
1 onion, minced
1 bay leaf
a little marjoram

Soak the dried shiitake (if using) in warm water for at least 30 minutes, then simmer in the soaking liquid for 30 to 40 minutes or until soft. Discard the stems, which are usually tough and dirty. Soak the dried porcini (if using) in warm water for 20 minutes. Drain, reserving the soaking liquid. Clean the fresh mushrooms at the last minute.

Meanwhile, make the fish stock, using the shrimp shells, the skin and bones from the sole, and perhaps another fish head that you have coaxed from the fishmonger. Cover these with the water, add the other stock ingredients, and boil for 1 hour, until the stock has reduced considerably. Strain and set aside. Prepare the fish: Cut the monkfish fillet into bite-sized chunks. Roll the sole fillets up and secure each roll with a wooden toothpick.

Use a pan that is deep rather than wide so that you will not need too much liquid to cover the fish. Melt the butter in the pan and sauté the monkfish for a minute. Add the rolled fillets of sole, the mushrooms, shrimp, and enough fish stock—to which you could add a little mushroom soaking liquid—to cover. Poach over a gentle heat for about 10 minutes or until the fish is cooked. Season to taste with salt and pepper.

Serve with freshly boiled potatoes or, better still, with a mound of buttered noodles.

SHRIMP WITH HORN OF PLENTY MUSHROOMS AND SAFFRON RICE

Horn of plenty mushrooms have some culinary peculiarities, such as becoming completely black when cooked. Here the tender little shrimp are an ideal combination with these mushrooms, making the dish both elegant to look at and extremely tasty to eat.

SERVES 4

10 OZ FRESH HORN OF PLENTY
  MUSHROOMS (CLEANED WEIGHT)
2/3 CUP CARNAROLI RICE
14 OZ RAW SMALL SHRIMP, PEELED
4 TBSP OLIVE OIL
1 SMALL ONION, FINELY SLICED
4 TBSP DRY WHITE WINE
1¹/2 TBSP BUTTER
A FEW SAFFRON STRANDS OR
  2 PINCHES POWDERED SAFFRON
1 TBSP LEMON JUICE
1 TSP MINCED PARSLEY
SALT AND PEPPER TO TASTE

Clean the mushrooms thoroughly. Cook the rice in abundant salted water for 15 minutes, then drain.

For the shrimp and mushrooms, heat the oil in a pan and sauté the onion until soft. Add the mushrooms and sauté for 5 minutes. Add the wine and cook to let the alcohol evaporate. Then add the shrimp and cook gently for 5 minutes longer.

Melt the butter in a clean pan with the saffron, lemon juice, and parsley. Add the hot drained rice and combine well. Check the rice and mushroom mixture for salt and pepper, then serve, either tossing the rice and shrimp mixture together, or mounding the shrimp mixture in the center of a small ring of rice.

FRIED SEAFOOD AND MUSHROOMS

In Italy, dishes that contain seafood and other ingredients are often cooked together to produce an interesting contrast. This recipe is a perfect combination of ingredients from sea and earth. It would be fantastic eaten with an aperitif, but also as a light first course accompanied by a green salad.

SERVES 4

4 OZ ST. GEORGE'S MUSHROOMS
5 OZ FRESH PORCINI
4 OZ RAW SMALL SHRIMP
4 OZ RAW MEDIUM SHRIMP
4 OZ WHITEBAIT
4 OZ SQUID OR SMALL OCTOPUS
2 EGGS, BEATEN
SALT AND PEPPER TO TASTE
OLIVE OIL FOR DEEP-FRYING
1 CUP DRY BREAD CRUMBS
ALL-PURPOSE FLOUR FOR DUSTING
2 LEMONS, QUARTERED

Clean the mushrooms and cut the larger ones in halves or quarters. Prepare all the seafood, cleaning and peeling as appropriate.
Season the beaten egg. Heat the oil in a pan to 350°–375°F, until a cube of bread dropped in browns in 30 seconds.
Dip the mushrooms first into the egg, then roll in the bread crumbs. Fry in the hot oil until golden, then remove and drain on paper towels, and keep warm. Then dip the fish into the flour and fry in the hot oil until golden.
Serve immediately, with the mushrooms and lemon quarters.

MUSHROOM-STUFFED SQUID

It is not so long since the idea of cooking mushrooms and fish together arrived in Europe. Eastern cultures, however, had always paired mushrooms with fish, especially in Thai, Japanese, and Chinese soups. More conventionally, the Europeans combined mushrooms with game and meat. This recipe is an interesting combination of two of my favorite foods. You could use any substantial mushroom instead of the sulfur shelf.

SERVES 4

7 OZ FRESH SULFUR SHELF
   MUSHROOMS
1$^1/_4$ LB MEDIUM-SIZED SQUID (YOU
   NEED AT LEAST 4, OR YOU COULD
   BUY MANY MORE SMALLER ONES)
$^1/_2$ CUP OLIVE OIL
1 GARLIC CLOVE, MINCED
$^1/_2$ TSP MINCED FRESH, HOT RED
   CHILI PEPPER
6 TBSP FRESH BREAD CRUMBS
1 TBSP MINCED PARSLEY
1 TBSP MINCED CILANTRO
2 EGGS
SALT AND PEPPER TO TASTE
$^2/_3$ CUP DRY WHITE WINE

Clean the mushrooms very well, then dice. Clean the squid and pull away the heads and tentacles. Mince the tentacles.
Put half the oil into a pan and sauté the garlic, chili, and squid tentacles briefly. Add the mushrooms to the pan and sauté until soft. Let as much moisture as possible evaporate. Season to taste, then let cool.
In a large bowl, mix together the mushrooms, bread crumbs, parsley, cilantro, and eggs. Season with salt. Now stuff the bodies of the squid with the mixture (very fiddly if you bought small squid), and hold each together with a wooden toothpick. Fry the stuffed squid in the remaining oil for 1 minute on each side, or until they begin to brown, then add the wine. Cook quickly to let the alcohol evaporate, then serve immediately, perhaps with some spinach.

SQUID WITH SHIITAKE AND JUDAS' EARS

The peculiar wild mushroom in this recipe perfectly complements the shiitake and squid. Auricularia, wild or cultivated, are much used in Chinese and Japanese cooking, but very little in the West. Indeed, this recipe leans toward the cuisines of the Far East in its use of spices and herbs. It is an interesting way of using mushrooms and could be accompanied by a little freshly boiled sticky rice.

SERVES 4

7 OZ FRESH SHIITAKE MUSHROOMS
5 OZ FRESH JUDAS' EAR
   MUSHROOMS, OR 2 OZ DRIED,
   SOAKED IN WARM WATER FOR 30
   MINUTES
1^1/$_2$ LB SQUID (CLEANED WEIGHT)
6 TBSP CORN OIL
1 TBSP PEANUT OIL
4 GARLIC CLOVES, MINCED
1 SMALL BUNCH GREEN ONIONS,
   MINCED
1^1/$_2$-OZ PIECE FRESH GINGER,
   PEELED AND MINCED
1 FRESH, HOT RED CHILI PEPPER,
   MINCED
1 TBSP CORNSTARCH, DISSOLVED IN
   2 TBSP WATER (OPTIONAL)
1 TBSP SOY SAUCE
1 TBSP RICE VINEGAR
JUICE OF 1 LIME
2 TBSP COARSELY CHOPPED CILANTRO
SALT TO TASTE

Clean the fresh shiitake, then trim the stems and slice the caps. Wash and rinse the Judas' ears, fresh or dried. Cut the squid body into rings and chop the tentacles.

In a wok or frying pan, heat the oils and stir-fry the garlic, green onions, ginger, and chili for a short while. Add the mushrooms and stir-fry for a couple of minutes more. Add the squid and stir-fry for 3 minutes, then add the cornstarch (if using), soy sauce, rice vinegar, and lime juice. Stir-fry for 2 minutes longer. Add salt and sprinkle with cilantro. Should you need more moisture, then use a little stock made with a cube—as every Chinese cook does (a little MSG won't kill you)!

OYSTERS WITH ZABAGLIONE AND WHITE TRUFFLE

This is the height of sophistication. Although it's very simple to prepare, it will impress, not least because it uses that exclusive fungus, the white truffle. You are most unlikely to find this in nature by yourself, because the collection of truffles, especially the white from Alba, is limited to specially licensed "trifolau." With the help of their trained dogs, they rummage through the Alba hills in the middle of the night (so as not to be seen) to get the most expensive food in the world. However, you only need a little per person. You could use black truffle, to reduce the cost of the dish, but it also reduces the effect.

SERVES 4

1 ALBA TRUFFLE, ABOUT 2 OZ
16 FRESH OYSTERS, SHUCKED AND
   LEFT IN THE DEEPER PART OF
   THE SHELL
1^1/$_2$ TBSP BUTTER
6 EGG YOLKS
^{2}/$_3$ CUP DRY WHITE WINE
JUICE OF ^{1}/$_2$ LEMON
A FEW DROPS OF TRUFFLE OIL
SALT AND PEPPER TO TASTE

Clean the truffle very carefully and, at the last moment, slice it very thinly with a "mandolino" (a special tool used to shave truffles). Arrange the oysters, 4 to a plate.
Preferably in a zabaglione pan (a copper bowl) over a pan of boiling water, or a double boiler, melt the butter, then add the egg yolks, wine, lemon juice, truffle oil, and some salt and pepper. Whisk until the mixture becomes almost stiff. Spoon this sauce over the oysters, then add a few thin slices of truffle.

CHAPTER FIVE
MEAT

Meat and mushrooms are the perfect partners.
Mushroom sauces provide succulent
accompaniments to plain grilled meat, and
mushrooms are an essential ingredient of meat
casseroles and stews. When testing ideas for
this book, I came across many new
combinations, some using variety meats,
a lot of which are traditional in many
diverse parts of the world, not just in
Italy. Game, red meat, and variety meats are
strong in flavor, but this can be matched
by the aromatic qualities of the most pungent
of mushrooms. More delicate meats such
as veal or chicken also have their fungal
counterparts in the subtlety of mushrooms
like chanterelles and parasols. There are
about 40 edible mushrooms described in
this book, of which three-fourths are wild
and one-fourth cultivated. Whatever meat you
like, you will certainly find one that goes with
this selection of fungi. Good luck!

CHICKEN CASSEROLE WITH TWO TYPES OF BOLETE

Chicken may be the most popular meat in the world, but very often it lacks flavor because it has been intensively-farmed. For this recipe you have to find the most wonderful chicken, organic and, if possible, reared outdoors. The two boletes will provide an irresistible combination to enjoy with some good friends. Bear in mind, though, that while the orange birch bolete always blackens when cooked, the porcini remains immaculately white.

SERVES 4

12 OZ MIXED FRESH PORCINI AND
   ORANGE BIRCH BOLETES
   (CLEANED WEIGHT)
1^1/$_2$ LB BONELESS CHICKEN PIECES
ALL-PURPOSE FLOUR FOR DUSTING
6 TBSP OLIVE OIL
1 MEDIUM ONION, MINCED
4 TBSP (^{1}/$_2$ STICK) BUTTER
1^1/$_2$ CUPS TOMATO PULP (FRESH OR
   CANNED)
A PINCH OF FRESHLY GRATED NUTMEG
1 SPRIG THYME
2 TBSP CHOPPED PARSLEY
^{2}/$_3$ CUP DRY WHITE WINE
SALT AND PEPPER TO TASTE

Clean the mushrooms and slice them. Dust the pieces of chicken in flour, then fry them in the oil until brown all over. Set aside.
Add the onion and butter to the oil, along with the sliced mushrooms, and sauté for a minute or two. Add the tomato pulp, nutmeg, thyme, and parsley, and cook for 2 minutes longer. Add the wine and some salt and pepper.
Return the chicken to the pan, along with any juices, and cook for 15 minutes. Serve with rice.

CHICKEN ROLLS WITH DUXELLES

This is an extremely simple recipe to create, providing you have some mushroom duxelles already made.

SERVES 4

4 LARGE, BONELESS CHICKEN
   BREAST HALVES
2 RECIPES WILD MUSHROOM
   DUXELLES (SEE PAGE 105)
4 TBSP (^{1}/$_2$ STICK) BUTTER
2 TBSP OLIVE OIL
JUICE OF 1 LEMON

Beat the chicken breasts with a meat pounder between two sheets of plastic wrap to flatten them a bit. Spread one-fourth of the duxelles over each breast, then roll up, securing with a wooden toothpick.
Fry in the butter and oil until brown all over, about 3 minutes on each side.
Pour the lemon juice over the chicken and serve with a little of the fat.
Accompany with steamed spinach and a potato purée.

CHICKEN WITH SHAGGY INK CAPS

These fungi appeared in my lawn just in time for this book! You shouldn't use or drink alcohol when cooking or eating them as they may cause a reaction, so I have used a very small amount for flavor. The problem disappears in cooking.

SERVES 4

14 OZ FRESH, YOUNG SHAGGY INK
   CAP MUSHROOMS
4 BONELESS CHICKEN BREAST
   HALVES, SKIN REMOVED
ALL-PURPOSE FLOUR FOR DUSTING
6 TBSP (³/₄ STICK) BUTTER
4 TBSP OLIVE OIL
5 TBSP MEDIUM-DRY SHERRY
4 TBSP DILL WEED
JUICE OF ¹/₂ LEMON
SALT AND PEPPER TO TASTE

Clean and trim the mushrooms.
Cut the chicken breasts into 4 pieces each, and pound them between pieces of plastic wrap until ¹/₃ inch thin. Dust the pieces with flour, then sauté in the hot butter and oil until brown on both sides. Remove the chicken to a plate.
In the same pan, sauté the mushrooms for a few minutes. Add the sherry and sauté for a few minutes to evaporate the alcohol. Return the chicken to the pan, along with any juices that have collected on the plate, and cook until hot. Add the dill weed, lemon juice, and salt and pepper to taste.

MUSHROOM AND CHICKEN CASSEROLE

How lucky my friend Ken Hom is to have visited the market at Yunam in China, where they grow and sell up to 200 different varieties of mushroom. With his kind permission I have taken from one of his books this interesting recipe, which is typical of that city. I hope he doesn't mind the addition of some dried morels.

SERVES 4

1 OZ DRIED SHIITAKE MUSHROOMS
1 OZ DRIED MORELS
1¹/₄ LB CHICKEN THIGHS, SKINNED
   AND BONED
2 TBSP PEANUT OIL
6 SLICES FRESH GINGER
1 TBSP DRY RICE WINE
1 TBSP DARK SOY SAUCE
2 TBSP SUGAR
1 CUP CHICKEN STOCK (SEE PAGE 104)
1 TSP CORNSTARCH

MARINADE
1 TBSP LIGHT SOY SAUCE
2 TBSP SAKÉ (RICE WINE)
1 TSP DARK SOY SAUCE
1 TSP TOASTED SESAME OIL
¹/₂ TSP SALT
1 TSP CORNSTARCH

Soak the dried mushrooms in warm water for 20 minutes. Discard the tough stem from the mushrooms; halve the shiitake and leave the morels whole. Cut the chicken into chunks about 3 x 1 inch. Marinate the chicken in the marinade ingredients for 20 minutes.
Heat the peanut oil in a wok or large pan and stir-fry the ginger for 2 minutes. Add the chicken and marinade, and stir-fry for 2 minutes longer. Pour the contents of the wok into a heavy casserole, then add the remaining ingredients except the cornstarch. Bring to a boil over medium heat, then simmer gently for 15 minutes, covered. Remove the lid and stir in the cornstarch mixed with 1 teaspoon water. Cook for 2 minutes longer. Discard the ginger and serve with plain boiled rice.

Karp Kalan Koli Curry

This recipe is from Mr. P. Ganeshan, who is a commis in the kitchens of The Park Hotel in New Delhi. Morels—known there as "gucchi" and found in Nepal, Kashmir, and Tibet—are the most popular, sought-after, and expensive mushrooms in India, though some years ago I got a bargain (see page 64).

Serves 4

8 boneless chicken breast
  halves (about 1³/₄ lb total)
butter
2 tbsp peanut oil
30 curry leaves
16 sprigs cilantro
salt

STUFFING
24 medium-sized dried morels,
  soaked in warm water for
  20 minutes
2 tbsp vegetable oil
¹/₄ cup minced onion
1 tbsp minced garlic
2 tbsp minced fresh ginger
1 tbsp minced fresh, hot green
  chili pepper
1 cup ground chicken
1 tbsp heavy or whipping cream
  (optional)

SAUCE
1¹/₂ cups packed grated fresh
  coconut
seeds of 5 cardamom pods
¹/₃ cup cashew nuts, soaked
  and drained
5 tbsp peanut oil
1¹/₂ lb onions, minced
1 tbsp fresh ginger paste
2 tbsp fresh garlic paste
1 tsp ground coriander
¹/₂ tsp cayenne pepper
¹/₄ tsp ground turmeric
2 cups fresh tomato puree

Preheat the oven to 400°F. Skin the chicken breasts and split nearly through horizontally. Open out, cover with a piece of plastic wrap, and pound to flatten. For the stuffing, drain the morels (reserving the soaking liquid). Mince half of them; cut the remainder into thin julienne strips (these will be used for the sauce and garnish). Heat the vegetable oil in a nonstick pan and sauté the onion, garlic, ginger, and chili to soften, then stir in the minced morels and the ground chicken. Cook until the chicken is well cooked, then add a little of the reserved soaking liquid and season with salt. Remove from the heat. If the mixture seems dry, add the cream.

Season the flattened chicken breasts with salt, then spread them with the stuffing mixture. Roll up the breasts tightly in pieces of buttered foil and twist the edges until the "packages" are firm.

For the sauce, combine the coconut, cardamom seeds, and cashew nuts in a mortar and grind them to a fine paste. Put the peanut oil into a heavy pan and heat it over medium heat until almost smoking. Add the minced onions and sauté until the onion is light brown. Add the ginger and garlic pastes, and keep stirring until the aroma of ginger and garlic is apparent. Stir in the coconut paste, then the coriander and cayenne, and stir for 2 minutes. Add the tomato puree and half the reserved soaking liquid. Bring the sauce to a boil and simmer gently for 20 minutes.

Meanwhile, put the chicken packages in a baking dish and bake for 20 minutes. To finish, heat the 2 tablespoons peanut oil and fry the curry leaves for a few seconds. Reserve half for garnishing, and add the other half to the sauce. Simmer the sauce for 5 to 6 minutes longer, then check the seasoning and consistency. Unwrap the chicken, add to the sauce, and stir gently to coat. Sauté the julienned morels in 1 tbsp butter for a minute or so, then add half to the sauce. Reserve the other half for garnishing.

Serve two pieces of chicken per portion with some sauce. Garnish with the remaining julienned morels, fried curry leaves and sprigs of cilantro.

CHICKEN WITH FRIED MUSHROOMS

Chicken and veal are common in Italian cooking, and many cuts are pounded thin. This makes the cooking time so short that you could almost consider dishes of this nature as "fast food." The egg coating here imparts a distinctive flavor, and the mushrooms make it very special.

SERVES 4

4 BONELESS CHICKEN BREAST HALVES,
   ABOUT 4 OZ EACH, SKIN REMOVED
2 TBSP ALL-PURPOSE FLOUR
1 TSP MINCED PARSLEY
   (OR CILANTRO, OR OTHER SOFT HERB)
2 EGGS, BEATEN
OLIVE OIL FOR FRYING
SALT AND PEPPER TO TASTE

MUSHROOMS
14 OZ CULTIVATED BLEWITS
4 TBSP ($^1\!/_2$ STICK) BUTTER
1 GARLIC CLOVE, MINCED
2–3 TBSP CHICKEN STOCK
   (SEE PAGE 104) OR WATER
1 TBSP CHOPPED PARSLEY

Clean the mushrooms, and quarter them if large.
Melt the butter in a frying pan, then add the garlic. Sauté for a few seconds. Add the mushrooms and sauté for 8 to 10 minutes. Stir in the stock or water, some salt and pepper, and the parsley.
Meanwhile, pound the chicken breasts between pieces of plastic wrap until $^1\!/_2$ inch thick. Dip into the flour to coat all over. Add the herbs and some salt and pepper to the beaten eggs.
Dip the floured chicken pieces into the egg mixture, then sauté in a little oil until brown on both sides. Serve with the mushrooms.

SUPREME OF DUCK WITH SAFFRON MILK CAPS

Duck is usually quite fatty, but if you use only the breast and discard the skin, it has all the flavor and no fat at all. This dish is fit for a prince from Eastern Europe, where they love the mushrooms used here, but I think the lesser mortals among us will appreciate it in just the same way.

SERVES 4

7 OZ FRESH SAFFRON MILK CAP
   MUSHROOMS, BLANCHED AND SLICED
$^1\!/_2$ OZ DRIED MORELS, SOAKED IN
   WARM WATER FOR 20 MINUTES
4 LEAN DUCK BREAST HALVES, ABOUT
   5–6 OZ EACH, SKINNED
3 TBSP OLIVE OIL
1 SMALL SHALLOT, MINCED
2 OZ PROSCIUTTO, CUT INTO SMALL
   STRIPS
2 CORNICHONS (SMALL GHERKINS),
   MINCED
1 TBSP BUTTER ROLLED IN FLOUR
2 TBSP DRY SHERRY
SALT AND PEPPER TO TASTE

Clean and trim the fresh mushrooms, then blanch in boiling water for a few minutes. Drain well and slice. Drain and trim the dried morels, reserving the soaking liquid for another dish.
Sauté the duck breasts in the oil for 5 minutes on each side until cooked. Remove to a plate and keep warm. Add the shallot and the prosciutto to the pan and sauté for a few minutes. Add the fresh mushrooms, the drained morels, and the cornichons. Cook for 5 minutes longer.
Return the duck to the pan with any juices that have collected on the plate. Stir in the butter and flour to thicken the sauce slightly, then cook over medium heat for 10 minutes. Stir in the sherry and season with salt and pepper. Heat for a minute or so, and serve warm.

ROAST PORK WITH FOUR MUSHROOMS

I like pork! It is one of the most flavorsome meats, succulent and versatile. Here I have combined it with three cultivated and one wild mushroom. I had considered initially using three oyster mushrooms in different colors, but when we were shooting the food pictures a friend came along with a huge sulfur shelf, just in peak condition! What would you have done in my place?

SERVES 6

1 BONE-IN PORK LOIN ROAST, ABOUT
4 LB, SKIN ON IF POSSIBLE, CHINE
BONE (BACKBONE) CUT THROUGH
1 TBSP SALT

BASTING MIXTURE
1 GARLIC CLOVE, MINCED
1/2 FRESH, HOT RED CHILI PEPPER,
MINCED
1 TBSP ROSEMARY NEEDLES,
MINCED
1 TBSP THYME LEAVES
2 TBSP OLIVE OIL

MUSHROOM "STEW"
1 3/4 LB MIXED FRESH MUSHROOMS
(2 TYPES OF OYSTER MUSHROOMS,
PINK AND YELLOW, SHIITAKE, AND
SULFUR SHELF)
6 TBSP OLIVE OIL
1 GARLIC CLOVE, MINCED
1 FRESH, HOT RED CHILI PEPPER,
SLICED
2/3 CUP DRY WHITE WINE
1/2 TBSP WHITE WINE VINEGAR
2 OR 3 GRATINGS OF NUTMEG
2 TBSP CHERVIL LEAVES
SALT AND PEPPER TO TASTE

Preheat the oven to 425°F. Rub the salt into the skin of the pork, then roast in the preheated oven for 40 minutes.

Meanwhile, combine the basting mixture ingredients. Take the meat out of the oven and baste with the basting mixture. Return to the oven and roast for 40 minutes longer (when done, the internal temperature should be 185°F).

Meanwhile, start the mushroom "stew." Clean the mushrooms well. Leave the oyster mushrooms whole if small, or cut in half if large. Slice the shiitake and sulfur shelf. Heat the oil in a wok, add the garlic and chili, and stir-fry briefly. Add the mushrooms and stir-fry for 5 minutes longer. Add the wine and vinegar, and cook gently for another couple of minutes. Just before serving add the nutmeg, some salt and pepper, and, lastly, the chervil.

Arrange the pork on a platter and surround it with the mushrooms. After carving, serve on hot plates.

SAUSAGE, LENTILS, AND FUNGI

One of the most popular Italian dishes in autumn and winter is cotechino with lentils. Cotechino is a cooking sausage made of pure pork, including the gelatinous parts such as ear and cheek. The long cooking time makes it succulent and delicious. The combination of lentils (Castelluccio are the best) and fungi makes this dish very appetizing.

SERVES 4

10 OZ LARCH BOLETE OR WOOD
  BLEWIT MUSHROOMS
2 COTECHINO SAUSAGES, EITHER
  PRE-COOKED OR RAW, ABOUT
  12 OZ EACH
$^1/_2$ CUP OLIVE OIL
2 GARLIC CLOVES, MINCED
8 CHERRY TOMATOES, CUT IN HALF
1 CARROT, FINELY DICED
1 CELERY STALK, FINELY DICED
1 CUP CASTELLUCCIO LENTILS OR
  LENTILLES DE PUY
UP TO 3$^1/_4$ CUPS CHICKEN STOCK
  (SEE PAGE 104)
1 SPRIG ROSEMARY, MINCED
SALT AND PEPPER TO TASTE

Clean the mushrooms, and cut into halves or quarters if large. Simmer the sausages in water for 30 minutes if pre-cooked, or 2 to 3 hours if raw.
Put half the oil in a pan, add half the garlic, and sauté for 30 seconds. Add the mushrooms and cook them until soft. Set aside.
In a heavy pan, heat the remaining oil and sauté the tomatoes, carrot, celery, and remaining garlic until soft. Add the lentils and stock as necessary: Castelluccio lentils will need less stock because they are ready in 20 minutes; Puy lentils need more because of their longer cooking time. Cook until the lentils are fully tender, 20 to 30 minutes. Add the rosemary and season to taste, then combine with the mushrooms, adding a spoonful of water if you think it necessary. Serve hot with slices of cotechino and, perhaps, some boiled potatoes.

SPRING LAMB WITH MORELS

I am passionate about eating seasonally, and the two major ingredients here could not be more seasonal. Spring lamb is wonderfully tender, and when combined with the fantastic shape, color, and flavor of the spring mushroom par excellence, the morel, you will create a dish to die for. At other times of year you can use dried morels (2 oz should suffice). You can use any other cut of lamb too, but you will probably need more—up to 1$^1/_4$ lb—because of trimming.

SERVES 4

14 OZ FRESH MORELS
1 BONED RACK OF LAMB, ABOUT 14 OZ
SALT AND PEPPER TO TASTE
4 TBSP OLIVE OIL
1 SMALL BUNCH GREEN ONIONS,
  COARSELY CHOPPED
1 SMALL SPRIG ROSEMARY, MINCED

Clean the morels. Leave them whole unless very large. Trim away any fat from the lamb, and cut it across into $^3/_4$-inch-thick medallions.
Salt the medallions and sauté them in half the oil to sear on each side. (I like them when they are still pink inside.) Set aside, keeping them warm. Add the rest of the oil to the pan and sauté the green onions for 5 minutes. Add the morels and rosemary, and cook for 10 to 15 minutes longer, until the morels are cooked. (If you are using dried morels, you can add a little of their soaking liquid.)
Return the lamb medallions to the pan, taste for seasoning, and warm through with the morels. Serve immediately.

SHOULDER OF LAMB WITH MUSHROOMS

This is one of the most loved recipes at the Neal Street Restaurant. My chef, Andrea Cavaliere, has developed the lamb side, while I took charge of the mushroom accompaniment. We may both be Italian, but we are living and working in Britain, thus I feel that this recipe is more British in inspiration than Italian. And, of course, it uses some of the food bounty of Britain—its wonderful lamb and the wild mushrooms that are everywhere (if you know where and when to look!). However, in the restaurant, I must admit that we serve the lamb with the unashamedly Italian polenta.

SERVES 6

7 OZ FRESH HEN OF THE WOODS
    MUSHROOMS (CLEANED WEIGHT)
$1/2$ OZ DRIED PORCINI, SOAKED IN
    WARM WATER FOR 20 MINUTES
4 SMALL SHOULDERS OF LAMB,
    BONED (HAVE YOUR BUTCHER DO
    THIS FOR YOU)
1 TBSP EACH OF CHOPPED
    PARSLEY AND ROSEMARY
1 TBSP CHOPPED GARLIC
ALL-PURPOSE FLOUR FOR DUSTING
$1/2$ CUP OLIVE OIL
1 MEDIUM ONION, MINCED
1 CELERY STALK, MINCED
1 TBSP BLACK PEPPERCORNS
2 CUPS CHICKEN OR VEGETABLE
    STOCK (SEE PAGE 104)
$1^{1}/4$ CUPS WHITE WINE
2 TBSP WORCESTERSHIRE SAUCE
SALT AND PEPPER TO TASTE

Clean the fresh mushrooms thoroughly, then separate into small lobes. Drain the porcini, reserving the soaking liquid, and mince. Remove most of the fat from the lamb shoulders, trimming them well. You want each piece to weigh about 7 oz. Lay the pieces, boned side up, on a work surface.

Combine the chopped herbs and garlic, season with salt and pepper, and divide among the pieces of lamb, spreading the mixture evenly on the meat. Fold each piece of lamb over, then roll and tie into an even shape with kitchen string. Dust with flour, then sauté in a casserole in the oil until brown on all sides, turning every few minutes.

Add the onion, celery, and peppercorns to the casserole and sauté briefly.

Add the stock, wine, and Worcestershire sauce. Cover with a lid and cook over gentle heat for 1 hour. Turn occasionally.

After an hour, much of the liquid will have evaporated, but there should still be enough to serve as a sauce. Add the mushrooms, fresh and dried, plus a little of the soaking liquid if necessary, and cook for 30 minutes longer.

Check the seasoning before serving. I like to serve the lamb with polenta flavored with Parmesan and butter.

Beef Wellington

To celebrate living in Britain for nearly 30 years, I have taken the two British ingredients that have most impressed me and united them in this fairly classic recipe. Because of my passion for mushrooms—and the plethora of mushrooms growing in the wild in Britain—they all had to be honored. The dish does require some preparation, I agree, but you can do this in advance, giving you time to receive your guests while the oven does the rest. It may be a long procedure, but it's well worth while!

SERVES 6–8

1 CENTER-CUT BEEF TENDERLOIN OR
   CHATEAUBRIAND ROAST, ABOUT
   2^1/$_4$ LB
2 TBSP BUTTER
3 TBSP OLIVE OIL
8 OZ PUFF PASTRY
1 RECIPE WILD MUSHROOM
   DUXELLES (SEE PAGE 105)
2 EGG YOLKS, BEATEN
SALT AND PEPPER TO TASTE

PANCAKE
^{1}/$_2$ CUP MILK
6 TBSP ALL-PURPOSE FLOUR
1 EGG, BEATEN
BUTTER FOR GREASING

SAUCE
^{1}/$_2$ CUP FINELY DICED CARROT
^{1}/$_2$ CUP FINELY DICED CELERY
1 SMALL ONION, MINCED
6 BLACK PEPPERCORNS, CRUSHED
3 BAY LEAVES
^{1}/$_2$ TSP THYME LEAVES
1 TBSP ALL-PURPOSE FLOUR
7 TBSP FULL-BODIED RED WINE
2 CUPS BEEF STOCK (SEE PAGE 104)
5 TBSP MADEIRA
2 TBSP BUTTER

Preheat the oven to 400°F.

Start by making the pancake. Put the milk, flour, egg, and a pinch of salt into a blender and process until the batter is smooth. Line a baking pan that is roughly 14 inches square with parchment paper and butter this well. Pour in the batter. Bake for 10 to 15 minutes until set. Let cool.

Sprinkle the beef with salt and pepper. Heat the butter and oil in a large pan, and sear the beef on all sides.

Roll out the pastry into a rectangular shape that will completely enclose the beef. Take the rectangular pancake and spread the duxelles on it. Place the beef on the pancake and gently roll the beef in the pancake. Transfer this very gently onto the rolled-out pastry, then wrap it up completely in the pastry, making sure that the top is sealed securely. Place on a greased baking sheet, brush with beaten egg yolk, and bake in the preheated oven for 25 minutes or until the pastry is golden (the meat will still be pink).

Meanwhile, using the same pan as the beef was browned in, combine the vegetables for the sauce, along with the peppercorns, bay leaves, and thyme. Sauté gently for a few minutes to soften. Stir in the flour, then add the wine and stir to loosen the meat juices from the bottom of the pan. Add the stock and bring to a boil, stirring, then continue to boil to reduce the sauce. Discard the bay leaves and pass through a fine sieve, or leave it as it is, although it will be a bit coarse. Stir in the Madeira and butter.

Remove the beef from the oven, slice, and serve on hot plates with some spinach or fine green beans (haricots verts), spooning some of the sauce over.

Beef with Shiitake

The combination of beef and mushrooms is well loved, and the shiitake, together with chili and cilantro, add a touch of Eastern promise and make this a truly memorable dish. If you wanted, you could use other mushrooms, such as king oysters.

Serves 4

4 TBSP OLIVE OIL
2 TBSP BALSAMIC VINEGAR
1 TBSP ENGLISH MUSTARD
SALT AND PEPPER TO TASTE
1 CENTER-CUT BEEF TENDERLOIN ROAST, ABOUT 1 LB

MUSHROOMS
14 OZ FRESH SHIITAKE CAPS
3 TBSP OLIVE OIL
2 TBSP FINELY SLICED GREEN ONION
1 GARLIC CLOVE, CRUSHED
1 FRESH, HOT RED CHILI PEPPER, MINCED
2 TBSP DRY RED WINE
2 TBSP CILANTRO LEAVES

Combine 2 tablespoons of the oil, the vinegar, mustard, and some salt and pepper. Marinate the meat in this mixture for a few hours.

Heat the remaining oil in a frying pan, add the beef, and carefully sear on all sides. Add some salt and pepper, then cook for about 10 minutes, ensuring the beef remains pink in the middle.

While the beef is cooking, clean and trim the mushrooms, and remove the stems. Put the oil into another frying pan and briefly sauté the green onion. Add the garlic and chili, followed by the mushrooms, and sauté for a few minutes. Add the wine and some salt and pepper, and cook for 5 minutes longer. Add the cilantro.

Serve the beef and mushrooms together, accompanied by bread, boiled rice, or potato purée.

Steak, Oyster, and Mushroom Pie

When I want to explore an interesting recipe from a country I don't know much about, I call a top chef from that country. Darina Allen, from Ireland, is a friend of mine and kindly provided this recipe—a strange combination of meat, shellfish, and fungi that is apparently part of the St. Bridget's Day festivities.

Serves 4

8 OZ FRESH MEADOW MUSHROOMS
4 TBSP (1/2 STICK) BUTTER
1 1/2 LB BEEF ROUND OR RUMP, CUBED
1 LARGE ONION, MINCED
2 TBSP ALL-PURPOSE FLOUR
2 1/2 CUPS GOOD BEEF STOCK (SEE PAGE 104)
12 LARGE, FRESH OYSTERS
SALT AND PEPPER TO TASTE

TOPPING
8 OZ PUFF PASTRY
1 EGG, BEATEN

Clean the mushrooms, then slice. In a large, heavy casserole, melt half of the butter. Season the beef, then brown on all sides. Remove the beef and reserve. Add the onion to the casserole and cook for 5 to 6 minutes. Add the flour and stir well, then cook for a minute before adding the stock. Return the meat to the casserole. Bring to a boil, cover, and simmer over low heat for 1 1/2 to 2 hours. Let cool. In another pan melt the remaining butter and sauté the sliced mushrooms. Season and set aside.

Preheat the oven to 450°F. Shuck the oysters, reserving the juices. Add the mushrooms, oysters, and their juice to the cooked meat and combine well. Let cool. Roll the pastry to fit the top of a deep pie or baking dish. Put the meat mixture in the dish and cover with the pastry, pressing it onto the rim of the dish to seal. Brush with beaten egg and bake for 10 minutes. Reduce the heat to 375°F and bake for 15 to 20 minutes longer, or until the pastry is puffed and golden. Serve immediately.

Osso Buco with Dryad's Saddle Mushrooms

That very special Italian dish "osso buco" is world-famous now, and everyone knows that the recipe's title refers to the cut of meat used. This is slices of veal shank in cross-section, with the marrow bone in the middle ("osso buco" means a bone with a hole). Traditionally, osso buco does not contain mushrooms, but in my opinion their addition makes the dish even more delicious!

SERVES 4

12 OZ FRESH DRYAD'S SADDLE
   MUSHROOMS
$^3/_4$ OZ DRIED PORCINI
$^1/_2$ OZ DRIED MORELS
4 THICK, MEATY SLICES VEAL SHANK,
   8 OZ EACH
ALL-PURPOSE FLOUR FOR DUSTING
4 TBSP OLIVE OIL
1 SMALL ONION, MINCED
$^2/_3$ CUP RED WINE
14 OZ CANNED ITALIAN PEELED
   TOMATOES, DRAINED OF HALF THE
   JUICE
SALT AND PEPPER TO TASTE

Clean the fresh mushrooms well, then slice them. Soak the two types of dried mushrooms in warm water for 20 to 30 minutes, then drain. Keep the soaking liquid for another dish. Discard the morel stalks.

Salt the veal and dust with flour. Heat the oil in a casserole and sauté, 2 pieces at a time, until brown on both sides. Remove from the casserole and set aside. In the same oil, sauté the minced onion until slightly brown, then add the dried mushrooms and wine. Boil to evaporate for a minute or so. Add the fresh mushroom slices, along with the tomatoes, salt and pepper. Cover the casserole and cook over low heat for 1½ hours or until the meat is meltingly tender. Serve with rice or gnocchi.

Veal Chops with Porcini

You can cook porcini with almost anything, because they impart such a wonderful flavor and a touch of luxury. The combination of the delicate veal paired with porcini makes an excellent main course, preceded perhaps by something like a light broth. I would accompany this dish with cubed new potatoes sautéed with garlic and rosemary.

SERVES 4

10 OZ FRESH PORCINI
4 VEAL LOIN CHOPS, ABOUT
   8 OZ EACH
ALL-PURPOSE FLOUR FOR DUSTING
4 TBSP ($^1/_2$ STICK) BUTTER
8 SAGE LEAVES
4 TBSP DRY WHITE WINE
4 TBSP EXTRA VIRGIN OLIVE OIL
1 GARLIC CLOVE, CRUSHED
2 TBSP MINCED FLAT-LEAF PARSLEY
SALT AND PEPPER TO TASTE

Clean the mushrooms well, then slice them.

Dust the chops with flour and shake off the excess. Melt the butter in a large pan and sauté the chops gently on each side until brown. Add the sage leaves and wine. Cook for a few more minutes, turning if necessary.

In another pan, sauté the mushrooms in the oil until they begin to brown, then add the garlic and parsley, and continue cooking for a couple of minutes. Season to taste.

Serve the chops with a little of the sage and wine sauce, and with the porcini and their juices.

Deviled Kidneys with Winter Chanterelles

Whenever "devil" is mentioned in a recipe, you can be sure of heat in some form or another. I leave it up to your own taste buds to control the degree of spice. The humble winter chanterelle seems to be perfect for this recipe because it exudes enough moisture, combined with the wine, to make a lovely sauce.

Serves 4

14 oz winter chanterelles
2 large potatoes (about 1¹/₂ lb total weight)
1¹/₂ lb veal kidneys (cleaned weight)
all-purpose flour for dusting
¹/₂ cup olive oil
2 garlic cloves, sliced
2 fresh, hot red chili peppers, chopped (with the seeds!)
5 tbsp medium Marsala wine
6–8 large sage leaves
juice of ¹/₂ lemon
salt and pepper to taste

Clean the mushrooms. Boil the potatoes in salted water, with their skins on, for 15 to 20 minutes, until nearly tender. Drain and let cool, then peel and cut into slices about 1 inch thick.

Cut the kidneys into slices ¹/₂ inch thick. Dust with flour, then sauté in a large pan in half the oil until crisp on both sides. Set aside.

Add the garlic and chili to the same pan and sauté them briefly, then add the mushrooms. Cook for 3 minutes, then add the Marsala, sage, and salt and pepper. Cook for 4 to 5 minutes. Return the kidneys to the pan, add the lemon juice, and combine well.

Meanwhile, fry the big slices of potato in the remaining oil until crisp and brown on both sides. Serve with the kidneys.

Sweetbread Medallions with Horn of Plenty

Not everybody likes variety meats, but sweetbreads, together with liver and kidneys, seem to be loved by most gourmets from around the world. In Italy, we also appreciate other parts of the animal like spinal cord, tripe, brains, spleen, and testicles, which we cook so that they become delicacies. One day, I will write an entire book about variety meats!

SERVES 4

12 OZ FRESH HORN OF PLENTY MUSHROOMS (CLEANED WEIGHT)
1$^1/_4$ LB VEAL SWEETBREADS
ALL-PURPOSE FLOUR FOR DUSTING
2 TBSP OLIVE OIL
4 TBSP ($^1/_2$ STICK) BUTTER
2 GARLIC CLOVES, MINCED
1 FRESH, HOT RED CHILI PEPPER, MINCED
3 TBSP DRY RED WINE
2 TBSP MINCED PARSLEY
1 TBSP MINCED MINT
JUICE OF 1 LEMON
SALT AND PEPPER TO TASTE

Clean the mushrooms well. Blanch the sweetbreads in salted water for 20 minutes, then drain and cool. Cut away all the muscle and nerves. Cut the sweetbreads into medallions and dust them with flour.

Heat the oil and butter in a large frying pan and sauté the sweetbread medallions over medium heat until brown on each side. Remove from the pan and keep warm.

Put the garlic, chili, and mushrooms into the same pan and sauté briefly. Add the wine, herbs, and some salt and pepper. Return the sweetbreads to the pan, add the lemon juice, and stir a little to flavor the meat. Serve either with toasted bread or with steamed rice.

VENISON CARPACCIO WITH RAW PORCINI

The term "carpaccio" today is generally used to describe raw meat or fish that is very thinly cut and cured instantly with lemon juice and oil. I introduced a carpaccio of venison, one of the healthiest red meats, to my restaurant, with enormous success.

You need venison tenderloin, the most tender part. Put the very thin slices between two sheets of plastic wrap and pound them gently to make them paper-thin. They are wonderful served with the raw porcini, also thinly cut from small, tender specimens. The fragrance of the two, accompanied by good bread, is very appetizing indeed, and as a dish it is very easy to make.

SERVES 4

10 OZ SMALL, FRESH PORCINI
  (CLEANED WEIGHT)
8 OZ VENISON TENDERLOIN, CUT IN
  $^{1}/_{4}$-INCH-THICK SLICES
JUICE OF 1 $^{1}/_{2}$ LEMONS
3 TBSP EXTRA VIRGIN OLIVE OIL
$^{1}/_{2}$ CUP MINCED PARSLEY
SALT AND PEPPER TO TASTE

Clean the mushrooms well and slice them finely.
Divide the very thin slices of venison among 4 plates, arranging them out to the rim.
Make a vinaigrette with the lemon juice, oil, and some salt and pepper, and sprinkle some of this onto the meat. Arrange the sliced mushrooms on top. Sprinkle with the remaining vinaigrette, then with the parsley and coarsely ground pepper. Eat as a first course with bread or grissini (breadsticks).

Rabbit Casserole with Winter Chanterelles

Wild mushrooms have a wonderful affinity with the lean, slightly sweet meat of rabbit. While many of us can collect edible mushrooms, it is less easy to shoot our own game. Luckily, farm-raised rabbit is widely available.

Serves 6

10 oz fresh winter chanterelles
  (cleaned weight)
1 rabbit, about 2 lb, quartered
all-purpose flour for dusting
salt and pepper to taste
$^1/_2$ cup olive oil
2 tbsp butter
10 medium shallots
10 garlic cloves (unpeeled)
2–3 bay leaves
2–3 whole cloves
1 sprig rosemary
1 tbsp thyme leaves
1 tbsp white wine vinegar
2 cups dry white wine
a little chicken stock
  (see page 104) as required

Keep the chanterelles whole, unless they are large, in which case cut in half. Dust the rabbit quarters with flour seasoned with salt and pepper. Heat the olive oil and butter in a frying pan and sauté the rabbit until brown all over. Set aside. Add the whole shallots and garlic cloves to the same pan and sauté briefly, then transfer to a casserole. Put the rabbit in the casserole, along with the bay leaves, cloves, herbs, vinegar, and wine. Season to taste. Cover and cook very gently for 40 minutes, adding a little stock if the mixture gets dry. At the last minute add the mushrooms and stir for a minute until cooked. Serve hot, either with boiled potatoes or rice.

Braised Rabbit with Mustard

The French often cook white meats in a wonderful stew, or "fricassee." You may find local variations, mostly made with chicken. This rabbit version with mushrooms, however, makes a really delicious autumn meal.

Serves 6

10 oz fresh, wild Agaricus
  bisporus or cremini mushrooms
$1^1/_2$ lb boneless rabbit, cut into
chunks
all-purpose flour for dusting
salt and pepper to taste
3 tbsp butter
4 oz bacon (or pancetta), cut into strips
12 small onions
1 garlic clove, crushed
1 bouquet garni (parsley, thyme,
  bay leaf)
$^2/_3$ cup dry white wine
1 cup chicken or beef stock (see
page 104)
2 tbsp Dijon mustard
1 tbsp minced parsley

Clean and trim the mushrooms. If large, quarter them. Dust the rabbit chunks with flour seasoned with salt and pepper.
Melt the butter in a large casserole until sizzling, add the rabbit, and brown on all sides. Add the bacon, cut into strips, the whole onions, and the crushed garlic, and cook for 5 minutes. Add the bouquet garni, wine, and mushrooms, and, after a few minutes, pour in the stock.
Bring to a boil, reduce the heat, then cook for 20 to 30 minutes longer or until the rabbit is tender. Stir the mustard into the sauce and taste for seasoning. Serve sprinkled with the parsley, with either boiled potatoes or bread.

LEFT Rabbit Casserole with Winter Chanterelles

PHEASANT BREAST WITH CAULIFLOWER MUSHROOM

I dedicate this recipe to His Royal Highness the Prince of Wales, because he once told me about his pleasure at having found this mushroom all by himself in the Balmoral woods. He was very impressed by the magnitude of the fungus, which, when weighed, was over 4 pounds. I don't know how the chefs of the royal household prepared it, but they must have done a good job for the Prince to mention it and to like it so much. I once saw a similar mushroom, dried, in a Chinese shop. You may be tempted by necessity to use this dried mushroom instead of the cauliflower mushroom.

SERVES 4

1 LB FRESH CAULIFLOWER
   MUSHROOM
4 LARGE PHEASANT BREAST HALVES
ALL-PURPOSE FLOUR FOR DUSTING
1/2 CUP OLIVE OIL
3 TBSP BUTTER
1 ONION, CUT LENGTHWISE
   INTO 6 WEDGES
4 BAY LEAVES
1 SPRIG ROSEMARY
10 JUNIPER BERRIES
3 1/2 CUPS BLUEBERRIES
1/2 CUP DRY WHITE WINE
6 SUN-DRIED TOMATOES, DICED
FRESHLY GRATED NUTMEG
SALT AND PEPPER TO TASTE

Cut the mushroom into chunks the size of an apricot.

Dust the pheasant breasts with flour. Heat the oil and butter in a pan, then brown the pheasant breasts on each side for 2 to 3 minutes, depending on thickness. Add the onion, bay leaves, rosemary, juniper berries, and blueberries. Cook for 5 minutes, then add the wine and tomatoes, and cook to evaporate the alcohol. Stir in the mushrooms, and continue cooking 7 to 10 minutes. Add salt and pepper and a pinch of nutmeg to taste.

Serve with a very buttery potato purée or with roast potatoes.

EXTRAVAGANZA OF GAME AND FUNGI

To me, this quartet of mushrooms represents the acme of the fungi world, and I like to combine them with the sublime flavors of four different game birds. If you can, use wild game birds for the dish. If this is impossible, then try to find ranched game birds, which have more flavor and less body fat than farmed birds. If you really want a feast of tastes, then add a little truffle, either shaved or in the form of oil, to the breasts. With the optional beet and balsamic salad, this is food nirvana!

SERVES 6

GAME

6 BREAST HALVES OF EACH OF THE FOLLOWING: PIGEON OR SQUAB, PHEASANT, QUAIL, AND PARTRIDGE
ALL-PURPOSE FLOUR FOR DUSTING
6 TBSP (³/₄ STICK) BUTTER
2 TBSP OLIVE OIL
2 TBSP BRANDY
1 TSP TRUFFLE OIL
2 TBSP GOOD AGED BALSAMIC VINEGAR
A LITTLE CHICKEN STOCK (SEE PAGE 104) OR LIQUID FROM SOAKING THE MORELS
SALT AND PEPPER TO TASTE

FUNGI

7 OZ FRESH ST. GEORGE'S MUSHROOMS
7 OZ FRESH PORCINI
7 OZ FRESH CHANTERELLES
3¹/₂ OZ FRESH MORELS, OR 1 OZ DRIED MORELS, SOAKED IN WARM WATER FOR 20 MINUTES
3 TBSP BUTTER
2 TBSP OLIVE OIL
JUICE OF ¹/₂ LEMON

BEET SALAD (OPTIONAL)

2 LB BEETS, FRESHLY BOILED
4 TBSP BALSAMIC VINEGAR
2 TBSP TORN CILANTRO LEAVES

First make the beet salad, if desired. When the beets are cool enough to handle, skin them and cut into thin slices. Sprinkle with the vinegar, cilantro, and some salt and pepper, then let cool completely.

Prepare the mushrooms by cleaning and trimming as appropriate. Cut the St. George's mushrooms into quarters. Leave the porcini whole if they are small; cut in half if larger. Halve the fresh morels. Drain the dried morels (if using), reserving their soaking liquid, and remove the stems.

For the birds, firstly dust the breasts with flour, then sauté them in the butter and olive oil until they are lightly browned. Start with the largest breasts, and cook the smallest and most tender—the quail—last. When all are browned, set them aside and keep warm.

Add the brandy, truffle oil, and balsamic vinegar to the pan. Boil to deglaze the pan and loosen all the cooking juices. Add some stock or water if needed and reduce to a liquid sauce. Adjust the seasoning. Return the breasts to the pan and keep warm.

To cook the mushrooms, heat the butter and oil in another pan. Add the morels, followed by the chanterelles, porcini, and, lastly, the St. George's mushrooms. Sauté briefly just to soften and lightly brown them. Add salt, pepper, and lemon juice to finish.

To assemble, arrange the breasts on a large platter and intersperse with the fungi, so the breasts look as if they are studded with jewels. Serve the gleaming red and green beet salad on the side. You will then need to open some bottles of an important red wine. Forget about the cost, and just enjoy!

LEFT ME WITH MY EXTRAVAGANZA OF GAME AND FUNGI

INDEX OF MUSHROOMS USED IN THE RECIPES

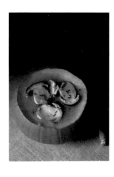

GLOSSARY

ADNATE (of gills) broadly attached to the stem

ADNEXED (of gills) narrowly attached to the stem

AGARIC large fungus family of the gilled group

ASCOMYCETES group of higher fungi whose spores are formed inside asci and are released by pressure

ASCUS (pl. asci) sac-like cell within which spores are formed

BASAL at or near the base

BASIDIA club-shaped cells on which spores are formed externally

BASIDIOMYCETES major group of higher fungi including agarics etc.,whose spores are formed externally on basidia

BOLETE mushroom with central stem and tubes/pores

CAP the upper part of the mushroom, usually the spore-bearing part

CHLOROPHYLL green pigments found in plants that trap energy from sunlight for use in photosynthesis

CONCENTRIC (of scales) pattern of circles on the cap

CONCOLOROUS same color as

CONVEX (of caps) rounded or domed

CROWDED (of gills) tightly packed together under the cap

CUTICLE the skin of the cap

DECURRENT (of gills) running down the stem

EPIGEAL/EPIGEOUS growing above ground

EXCENTRIC (of stems) cap central to the stem

EXOPERIDIUM outer layer of the spore case in puffballs and similar

FIBRILLOSE covered with small fibers

FREE (of gills) detached from stem

FRONDOSE (of trees) broad-leaved or deciduous

FRUIT-BODY the actual fungus growing from the mycelium

FUNGUS fruit-body formed by the meeting of hyphae, lacking chlorophyll and usually producing spores

GASTEROMYCETES group of Basidiomycetes where spores mature within the fruit-body, e.g. puffballs

GENUS a group of related species demonstrating common characteristics

GILLS blade-like strips of tissue that radiate on underside of cap of certain fungi, bearing little sacs in which spores are produced, e.g. in agarics. Also known as lamellae

GLEBA spore-bearing fleshy tissue within Gasteromycetes

HYMENIUM spore-bearing fertile layer of asci, basidia, etc.

HYPHA (pl. hyphae) minute individual filament from which mycelium and fruit-body are formed

HYPOGEAL/HYPOGEOUS growing underground

INROLLED with cap curling in toward the stem (as with Lactarius)

LAMELLAE gills

LATERAL (of caps) growing laterally, at the sides

MYCELIUM complex of hyphae: the vegetative portion of a fungus growing into the nutritive substrate/material

MYCOLOGIST one who studies the world of fungi

MYCOPHAGIST one who likes to eat fungi

MYCOPHILE a lover of mushrooms

MYCORRHIZA symbiotic association of the mycelium with plant and tree roots

PARASITIC drawing nutrients from living material/organisms

PERIDIUM outer skin; wall of the spore case in many Gasteromycetes

POLYPORE woody-textured fungus with tubes on underside of cap strongly attached to the flesh and built by millions of pores

PORES the mouths of the tubes in boletes and polypores

POROID consisting of pores

RETICULUM net-like mesh pattern on stem of some boletes

RHIZOMORPH a root-like or string-like bundle of mycelial hyphae

RING remnant of a veil, present around stem of some agarics

SAPROPHYTIC living on dead matter

SCABROUS rough granular or scaly texture on stem surface

SESSILE having no stem

SINUATE (of gills) notched to the stem

SPAWN mycelium produced artificially for the purpose of cultivating mushrooms

SPORE the single reproductive unit of a fungus

STEMS the stalk or foot of a fungus, which supports the cap

SYMBIOSIS growing association with certain types of trees

TUBES sponge-like spore-producing layer, e.g. of boletes

UMBO central swelling on cap of many agarics

VEIL protective membrane enclosing entire fruit-body (universal veil), e.g. in amanitas, or joining cap cuticle to stem (partial veil,) e.g. in agarics

VISCID slimy or wet

VOLVA remains of universal veil forming cup-like sac around stem base, also called "skirt", e.g. in amanitas

RECOMMENDED READING

● G.C. Ainsworth, INTRODUCTION TO THE HISTORY OF MYCOLOGY (Cambridge University Press, 1976)
● Darina Allen, THE FESTIVE FOOD OF IRELAND (Kyle Cathie, 1992)
● David Arora, MUSHROOMS DEMYSTIFIED (Ten Speed Press, 1979)
● F.H. Brightman, THE OXFORD BOOK OF FLOWERLESS PLANTS (Peerage Books, 1966)
● Renato Brotzu, GUIDA AI FUNGHI DELLA SARDEGNA (Editrice Archivio Fotografico Sardo, 1988)
● Bruno Cetto,I FUNGHI DAL VERO, 5 vols (Arti Grafiche Saturnia-Trento, 1970)
● S.T. Chang & W.A. Hayes, THE BIOLOGY AND CULTIVATION OF EDIBLE MUSHROOMS (Academic Press, 1978)
● S.T. Chang & P.G. Miles, EDIBLE MUSHROOMS AND THEIR CULTIVATION (CRC Press, 1989)
● Heinz Denckler, DAS PILZ BUCH (Heyne Verlag, 1982)
● Colin Dickinson & John Lucas, COLOR DICTIONARY OF MUSHROOMS (Orbis, 1982)

● Manfred Enderle & Hans E. Laux, PILZE AUF HOLZ (Kosmos, 1980)
● Louise Freedman, WILD ABOUT MUSHROOMS (Aris Books, 1988)
● Sara Ann Friedman, CELEBRATING THE WILD MUSHROOM – A PASSIONATE QUEST (Dodd, Mead & Co., 1986)
● E. Garnweidner, PILZE (GU Compass, 1993)
● Jane Grigson,THE MUSHROOM FEAST (Michael Joseph, 1975)
● Hans Hvass, MAD SVAMPE I FARVER (Politiken Forlag, 1973)
● Ying Janzhe, Mao Xiaolan, M.A.Qiming, Zong Yichen & Wen Huaan, ICONS OF MEDICINAL FUNGI FROM CHINA (Science Press, 1987)
● Katsuji Komiyama, KINOKO (Nagaoko Shoten, Tokyo, 2002)
● A. Krasheninnikoya, RUSSIAN COOKING (Mir Publishers, 1978)
● J.E. Lange & M. Lange, BLV BESTIMMUNGS-BUCH (BLV Verlagsgesellschaft, 1982)

● Hans E. Laux, ESSBARE PILZE UND IHRE GIFTIGEN DOPPELGÄNGER (Kosmos, 1985)
● Carin Lindh, GOTT MED SVAMP (Bokförlaget Semic, 1983)
● Gisela Lockwald, PILZGERICHTE NOCH FINER (IHW Verlag, 1999)
● Marcel Loquin & Bengt Cortin, CHAMPIGNONS COMESTIBLES ET VÉNÉNEUX (Fernand Nathan, 1975)
● Riccardo Mazza, I FUNGHI (Manuali Somzogno, 1994)
● Orson K. Miller, MUSHROOMS OF NORTH AMERICA (E.P. Dutton, 1978)
● Roger Phillips, MUSHROOMS AND OTHER FUNGI OF GREAT BRITAIN AND EUROPE (Pan Books, 1981)
● Emil Reimers, KOSTILCHES AUS DER PILZKUCHE (BLV VerlagsGesellschaft, 1982)
● Roland Sabatier, LE LIVRE DES CHAMPIGNONS (Gallimard Editions, 1987)
● Paul Stamets,GROWING GOURMET AND MEDICINAL MUSHROOMS (Ten Speed Press, 1993)

INDEX

AUTHOR'S ACKNOWLEDGMENTS

Alison Cathie—for publishing, Alastair Hendy—for superb photos, Susan Fleming—for invaluable editing, Priscilla—for her patience, Kate Fry—for helping to cook, Giselle Cody—for understanding my English, Mrs. Tee, Yuki Sugiura, Wild Harvest (fungi), Miho & Michiya Uchida, Hugh Owens, Jane O'Shea, Hilary Mandleberg, Mary Evans, Tim Livesey (fungi), Hans Baumann, Giuseppe,Tim Neat (fungi), Tim Wisley (fungi), Dru McPherson (fungi), Roger Phillips, Flavio Giacoletto, Enzo Zaccharini, Enza Bettelli, Sumir Sarabhai, Roman Mauro, Diana & Tim Bateman, Tartuflanghe, Domenica Bartolusso, Ros Ellis, Professor Roy Watling—for mycological supervision, Giuseppe Meuro, Constanza Guimares, Mushroom Bureau (www.mushroom-uk.com), Urbani Tartufi, Priya Paul, Natasha Kilcoyne, The French Garden, Kent Down Mushrooms, Ken Hom, Darina Allen, Andrea Cavaliere, Asami Sarabhai, David Thomas, Paul Masuda.

PICTURE CREDITS

10–18 Alastair Hendy; 20 Roger Phillips; 21 above David E. Thomas; 21 below Roger Phillips; 22 Roger Phillips; 23 Alastair Hendy; 24 Roger Phillips; 25 above left Roger Phillips; 25 below left David E. Thomas; 25 above right David Thomas; 26 Roger Phillips; 27 above Felix Labhardt/Bruce Coleman; 27 Roger Phillips; 28 Alastair Hendy; 29 left Roger Phillips; 29 right Roger Phillips; 29 below right David E. Thomas; 30 David E.Thomas; 31 Roger Phillips; 32 above David E. Thomas; 32 below Roger Phillips; 33 below Roger Phillips; 33 top David E. Thomas; 34 Roger Phillips; 35-36 Alastair Hendy; 37 Roger Phillips; 38 Roger Phillips; 39 top Alastair Hendy; 39 below David E. Thomas; 40 Roger Phillips; 41 Roger Phillips; 42 Roger Phillips; 43 Alastair Hendy; 44 Alastair Hendy; 45 Roger Phillips; 46 above Roger Phillips; 46 below David E. Thomas; 47 Alastair Hendy; 48 top David E. Thomas; 48 below Roger Phillips; 49 top and right Roger Phillips; 49 below David E. Thomas; 50 above left Roger Phillips; 50 above right Roger Phillips; 50 below David E. Thomas; 51 left Alastair Hendy; 51 above Roger Phillips; 52 Roger Phillips; 53 above Roger Phillips; 53 below David E. Thomas; 54 Roger Phillips; 55 Alastair Hendy; 56 above Alastair Hendy; 56 below Alastair Hendy; 57 Roger Phillips; 58 above Roger Phillips; 58 below David E. Thomas; 59 Alastair Hendy; 60 David E. Thomas; 61 above Alastair Hendy; 61 below Roger Phillips; 62 above Alastair Hendy; 62 below David E. Thomas; 63 top David E. Thomas; 63 below Roger Phillips; 64 Roger Phillips; 65 Alastair Hendy; 66 left Hans Reinhard/Bruce Coleman; 66 right Roger Phillips; 67 above left David E. Thomas; 67 above & below right Roger Phillips; 68 Alastair Hendy; 69 above left & right Roger Phillips; 69 below David E. Thomas; 70 Roger Phillips; 71 Roger Phillips; 72 Alastair Hendy; 73 above Alastair Hendy; 73 below Roger Phillips; 74 left Alastair Hendy; 74 right Roger Phillips; 74 below Roger Phillips; 75 Roger Phillips; 76 Alastair Hendy; 78 Roger Phillips; 79 Alastair Hendy; 80 Alastair Hendy; 82 Alastair Hendy; 83 left Roger Phillips; 83 right Alastair Hendy; 84 Alastair Hendy; 85 Dr. Paul S. Masuda; 86 Alastair Hendy; 87 Alastair Hendy; 88 Alastair Hendy; 89 Alastair Hendy; 90 Alastair Hendy; 91 above Mushroom Gourmet/www.14u.co.nz; 91 below Alastair Hendy.

All the remaining photographs were taken by Alastair Hendy.